D0907373

Scenic Driving
THE OZARKS

Help Us Keep This Guide Up to Date

Every effort has been made by the author and editors to make this guide as accurate and useful as possible. However, many things can change after a guide is published—establishments close, phone numbers change, hiking trails are rerouted, facilities come under new management, etc.

We would love to hear from you concerning your experiences with this guide and how you feel it could be made better and be kept up to date. While we may not be able to respond to all comments and suggestions, we'll take them to heart, and we'll also make certain to share them with the author. Please send your comments and suggestions to the following address:

The Globe Pequot Press
Reader Response/Editorial Department
P.O. Box 480
Guilford, CT 06437

Or you may e-mail us at:

editorial@GlobePequot.com

Thanks for your input, and happy travels!

A FALCON GUIDE®

Scenic Driving

THE OZARKS

INCLUDING THE
OUACHITA MOUNTAINS

Second Edition

DON KURZ

FALCON®

GUILFORD, CONNECTICUT
HELENA, MONTANA
AN IMPRINT OF THE GLOBE PEQUOT PRESS

ISBN 0-7627-3034-X
ISSN 1548-1581

Manufactured in the United States of America
Second Edition/First Printing

Contents

THE SCENIC DRIVES

This book is dedicated to Paula and Molly, for their patience and understanding of my need to travel and see new landscapes; and to my parents, Ken and Milly, who taught me to live up to my commitments and to do the best job I can.

Preface

This book was first published eight years ago, with another printing four years later when I revised the drives and added a new one. Now, four years later again, the process has been repeated and a new drive added. With each revision, I re-drove every route making additions and deletions along the way. In each four-year cycle, it is amazing to me how fast features change, including street names, new highways, new exhibits, and new points of interest to explore. Please keep an open mind while using this book because you will undoubtedly encounter something new, different, or missing along your travels that have occurred since the last printing.

I hope you enjoy these scenic drives through our wonderful Ozarks and Ouachitas!

Acknowledgments

My sincere appreciation goes to several people from the public and private sector whom I met along this journey. Their information and advice helped me produce a better book. My thanks goes to Tom Foti, who shared with me his favorite Arkansas drives.

My special thanks goes to Chris Cauble, former Vice President of Publishing for Falcon Publishing, who suggested this project, and to Megan Hiller for seeing the first edition through the editorial and production processes. Much appreciation also goes to Leeann Drabenstott for her close attention to detail in editing the revision of this book and now to The Globe Pequot Press, for giving me the opportunity to do a second edition.

Introduction

The Ozark region is one of the most identifiable in the United States. You don't have to visit the area to be able to picture rugged, wooded landscapes with clear-flowing streams and abundant wildlife. The Ozarks is a region of geographic contrasts: from unbroken woodlands to crop fields and pastures; broad, slow-moving rivers to swift mountain streams; nearly level plateaus and river valleys to dramatically rugged terrain; and sloughs and swamps to some of the driest forests in eastern North America.

The Ozark region extends across five states but lies mainly within Missouri, Arkansas, and Oklahoma. Its northwestern boundary just nicks southeastern Kansas. In the geologic past, the Mississippi River carved through the eastern Ozarks, isolating a portion of the highlands in what is now Illinois. The total geographic extent of the Ozarks is approximately 50,000 square miles, an area the size of Florida.

This book also includes the Ouachita Mountains. This region, which covers 22,500 square miles, stretches across part of the midsections of Arkansas and Oklahoma. Although it was formed by the same process that created the Ozarks, its east-west trending mountains, with their craggy ridges, steep slopes, and narrow valleys, have always been considered separate from the Ozarks.

These regions were historically inhabited by the Osage, Illinois, Caddo, and Quapaw Indian nations. The Osages occupied most of the interior and western Ozarks, the Illinois lived along the Mississippi River border, the Caddos covered the southern half of the Ozarks and the Ouachitas, and the Quapaws hunted in the southeastern hills of the Ozarks and Ouachitas. European settlement of the region began as a result of the French mining for lead and iron ore in the area between Ste. Genevieve and Potosi, Missouri. Later, settlers of Scotch-Irish descent from Tennessee, Kentucky, and nearby parts of the southern Appalachians moved into the Ozarks and Ouachitas. The rugged terrain made education, socializing, and travel difficult, and modernization came slowly. In spite of these obstacles—or perhaps because of them—the hill people, or "hillbillies," became known as honest, kind, skilled craftsmen perservering to wrest a living from the rugged hills. The term *hillbilly* was first used during the Great Depression to describe the individuals living in poverty in these mountain districts deep in the heart of the Ozarks. Since then, training, education, and employment have made this image a thing of the past—except for the occasional caricature displayed on roadside advertisements.

The formation of the Ozarks and the Ouachitas goes back about 300 million

Impressive limestone bluffs of Pine Hills overlook vast wetlands at LaRue Swamp.

years; to when the continents of South America and Africa drifted up from the south and collided with the North American plate. This process, which lasted more than 200 million years, uplifted a high, flat plateau called the Ozarks. Just to the south, where the impact of the collision was stronger, the rock wrinkled like an accordion and sometimes folded over, forming the long ridges of the Ouachita Mountains. These east–west trending mountains are unique in the United States. The Sierras, Rockies, and Appalachians are all north–south trending mountains formed by previous collisions of continental plates from the east and west.

The mountains of the Ozarks and Ouachitas offer far-reaching views unparalleled in the midcontinent region. The most dramatic relief in the Ozarks occurs in the Boston Mountains, with their elevations of up to 2,500 feet; however, the highest point in the Midwest is Mount Magazine in the Ouachitas, at 2,753 feet. This mountain stands as a sentinel above the Arkansas River valley and is considered part of the Ouachitas. The oldest rock in the midcontinent region is found in the St. Francois Mountains in the eastern Ozarks. Here, exposed igneous rocks of volcanic origin date back two to three billion years.

The falls at Kings Bluff plunges 100 feet down a sheer sandstone cliff.

The Ozarks and Ouachitas are divided into geographic regions based on geology, soils, topography, and plant and animal communities. Although specialists divide the Ozarks and Ouachitas into finer detail, for the purposes of this book, the Ozarks are composed of the Springfield and Salem plateaus, the St. Francois and Boston Mountains, and the Ozark Border. The Ouachitas consist of the Arkansas River valley and the Ouachita Mountains. These geographic regions are discussed and their interesting features described as they are encountered along the drives.

The geology of the Ozarks and the Ouachitas is complex and fascinating. Travelers may encounter a variety of rocks including igneous, dolomite, limestone, chert, shale, and sandstone. Because different bedrocks erode at varying rates, their weathering produces different shapes. The Ozarks and Ouachitas display a diverse array of interesting features including mountains, hills, knobs, mounds, shut-ins, waterfalls, rapids, bluffs, narrows, cutoffs, lost hills, faults, sinkholes, caves, springs, arches, bridges, tunnels, and isolated rock prominences.

The varied topography and numerous bedrock and soil types give rise to a great variety of terrestrial and aquatic natural communities. The scenic drives in this book lead to forests, savannas, prairies, glades, cliffs, caves, fens, swamps, marshes, springs, creeks, and rivers. There are numerous opportunities to observe and enjoy a diversity of plant and animal life when visiting these habitats. The Ozarks and Ouachitas are renowned for providing beautiful displays of roadside wildflowers and fall colors along with occasional glimpses of interesting and unique wildlife. Although it is common to see deer, turkeys, foxes, coyotes, beavers, vultures, herons, songbirds, snakes, and lizards, rare occasions might also include sightings of bald eagles, ospreys, prairie chickens, bears, and river otters. There are also elk and bison that have been introduced into specific areas, as well as some rare sightings of mountain lions in the more rugged regions.

BEFORE YOU BEGIN

Scenic Driving the Ozarks contains thirty-three drives that provide the traveler with the opportunity to experience the wonders of this unique region. The drives cover more than 1,600 miles of highways and back roads. Varying from 5 to 95 miles in length, the routes were chosen for the quality of their scenery, natural features, recreational activities, and historic significance. Points of interest along the way are highlighted in **bold type** in the text.

The highways and gravel roads are passable by all types of vehicles unless otherwise noted. A few sections of road are steep and winding and demand extra caution from the motorist. Avoid low-water crossings that appear flooded and fast

A view of Hot Springs National Park from Hot Springs Mountain Tower.

moving. Some scenic views offer no safe pulloffs, so it is best to keep moving to the next designated stop. Distances in this guide were measured using a vehicle odometer and may vary slightly from distances given by highway signs or other odometers. Be aware of highway signs, junctions, and other vehicles while traveling the sometimes busy roads. Be alert for wildlife on the road. Snakes and turtles are especially vulnerable during the day, while armadillos, opossums, raccoons, skunks, and deer are more active at night.

The weather in this region is very changeable throughout the year and is especially fickle in the winter. The Ozarks average up to 15 inches of snow per year, but it usually lasts only a few days. Freezing rain, although uncommon, can create very hazardous road conditions for up to a day or two. The most popular times to travel are during the spring, summer, and fall. Spring rain brings waterfalls and wildflowers. Summer offers opportunities for families to share in outdoor activities. Autumn brings lower temperatures and lower humidity, plus a spectacular palette of fall colors. Some of the higher elevations, especially in the Ouachita Mountains, experience fog on occasion, but it usually burns off by midday.

Unlike the situation in many western states, there is usually enough activity on most of the roads in the Ozarks and Ouachitas to minimize the chances of being stranded for long periods of time. Having a vehicle in good condition and with plenty of gas helps to avoid possible problems on the road. Travelers should carry water, especially in the summer. Unfortunately, vandalism is always a possiblity wherever you travel, so be sure to conceal all valuables out of sight when parking your vehicle for any length of time. The drives in this book pass through public and private lands. Respect private property by not trespassing, and never litter. Allow others to enjoy the beauty of clean, uncluttered settings.

These drives offer plenty of opportunities to see the best of what the Ozarks and the Ouachitas have to offer. The routes were chosen for leisurely travels; to really benefit from the experience, consider involving at least one overnight camping or lodging stop. These drives take on different appearances in different traveling seasons. A scenic drive in springtime can be totally different when revisited in the fall. These drives may also be traveled in reverse, adding another new perspective.

The amount of time it takes to explore each special feature is up to you. The Ozarks and the Ouachitas offer unique and memorable experiences that will draw you back time and time again, for regardless of when they are traveled, every stop is a reward in itself.

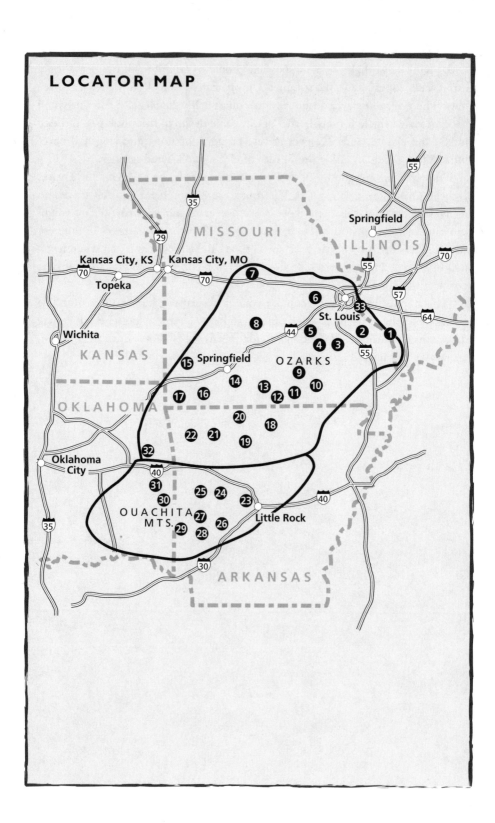

LOCATOR MAP

MAP LEGEND

Scenic Drive (paved)

Scenic Drive (gravel)

Interstate

Other Roads

Hiking Trail

State Boundary

Forest/Reservation
Boundary

Lake

River or Creek

Interstate

U.S. Highway

State and County Roads

Forest Road

Campground

Mountain

Pass or Saddle

Point of Interest

Scale and Orientation

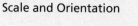

Scenic Drive Location

River and Hill Country

CAPE GIRARDEAU TO GRAND TOWER, MISSOURI/ILLINOIS

GENERAL DESCRIPTION: A 70-mile drive starting in Cape Girardeau and following the eastern Ozark border on both sides of the Mississippi River.

SPECIAL ATTRACTIONS: Cape Girardeau, Conservation Southeast Regional Office, Mississippi River, Trail of Tears State Park, Port Cape Girardeau, Cape River Heritage Museum, Red House Interpretive Center, Glenn House, Union County Conservation Area, Trail of Tears State Forest, Ozark Hills Nature Preserve, LaRue–Pine Hills Ecological Area, Clear Springs/Bald Knob Wilderness Area, and Grand Tower; scenic views, hiking, camping, fall colors, spring wildflowers, hunting, and fishing.

LOCATION: Eastern Ozarks. The drive begins on the northwest side of Cape Girardeau at the junction of U.S. Interstate 55 and U.S. Highway 61.

DRIVE ROUTE NUMBERS: U.S. Interstate 55, U.S. Highway 61, Missouri Highway 177, Illinois Highways 146 and 3, and Forest Roads 236 and 345.

CAMPING: Trail of Tears State Park has 35 basic campsites in wooded riverside hills, 12 campsites with electrical hookups, and 8 campsites with electricity and sewer hookups located near the river. Campgrounds include modern rest rooms, laundry facilities, hot showers, and a dumping station. Two primitive camping areas bordering the Peewah Trail are available for use by backpackers. Pine Hills Campground has 12 Forest Service campsites with water and pit toilets. Grapevine Trail Campground has 5 basic campsites with water and pit toilets. Trail of Tears State Forest in Illinois has 4 basic camping areas with pit toilets. Grand Tower has a campground at Devil's Backbone Park with rest rooms, showers, electricity, and water.

SERVICES: All services at Cape Girardeau. Gas and food at East Cape Girardeau, McClure, Ware, and Grand Tower.

NEARBY ATTRACTIONS: Bollinger Mill State Historic Site, Grand Tower Natural Area, Steam Train Ride, and Jackson (in Missouri); Cache River State Natural Area (in Illinois).

THE DRIVE

Located on the easternmost edge of the Ozarks, this drive follows the rugged river hills and floodplain of the Mississippi River. The Ozarks extend about 10 miles into Illinois. This section of the Ozarks was once part of a much larger

To Chester

7. Grand
6. Tower

Grand
Tower
Island

Big Muddy River

345

LARUE-PINE HILLS ECOLOGICAL AREA

279

236

CLEAR SPRINGS/BALD KNOB
WILDERNESS AREA

SITES

1. Conservation Southeast
   Regional Office
2. Cape Rock
3. Union County
   Conservation Area
4. Pine Hills Campground
5. Winters Pond
6. Tower Rock
7. Devil's Backbone Park
8. Trail of Tears State Park

5.

Mississippi

Wolf
Lake

4.

3

ILLINOIS

To
Trail of Tears
State Forest

To I–55

177

8.

River

N

Ware

3.

146

To
Jonesboro

MISSOURI

0 Kilometers 5
0 Miles 5

To St. Louis

East Cape
Rock
Drive

Reynoldsville

To
Jackson

1.

Broadway

55 61

177

2.

Devils Island

Cape Girardeau

K

McClure

To Grapevine
Trail Campground

East Cape
Girardeau

146

3

To Sikeston

To Cairo

Ozarks millions of years ago until a new, southward-flowing river system formed and cut deep into the landscape. The geology, plants, and animals are basically the same on both sides of the Mississippi River, but the Illinois side is forever isolated. The river is still a dominating force on the landscape, and this drive provides opportunities to see it in action.

CAPE GIRARDEAU

Begin the drive just north of Cape Girardeau at the junction of I–55 and US 61 and head south on US 61 for about a mile. Turn left at the first lane crossover and enter **Cape Girardeau County Park.** The first stop is the **Conservation Southeast Regional Office** operated by the Missouri Department of Conservation. Open from 8:00 A.M. to 5:00 P.M. Monday through Friday, the center offers publications and brochures on activities in the area. Just north of the building, a half-mile paved trail winds through woods and over a creek, affording close-up views of plants and animals characteristic of the region. Nearby, a new Conservation Nature Center is under construction with a scheduled completion in 2005.

Return to US 61, which also bears the city street name of Kingshighway, and follow it into town. After about 3 miles, turn left onto Broadway Street at the traffic light. Follow Broadway, passing Southeast Missouri State University, and in about 2 miles you will find Cape Girardeau Convention and Visitors Bureau at 100 Broadway. The people there can supply you with brochures and maps to guide you to interesting areas of the city. The bureau will soon be moving to a new location just south of the new bridge over the Mississippi River and will be part of what is now called the Southeast Missouri State University River Campus. This building complex was the former Evangilization Center, St. Vincents College, founded in 1843, which is located at the intersection of Lorimore and Morgan Oak along MO 177. At the intersection of Broadway and Main, follow MO 177 north through a residential part of town. (Along the way, a short side trip on Main Street leads to the Red Star Public Fishing Access, which offers a close view of the Mississippi River.) After 1.5 miles, turn right onto East Cape Rock Drive. Follow it for about 2 miles, past the city water plant to a promontory overlooking the Mississippi River.

The view from **Cape Rock,** also called the Mississippi River Scenic Overlook, is the best in the city. You can look up, down, and across the mighty Mississippi; observe the Illinois floodplain with its cottonwood and willow trees; and view the distant hills of the Illinois Ozarks. This view was also appealing to Jean Baptiste Girardot, a French soldier stationed at Kaskaskia, Illinois, who in 1720 stood on this point and envisioned a trading post. He noticed the current of the river striking the base of this prominent outcrop and making a cove or "cape" just downstream that could provide shelter for boats. The site was the perfect spot for trappers and river travelers to stop. The area soon became known by voyagers traveling the Mississippi as Cape Girardot, which later was modified to "Girardeau." But Girardot was a trader, not a settler, and it is not known just how long he remained at the trading post. In the late 1800s much of this promontory was removed to create riverfront space for the Frisco Railroad tracks.

The man credited with settling the area around the rock promontory is Louis Lorimier. In 1792 he was commissioned by the Spanish governor general to establish a trading center in the area for himself and the Indians. Over time, **Cape Girardeau** became one of the most populated and important districts west of the Mississippi River, not excepting St. Louis. The town prospered between the arrival of the steamboat in 1835 and the Civil War. During the war, Cape Girardeau was occupied by Union soldiers who erected four forts to protect the city and river. One minor conflict occurred west of town, with both sides claiming victory, but Cape Girardeau was spared the devastation of total war. The city is rich in history. As the site of Southeast Missouri State University, Cape Girardeau has been the educational and commercial center of southeast Missouri for more than a hundred years.

At this point of the drive you have a decision to make. You can continue on Cape Rock Drive, which wraps around the "Cape" affording a closer view of the river and barge traffic, and proceed to MO 177, which leads 10 miles to **Trail of Tears State Park** as a side trip. Alternatively, you can return to East Cape Rock Drive and then MO 177 south to continue the main drive. Trail of Tears State Park is an exceptional state park with beautiful forested hills that are spectacular in the spring, when dogwoods bloom, and in the fall, when there is a myriad of beautifully colored foliage. The state park contains a nature center with exhibits and on-duty naturalists. There are several trails that wind through oak, tulip tree, and beech-maple forests and a scenic overlook that rivals Cape Rock. The park is named for the 13,000 Cherokee Indians who were forced to march from their homeland in the southeastern United States to a reservation in Oklahoma during the winter of 1838–1839. One of the groups that crossed the Mississippi River did so here, where the park now stands. The nature center has exhibits telling the story of this sad chapter in America's history. Beginning at the bridge over the Mississippi River and along IL 3, you will notice several TRAIL OF TEARS AUTO TOUR ROUTE signs. A more detailed explanation of this historic designation is provided in Drive 5.

Returning to downtown Cape Girardeau by way of MO 177, turn left at

Broadway and park along Water Street. Walk through one of the gates along the flood wall and stroll along the river walk. Evenings are particularly relaxing times to watch the river's never-ending journey down to the Gulf of Mexico.

Just about a block south on Water Street, **Port Cape Girardeau** stands much the way it did when it was occupied by Ulysses S. Grant during the Civil War. The construction of the building dates back to before 1836, a fact that establishes this as one of the oldest buildings west of the Mississippi. Although you can't buy 3-cent Coca-Colas now, as an old sign on the building advertises, the restaurant inside offers a delicious barbecue menu that is hard to beat.

If you walk south along the city-side of the Mississippi River flood wall, you will come upon the **Missouri Wall of Fame.** This 500-foot mural portrays the images of forty-five famous Missourians. The center panel is dedicated to the Missouri State flag. Just 200 feet south of the Missouri Wall of Fame, the Red House Interpretive Center represents the house, trading post, and seat of government where Louis Lorimier, founder of Cape Girardeau, entertained Meriwether Lewis on November 23, 1803.

There are numerous historic buildings in the downtown area of Cape Girardeau. For more information visit the **Cape River Heritage Museum** located at the corner of Independence and Frederick Streets. Take MO 177 south from Broadway 2 blocks and turn right (west) on Lexington for 5 blocks

One of the oldest buildings west of the Mississippi River,
Port Cape Girardeau dates back to before 1836.

to Fire Dept. #1 Headquarters, Cape River Heritage Museum. This two-story brick building is open Friday and Saturday from 11:00 A.M. to 4:00 P.M. There is a small admission charge. It is open at other times by appointment; call (314) 334–0405 or 334–3802.

Follow MO 177 south, and after a few city blocks notice the historic **Glenn House** on the right. The two-story Victorian home, built in 1883, is open for tours Saturday and Sunday from 1:00 to 4:00 P.M. May through October. Tours are also available by appointment; call (573) 334–1177. Turn left at the next intersection and drive over the new Mississippi River Bridge. Beginning at the bridge and along IL 146, you will notice several TRAIL OF TEARS AUTO ROUTE signs along this drive. A more detailed explanation of this historic designation is provided in Drive 5.

Proceed on IL 146, through the town of **East Cape Girardeau** for 3 miles. Notice the depressions in the nearby fields, some of which hold water. These are remnants of the Great Flood of 1993, when the rain-swollen Mississippi River broke through a levee upstream and sought out a new high-water course. Parts of the highway were destroyed by the force of the river, and many Illinois residents who depended on work in Cape Girardeau were subsequently unable to drive to their jobs. It was several months before the highway could be repaired.

Turn left at the junction of IL 3 and proceed 0.6 mile. On the left, a rest stop provides information on the Great River Road with a map showing attractions on the Illinois side of the river. A monument explains early exploration on the river.

McCLURE TO WOLF LAKE

Continue north on IL 3 and proceed to **McClure.** This town was established in 1896 and at one time supported a canning factory, five general stores, three churches, a hotel, and a restaurant. A sign for the **Grapevine Trail** is posted at an unnamed road heading east out of town. A Forest Service campground is located 4 miles down that road.

Continue on IL 3 for 3 miles and enter the small community of **Reynolds-ville,** which once maintained a ferry across the Mississippi River just west of town.

After another couple of miles on IL 3, turn right at the entrance to **Union County Conservation Area.** In late fall and throughout the winter months, this refuge drive offers excellent opportunities for viewing Canada geese and bald eagles. The eagles come to feed on the geese that are sick and injured. About 85,000 geese use the refuge, making it one of the few places in Illinois where so many geese can be closely observed and photographed.

Follow the refuge drive to IL 146 and turn left, returning to IL 3. (If you turn right on IL 146 and go 8 miles east to Jonesboro, you will find signs leading to the Forest Service's Jonesboro Ranger Station. Maps and brochures are available at the office, which is open during business hours.) Proceed north on IL 3; pass through the community of **Ware** and continue 5 miles to **Wolf Lake.** A fairly prosperous community, Wolf Lake's main employer is the Trojan Powder Company, a gunpowder manufacturer. The town is named for a lake at the base of Pine Hills. Take State Forest Road 1135 North leading east from town. Follow the directional signs to Pine Hills (half a mile) and Trail of Tears State Forest and State Nursery (4 miles).

Trail of Tears State Forest is operated by the Illinois Department of Natural Resources. The site superintendent's office provides several maps and brochures on recreational activities in the area. Although 120 acres of the state forest are devoted to growing nursery trees, the remaining 5,000 acres provide picnicking, trails, camping, and hunting. A drive through the 222-acre **Ozark Hills Nature Preserve** offers opportunities to see such unusual plants as red buckeye, wild azalea, and cucumber magnolia. However, the narrow road is not recommended for motor homes or vehicles pulling trailers.

The nature preserve is reached by taking State Forest Road 1135 North half a mile beyond the entrance road to the nursery office and turning right on the South Forest Road. Just to the left is a sign for the Ozark Hills Nature Preserve and an entrance road that follows about a 3-mile loop drive around the perimeter of the nature preserve. The drive ends back at State Forest Road 1135 North. To the right, you will see another entrance on the opposite side of the blacktop that begins the 4-mile North Road loop. This gravel road offers another route to take through the Ozark Hills leading to a great view of the surrounding area, including the Bald Knob Cross.

Return to the entrance to the **Pine Hills,** which is half a mile east of Wolf Lake. A gravel road, FR 236, also called Pine Hills Road 55E, passes towering stands of American beech, tulip tree, and white oak that are of old growth dimensions. At 0.6 mile, **Pine Hills Campground** is visible on the right. Between its two camping sections, White Pine Trail heads northeast for a moderate 3-mile, one-way hike that ends just south of a picnic area called Allen's Flat. You can return by way of the trail or walk 2.5 miles back to the campground along FR 236.

LaRUE-PINE HILLS

Continue on FR 236 and in about 2 miles the road begins to climb to the top of the Pine Hills. Along the way, a sign marks the boundary of the **LaRue–Pine Hills Ecological Area.** This designation was the first of its kind in the national forest system. It is said that there are more plant and animal species in this 3,000 acres than in any other area of similar size in the nation. This specially designated area contains more than 1,150 species of plants, which is more species than occur in all of the Great Smokey Mountains National Park. There are also 41 mammal, 24 amphibian, 35 reptile, and 173 bird species that inhabit the area. The diversity of the plant and animal life correlates with the diversity of habitats or natural communities found here, ranging from high, wooded ridges; steep, moist-to-dry slopes; and 350-foot bluffs to a vast floodplain of swamp and bottomland forest. There are more habitats here than in any other place in the Ozarks. To celebrate this outstanding landscape, a LaRue–Pine Hills Appreciation Day is held biannually with field trips and nature talks by botany, zoology, and geology interpreters. Check with the Jonesboro Ranger District for more information.

In less than half a mile, **Allen's Flat** provides picnic tables and pit toilets. No scenic views are available here. Just beyond Allen's Flat, **McGee Hill** picnic ground has picnic tables and pit toilets. Continuing on the main road and just below McGee Hill, a scenic overlook provides one of the finest views of the Mississippi River valley. LaRue Swamp is below, and, in the distance, you can see the Missouri Ozarks. **Crooked Tree Trail** is 1.3 miles north of McGee Hill on FR 236. From the signed pullout, there is a short (0.2-mile) trail leading to a bench overlooking the valley.

Just beyond the Crooked Tree Trail pullout, you'll find the South Hutchins Creek Road and the sign for the Clear Springs Wilderness, Shawnee National Forest. The wilderness area, which has a total of 4,730 acres, was approved by the United States Congress and designated in 1990. Trail access to the area is located farther down FR 236.

Saddle Hill vista is next, only half a mile from Crooked Tree Trail. Unfortunately, the view is being closed in by tree growth. **Pine Ridge** is 0.7 mile beyond Saddle Hill. A short trail leads to a valley overlook and a stand of shortleaf pine, the namesake of the ecological area. Shortleaf pine is endangered in Illinois and exists in only two areas in the Illinois Ozarks. It is much more common in the Ozarks of Missouri, Arkansas, and Oklahoma.

In another 0.2 mile on FR 236, **Government Rock** provides a 0.1-mile hiking trail to an old fireplace and view of the lowlands. Beyond Government Rock at 0.2 mile, Old Trail Point offers a view of the Mississippi River valley.

Proceed on FR 236 for 0.4 mile to the head of the Godwin Trail and the **Clear Springs/ Bald Knob Wilderness Area.** The trail extends 6 miles east to Bald Knob blacktop road, which is 3 miles southwest of Alto Pass. There are some confusing turns along the way, and it is best to use a topographic map or consult the Jonesboro Ranger Station for trail conditions.

Follow the road to **Inspiration Point,** which is 0.3 mile north of the wilderness trailhead. An easy quarter-mile walk leads to great views of the Mississippi River valley, including LaRue Swamp and the Big Muddy River bottoms. It is best to stay on the trail because the steep, cherty slopes are unstable, especially along the bluff. The trail continues another half mile through a north-facing cool valley with large beech trees to **McCann Springs Picnic Area.**

If you continue on FR 236, the road will immediately descend out of the Pine Hills, past McCann Springs Picnic Area, to the intersection of FR 345. Turn left and enter **LaRue Swamp.** After 0.3 mile, turn right and take a side trip on the levee road. Go a few hundred yards and turn around. Be prepared for a spectacular view of the Bailey limestone bluffs rising 350 feet above the valley floor. At the top is Inspiration Point. Return to FR 345 and turn into the entrance of **Winters Pond.** This 0.3-acre depression was created when fill

A sheer limestone cliff towers over a levee road and nearby LaRue Swamp.

material was taken to help build the levee. Picnic tables and a boat launch are provided here. You can view interesting swamp vegetation from the water's edge, or you can launch a canoe or boat to explore the extensive swampland. Winters Pond is a good place to park and walk along the level, 3-mile road. This road is closed to all but foot traffic during the last three weeks of April and the last three weeks of October. Limiting traffic this way helps protect the amphibians and reptiles as they migrate between their winter retreats at the base of the bluffs and their summer homes in the swamp. The swamp is dominated by pumpkin ash around the margins (look for swollen buttresses at the base), buttonbush, swamp loosestrife (with its arching stems), American lotus, yellow pond lily, and, of course, a carpet of duckweed.

The road affords excellent views of LaRue Swamp, a spring at the base of the bluff, dense bottomland hardwood forest, massive limestone bluffs supporting small grassy openings on top, and beautiful displays of wildflowers in the spring.

GRAND TOWER

Continue on the gravel road as it turns and heads west; use caution as you approach the double railroad crossing. At IL 3, turn right to head north to

Tower Rock stands sentinel against the swift waters of the Mississippi River.

Grand Tower and cross the Big Muddy River. The land west of the road is Grand Tower Island, which is part of Missouri. Late in the 1800s, the main channel of the Mississippi River took a westward course, thereby isolating this part of Missouri. After another couple of miles, turn left onto Grand Tower Road and proceed a half mile west to Front Street. The town was surveyed and platted in 1867 and named for the prominent rock outcrop on the far side of the river. This rock outcrop of Bailey limestone, now called **Tower Rock,** is a designated Missouri State Natural Area. It was first recorded and described in 1673, when the French explorers Joliet and Father Marquette penetrated the region. Around 1680 La Salle noted the stately grandeur of the "Grand Tower," which has for thousands of years withstood the continual torrents of the mighty Mississippi.

On the north side of Grand Tower, **Devil's Backbone Park** offers camping, hiking along Devil's Backbone, and strolls along the sandy beach. Walk north of Devil's Backbone to the natural gas pipeline that extends across the river. The pipeline is said to be the longest suspended pipeline in the world. Devil's Bake Oven, a prominent rock formation with a shallow, south-facing cave, rises at the base of the pipeline. A trail winds its way to the top for a great view of the Mississippi River.

Great River Settlements

STE. GENEVIEVE TO FULTS HILL PRAIRIE, MISSOURI/ILLINOIS

GENERAL DESCRIPTION: A 28-mile drive through historic French settlements along the Mississippi River with a side trip to picturesque sandstone outcrops and canyons.

SPECIAL ATTRACTIONS: Ste. Genevieve, Great River Road Interpretive Center, Felix Valle House State Historic Site, Pickle Springs Natural Area, Hawn State Park, Mississippi River (may be closed to ferry traffic during high waters, especially in spring), Modoc Rock Shelter, Fort de Chartres, Prairie du Rocher, Fults Hill Prairie Nature Preserve, and Maeystown; scenic views, hiking, camping, fall colors, hill prairies, and weathered sandstone features.

LOCATION: Northeastern Ozarks. The drive begins at the junction of U.S. Interstate 55 and Missouri Highway 32.

DRIVE ROUTE NUMBERS: Missouri Highways 32, 144, and AA and Illinois Highway 155.

CAMPING: Hawn State Park has 50 campsites, including 17 with electrical hookups. The camping area includes modern rest rooms, hot showers, laundry facilities, a dumping station, and playground equipment.

SERVICES: All services at Ste. Genevieve and Maeystown. Gas and food at Prairie du Rocher.

NEARBY ATTRACTIONS: Amidon Memorial and Magnolia Hollow conservation areas and Ball Mill Resurgence Natural Area (in Missouri); Fort Kaskaskia State Park (in Illinois).

THE DRIVE

Before entering the town of Ste. Genevieve, take a side trip to **Pickle Springs Natural Area.** It is truly one of the most interesting areas in the Ozarks; a well-designed 2-mile trail system takes you to outstanding features of sandstone outcrops.

To get to Pickle Springs Natural Area, take MO 32 at the junction of I–55 and drive west. Proceed through the small communities of New Offenburg

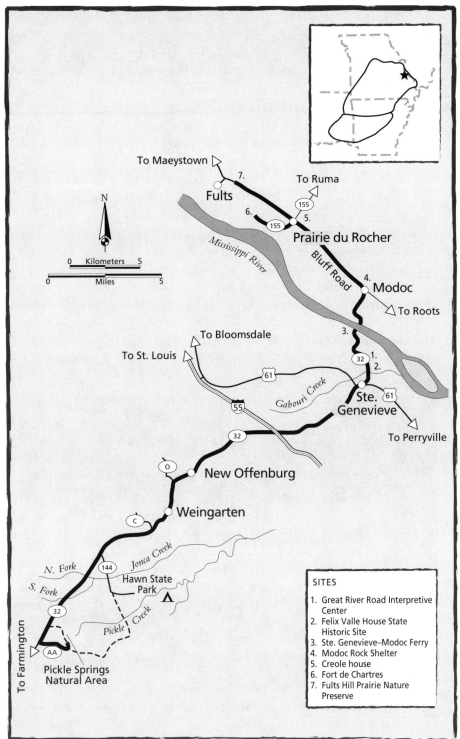

To Maeystown

7.

Fults

To Ruma

6.

155

5.

155

Prairie du Rocher

N

Mississippi River

Bluff Road

4.

Modoc

To Roots

0 Kilometers 5

0 Miles 5

To Bloomsdale

To St. Louis

3.

32

1.

2.

61

Ste. Genevieve

61

To Perryville

Gabouri Creek

55

32

O

New Offenburg

C

Weingarten

Jonca Creek

N. Fork

144

Hawn State Park

S. Fork

32

Pickle Creek

AA

To Farmington

Pickle Springs Natural Area

SITES

1. Great River Road Interpretive Center
2. Felix Valle House State Historic Site
3. Ste. Genevieve–Modoc Ferry
4. Modoc Rock Shelter
5. Creole house
6. Fort de Chartres
7. Fults Hill Prairie Nature Preserve

and Weingarten. After about 11 miles you will meet MO 144, which leads to **Hawn State Park.** The 3,271-acre state park offers two trails that explore oak-pine forests, savannas, rock outcrops, and Pickle Creek. Hawn State Park is downstream from Pickle Springs Natural Area, and there are plans for a trail connecting the two areas. Information on recreational activities at the park can be obtained at the superintendent's office.

Continue on MO 32 another 4.8 miles and turn left on MO AA. Proceed another 1.5 miles, turn left on Dorlac Road, follow it about 0.2 mile, and pull into the parking lot of Pickle Springs Natural Area. The sandstone bedrock here has been sculptured by the forces of wind, rain, and ice. The resulting narrow fissures, rock pillars ("hoodoos"), gigantic boulders, arches, and box canyons were formed over more than 500 million years of geologic time. This is the oldest sedimentary rock in the Ozark region. Imagine a time when land animals and plants had not yet appeared: Vast seas covered most of what is now the United States, and marine invertebrate animals and primitive fish ruled the waters. Active and inactive volcanoes protruded above the ocean, and rain and waves continually pounded them, breaking their igneous rock down into fine sediments. This sand was eventually covered by additional sediment, cementing it all together to form sandstone. Today this sandstone, the Lamotte, crops out in just a small portion of the St. Francois Mountains region of the Ozarks.

Double Arch is one of the many unique sandstone features found at Pickle Springs Natural Area.

A trail leads from the parking lot along a gentle to moderately diff
through special places like The Slot, Cauliflower Rocks, Double Ar
Canyon, and Headwall Falls, to name a few. Be sure to obtain a trail booklet at
the trailhead for complete descriptions. The natural area, named after William
Pickles who owned the land in the mid-1800s, exhibits a wide array of plant
life. Mosses and lichens form colorful patterns on the rocks while ferns thrive
in moist nooks and crannies. Wild azaleas are a special treat, blooming in early
May, and box canyons display waterfalls during spring runoff and after heavy
rains. Listen for pine warblers in spring and watch for wild turkeys any time
of year.

STE. GENEVIEVE

Return to MO 32 and head for **Ste. Genevieve,** the first permanent European settlement west of the Mississippi River. Upon entering town, follow the
signs to the historic downtown area, which is reached by bearing right on MO
32 and crossing over US 61. The road now becomes Center Drive and shortly
changes into Fourth Street. Cross over the railroad tracks and turn right onto
Market Street at the first stop sign. Proceed 3 blocks to the **Great River Road
Interpretive Center.** Parking is available behind the building. This is a good
place to explore exhibits depicting historic events and obtain tourist information, including maps and brochures. While at the interpretive center, ask for
directions to the Bequette-Ribault House. Dated 1778, it is one of four known
surviving structures of pole and soil construction in America.

Ste. Genevieve was founded around 1735 by French Canadians who moved
into the Mississippi Valley to avoid British rule in Canada. They settled first on
the east side of the river at Kaskaskia, then moved across the river when prospec-
tors discovered lead at Mine La Motte in Madison County, 30 miles to the west.
After St. Louis became established upstream, the two settlements competed for
river trade. St. Louis finally emerged predominant, because it had a better geo-
graphical location for commanding trade on the Missouri, the upper Mississippi,
and the Illinois Rivers. Ste. Genevieve declined as St. Louis grew.

Today Ste. Genevieve is an architectural treasure trove. Houses and buildings
from the 1700s, 1800s, and early 1900s make a tour of Ste. Genevieve a fascinating walk through history. Many of the original log cabins of the early settlers still
stand. As you walk or drive through the town, you will notice that many private
homes have plaques bearing their construction date. There are presently eighty-
nine historic properties listed in Ste. Genevieve's preservation ordinance record.
Because there are so many wood, brick, and stone buildings to see, you may want
to ask the staff at the interpretive center for advice based on your interests.

Ste. Genevieve's Bolduc House, originally constructed in 1770 by Louis Bolduc, was moved and rebuilt after a major flood in 1875.

A "must" visit is the **Felix Valle House State Historic Site** on Merchant and Second Streets. Built in 1818, the home is decorated with furnishings of the period; tours are provided by guides in period costume. The building was also used by a trading firm, and today's visitors can enjoy the Menard and Valle Store, stocked with the trade goods and furs that would have filled its shelves in 1830.

Along the streets closer to the Mississippi River floodplain, you will notice remnant sandbags and rebuilt levees, all reminders of the Great Flood of 1993. Ste. Genevieve received international attention when the floods of that year threatened the town and, in some cases, engulfed buildings along the bottoms. During the "Summer of the Sandbag," more than 1,500 volunteers from across the country came to fill and stack more than 98,000 sandbags on water-soaked levees. There has been a long-standing feud between the "Mother of the West," as Ste. Genevieve is known, and the "Father of Waters"—in 1993 the historic community held its own. That summer the river crested at 49.67 feet during what the U.S. Army Corps of Engineers described as a "500-year flood" (meaning a flood of this intensity occurs, on an average, only once every 500 years). Extraordinary efforts to save the historic buildings paid off: Only four of the eighteenth- and nineteenth-century buildings were inundated by the flood.

Floods have grown more destructive and have reached higher water levels mostly as the result of man's efforts to contain the river. The massive levee system along most of its length confines the Mississippi River for the sake of flood control, commercial navigation, agriculture, and hydropower generation. When the river swells, as it did in 1993, there are no safety valves to relieve the pressure. Before the levees were built, marshes, sloughs, lakes, and backwater areas were the overflow points where the river released some of its energy. These critical areas have now been cut off by the levees, drained, and filled for agriculture, a process that also eliminated important habitat for many kinds of wildlife. The Corps of Engineers and other government and state agencies are beginning to rethink and study some of these issues. Much work is still needed to properly address this problem.

The rest of the drive is on the Illinois side of the Ozarks, which can be reached by taking a ferry across the Mississippi River. Follow the ferry crossings signs through town to the river, about 2 miles away. If you have not been on a ferry before, it is a pleasant experience. The **Ste. Genevieve–Modoc Ferry** is in operation from 6:00 A.M. to 6:00 P.M. except on Sunday and holidays, when it is open from 9:00 A.M. to 6:00 P.M. The fee is $6.00. On the rare occasions when the river rises above 28.5 feet, the entrance ramps are closed due to high water. The ferry holds up to nine vehicles, and motor homes are allowed.

MODOC TO FULTS HILL PRAIRIE NATURE PRESERVE

On the other side, the road leads to Modoc, a distance of 3.4 miles. Follow the river road through Modoc and head north on Bluff Road. After another 1.5 miles, pull off on the right side of the road at the base of a bluff. This is the **Modoc Rock Shelter,** a national prehistoric site. The bluff is Aux Vases sandstone, parts of which are stained by iron oxides. *Aux Vases* is French for "of slime/mire/ooze"; a possible reference to the staining of the rock or the fact that this formation is a petroleum reservoir at some locations. At the base of the cliff is a rock shelter of archaeological significance. Excavations have uncovered many Indian artifacts whose age makes this the earliest known human habitation east of the Mississippi River. Skeletons from here were found to have been buried between about 6219 and 2765 B.C., and artifacts have been dated to 8000 B.C. An interpretive sign describes the historical uses of the rock shelter.

Continue on Bluff Road another 1.6 miles to **Prairie du Rocher,** which means "Prairie on the Rock." Notice the prairie grasses dominating the openings above the limestone cliffs. (For a better view, drive west into town and look back at the cliffs.) Later in the drive, you will have a chance to visit a hill prairie that has been designated a state nature preserve. Prairie du Rocher was founded by French settlers in 1722 and is Illinois's oldest town. A **Creole house** dating back to 1800 is featured in the town, along Bluff Road.

Proceed another 2.3 miles and turn left on IL 155 for 4 miles to **Fort de Chartres.** The fort is named in honor of Louis duc de Chartres, son of the regent of France. An earlier fort, which was closer to the Mississippi River, was completed in 1720. It consisted of a fence of squared logs surrounded by a dry moat. The fort, subject to frequent flooding from the river, deteriorated rapidly. A second fort, more inland from the river, was built in 1725 and served until 1742. Since the 1730s, French leaders had discussed building a stone fort to protect their interests on the Mississippi River. After much disagreement and delay, construction finally began on a new fort only a short distance from its predecessor. Stone was quarried and hauled from the bluffs north of Prairie du Rocher.

The stone Fort de Chartres served as France's Illinois Country headquarters for only ten years. In 1763 France surrendered Illinois and most of its North American possessions to Great Britain in the Treaty of Paris, which ended the Seven Years' War. British troops took possession of the fort in 1765. They showed little interest in maintaining the fort, and by 1772 the south wall and bastions had collapsed into the Mississippi River. The fort continued to deteriorate. By 1900 none of the wall existed above ground level, since much of it had either been silted in or carted off for other building use. In 1913 the Illinois legislature authorized purchase of the stone fort site, and by the 1930s the Works Progress Administration (WPA) had reconstructed the gateway and two stone buildings.

Fort de Chartres was also inundated by the flood of 1993 when water levels reached 13 feet. Damaged areas have been repaired and visitors can investigate the various buildings, a museum, and a gift shop that carries an impressive array of books, crafts, and items of the period. Check the special events schedule for festivals and reenactments held during the year.

Return on IL 155 to Bluff Road and turn left, heading north. For the next few miles, look for large limestone mines tunneled into the cliff face. Called St. Louis limestone, this rock is high in calcium and makes excellent road rock. About 4 miles from IL 155, a small parking lot on the left marks the beginning of a marsh called **Kidd Lake Nature Preserve.** Continuing north on Bluff Road, notice the extensive marsh on the west side of the road dominated with cattails and bullrushes that provide cover and nesting for marsh wildlife. In another mile, an entrance and sign on the right indicate that you are at **Fults**

At historic Fort de Chartres, a gift shop and concession features books and crafts depicting life in the eighteenth century.

Hill Prairie Nature Preserve. Dedicated in October 1970 as the thirtieth Illinois Nature Preserve, the 532-acre tract is owned and managed by the Illinois Department of Natural Resources. Fults Hill Prairie lies within the rugged topography of the northern section of the Illinois Ozarks.

The site contains the largest assemblage of the highest quality loess hill prairies along the Mississippi River. Loess is a German term for the wind-deposited silt that is usually derived from glacial activity. Although no glacier has ever touched this area, 200,000 years ago the Illinoisan glacier came within 3 miles of overtopping the bluff on its southward path. Glacial meltwaters from the Illinoisan and from the more recent (10,000 to 40,000 years ago) Wisconsinan glacial period had a remarkable influence on this land. The tremendous meltwaters from the glaciers helped to scour the Mississippi River valley, ever-enlarging the cliff face. In the winters, when the glaciers stopped melting and the waters receded, winds from the northwest would whip across the dry 4-mile riverbed, creating clouds of fine silt. As the winds lifted over the cliff face, heavier particles of silt dropped out, depositing hundreds of feet of loess. Over time some of the silt wore away, but prairie plants, which are adapted to steep slopes and hot, dry, westerly exposures, colonized the soil and slowed erosion.

Hill prairies are rare worldwide. They occur along the eastern side of the Mississippi River valley from Wisconsin to southern Illinois; along the eastern side of the Missouri River from Council Bluffs, Iowa, to just north of Kansas City, Missouri; along the Rhine River in Germany; and along the Yellow River in China.

Two paths lead from the parking lot: one north, the other south. Steps on the south trail lead to a small hill prairie and overlook. However, if you have more time, take the northern path; it is the most rewarding. The first 200 feet are just like climbing steps—take it slow and easy. The trail passes through stands of walnut, sugar maple, honey locust, flowering and gray dogwood, white oak, red oak, slippery elm, box elder, and hickory. Watch out for poison ivy. The first opening is a limestone glade. The southern exposure is ideal for glade-loving Ozark animals like the plains scorpion, coachwhip snake, and narrow-mouthed toad. This is a natural area; please leave the rocks in place and wildflowers to bloom for others to enjoy. The dominant grasses are little bluestem, side-oats grama, Indian grass, and big bluestem. Wildflowers, particularly many diverse members of the sunflower and legume families, are abundant throughout the season.

Continue up the path through a wooded area where the trail soon opens onto a hill prairie. It differs from the rocky limestone glade by having a deep layer of loess. Follow the path west along the ridge for a spectacular view of the Mississippi River valley. Many visitors are content to sit here and enjoy the view from this point. If you decide to go farther, the route does lead down to the cliff's edge, so exercise great caution, because it is a long drop to the bottom.

If you choose, you can continue your drive by stepping back in time and exploring the nineteenth-century German village of **Maeystown.** From the nature preserve, continue north on Bluff Road, passing what is left of the community of Fults after the Great Flood of 1993. After 5 miles, cross over Chalfin Bridge and turn right, following the signs to Maeystown. Founded by Jacob Maeys in 1852, the village was settled by German immigrants predominantly from the former Bavarian Rheinpfalz. Sixty historically significant buildings still exist, including Maeys's log house; the original 1865 stone church; Zeitinger's Mill; and various outbuildings, barns, and smokehouses made of limestone, brick, and wood. Gift and bakery shops, a general store, a restaurant, and a bed-and-breakfast are also featured. Maeystown was listed on the National Register of Historic Places in 1978.

3

Mineral Mines

BONNE TERRE TO MILLSTREAM GARDENS, MISSOURI

GENERAL DESCRIPTION: A 33-mile drive that begins at Bonne Terre and travels through the historic mining region to the scenic granite shut-ins of Millstream Gardens Conservation Area 9 miles west of Fredericktown.

SPECIAL ATTRACTIONS: Bonne Terre Mine, Mineral Mines State Historic Site, Silver Mines Recreation Area, and Millstream Gardens Conservation Area; scenic views, hiking, camping, fishing, canoeing, kayaking, off-road-vehicle (ORV) trails, and geology.

LOCATION: Northeastern Ozarks. The drive begins at the junction of U.S. Highway 67 and Missouri Highway 47 at the Bonne Terre exit.

DRIVE ROUTE NUMBERS: U.S. Highway 67 and Missouri Highways 72, 47, 32, and D.

CAMPING: St. Francois State Park is 4 miles north of Bonne Terre on U.S. Highway 67. The park offers 47 basic campsites

and 63 improved sites with modern facilities. St. Joe State Park, along the south edge of Park Hills, provides 35 basic campsites, plus 15 modern ones that are primarily for ORV users. A daily fee is charged for camping at both state parks on a first-come, first-served basis. Mark Twain National Forest's Silver Mines Recreation Area, located south of Missouri 72 along Missouri Route D, offers 91 campsites.

SERVICES: All services at Bonne Terre, Deslodge, Leadington, Park Hills, Farmington, and Fredericktown.

NEARBY ATTRACTIONS: Washington, Elephant Rocks, Hawn, and Taum Sauk Mountain state parks; Hughes Mountain and Pickle Springs natural areas and Amidon Memorial Conservation Area (Missouri Department of Conservation); the Ozark Trail; and Marble Creek Recreation Area and Rock Pile Mountain Wilderness Area (in Mark Twain National Forest).

THE DRIVE

This drive begins in the Ozark border's rolling, wooded hills and their broad, open valleys and clear streams. This area is part of the largest lead-producing region in the world. The hills become more pronounced and rugged as you head south. Here, US 67 edges along the eastern flank of the St. Francois Mountains, a landform that contains the oldest exposed rock (two to three billion years old) in the midcontinental region. Most of the rock is covered by

To 55

A
St. Francois
State Park

67

To 21 ◄ 47
Bonne Terre

Deslodge

To Potosi ◄ 8

Mineral Mines
State Historic Site

Park Hills
Leadington

32
To Bismarck

A
St. Joe
State Park

Farmington To 55
32

N

0 Kilometers 5
0   Miles   5

St. Francis River

Knob Lick
Mountain

67

Millstream Gardens
Conservation Area

To Ironton ◄ 72

A

To 72 ◄ D

72 To Jackson

Fredericktown

Silver Mines
Recreation Area

To Poplar Bluff

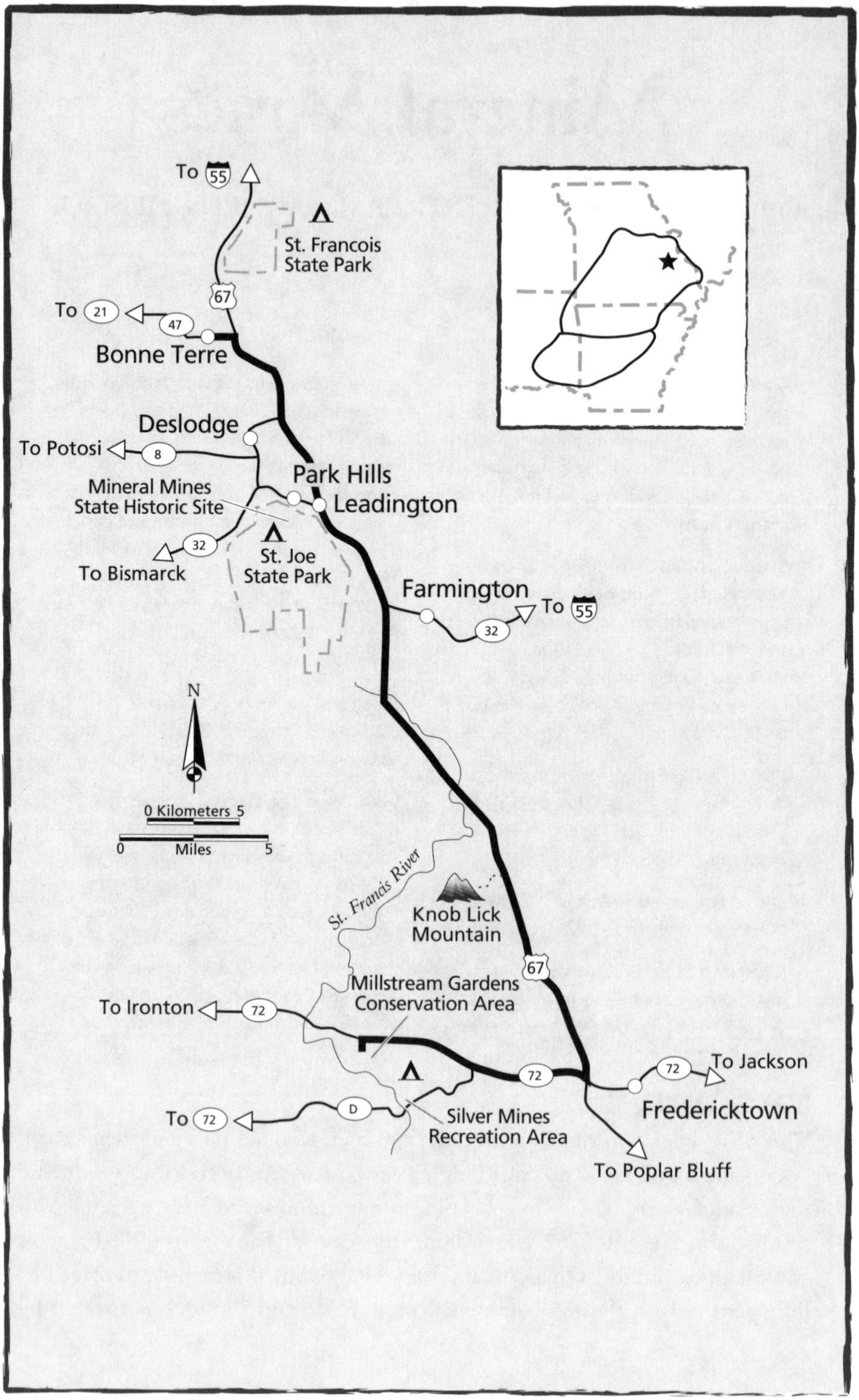

dense forests of oak and pine, but grassy openings called glades and boulder-strewn streams known as "shut-ins" provide interesting places to explore the geologic past.

BONNE TERRE TO PARK HILLS

Start the drive at the intersection of US 67 (a four-lane route) and MO 47. Take the exit ramp west onto MO 47 and proceed into the town of **Bonne Terre.** The French called this area *La Bonne Terre,* "the good earth," in reference to its mineral wealth. Bonne Terre is the oldest of a series of closely spaced lead-mining towns. In 1864, 946 acres were purchased by the newly incorporated St. Joseph Lead Company of New York. The next year a company store was established to supply the miners and their families with necessities. A post office was built the following year. Mining was confined to digging from 4 to 8 feet below the surface to extract horizontal sheets of lead. It was not until the introduction of the diamond drill in 1869 that larger amounts of lead ore could be extracted from deep below the surface. For more than a hundred years, lead mining and smelting dominated the communities in the area in what is today known as the Old Lead Belt. There are nearly 1,000 miles of multilevel mine tunnels in this region, testifying to the many operations in this area. In 1976, after the mines played out, the renamed St. Joseph Mineral Corporation moved its offices to Viburnum, in what is known as the New Lead Belt.

Signs of past mining activities can still be seen in Bonne Terre. One-half mile west on MO 47, a large, bare hill of "chat," or mine tailings, can easily be seen to the north. Go another half mile and enter the parking lot of the **Bonne Terre Mine.** This replica of an 1864 mining town sits atop the first underground lead mine in Missouri. Commercially guided tours lead you into underground rooms, some as high as 200 feet and in some places filled with water as deep as 400 feet. Bonne Terre Mine is on the National Register of Historic Places.

On Main Street you will find the **Bonne Terre Memorial Library.** To get there from Bonne Terre Mine, turn right onto Park Avenue (MO 47). At the first intersection turn right on Allen, go 1 block and turn right on Main, and proceed to the first intersection. The library is on the far right-hand side of the intersection. Established in 1867 and moved to its present location in 1904, the library, built of Bedford limestone, is one of the oldest in Missouri. A clock, handmade in England in the late 1700s, decorates the entrance. The adjacent **Shepard House** was built by Cornish miners in about 1865. Tours are provided, and a museum is located on the second floor. While at the Shepard House, which also serves as the Visitor Center/Chamber of Commerce, ask about other places to visit in the area. To continue the drive, return to US 67 and proceed south. Notice the roadcut at the highway intersection; it is Bonne Terre dolomite, the rock from which layers of lead were once mined. This dolomite, which was formed about 500 million years ago, is composed primarily of magnesium carbonate. This tan dolomite differs from limestone in that limestone is made of calcium carbonate and is whitish.

Return to US 67 and head south. Notice the first of several TRAIL OF TEARS AUTO ROUTE signs along this highway. An explanation of this historic designation is provided in Drive 5. After 6 miles on US 67 south, take the MO 32 exit ramp. Turn right on MO 32 and follow the signs to the **Missouri Mines State Historic Site,** approximately 1 mile west. You are now in the south part of the city of Park Hills which, prior to January 1994, was composed of the towns of Flat River, Esther, Elvins, and Rivermines. The citizens of these four financially strapped communities voted to pool together their duplicate resources and emerge with increased services, a stronger tax base, and a projection of future growth and development.

Plan to spend a couple of hours at the Mineral Mines State Historic Site. A guided tour will take you through old Federal Mill Number 3. Closed in 1972, this complex consisted of twenty-five buildings whose operations were aimed at crushing, grinding, and concentrating lead ore. Prior to its closure, the Fed-

Bonne Terre Memorial Library, built of Bedford limestone,
continues to operate on funds donated by the local community.

eral Mill became the largest operation of its kind in the world. In 1976, 8,244 acres of land, including the mill complex, were donated to the state of Missouri and became St. Joe State Park. The mill complex became a state historic site soon after in 1980. Within the old mill there are exhibits on geology, mineral resources, and an outstanding array of mineral specimens; this museum has been rated one of the best in the Midwest. Selected pieces of restored underground mining equipment are also on display. Ask to see the videotape that explains mining history and technology.

FARMINGTON TO FREDERICKTOWN

Return to US 67 and proceed south. In about 4 miles there is an exit ramp to **Farmington.** The town has a variety of stores and places to eat.

Five miles beyond the Farmington exit, you cross over the St. Francis River. Notice the roadcut to the right of the highway. The pink rock is granite overlain by the yellow sandstone. The granite is your first contact with the St. Francois Mountains.

Proceed another 5 miles and then turn onto a small road on the right. It is easy to miss, so be prepared to turn onto the side road after a long climb up a large hill called **Knob Lick Mountain.** The side road immediately branches, so be prepared to turn right. A wooden sign designating Knob Lick Lookout Tower is then visible. Follow the road, which eventually turns to gravel, for 1 mile to the top of the large hill. The last part of the road is rather steep but can be handled by most vehicles. A walk from the parking lot leads to the lookout tower. A sign warns you to climb at your own risk. No more than five people should be on the tower at one time. A moderately strenuous climb to the top affords a commanding panoramic view of the countryside. The distant hills to the south and west are also part of the St. Francois Mountains. Below the parking lot, the moss-covered ground thins to expose large areas of granite. Here, drought-adapted plants survive in a desertlike environment called a glade. Take the time to walk around and inspect the boulders and open pavement. Post oak and blackjack oak grow immediately upslope, where the soil is a little deeper. These trees are stunted and slow-growing because of the poor conditions. Many are more than a hundred years old; however, most rarely reach a second century.

Return to US 67 and head south another 7 miles to the Fredericktown exit. Turn right onto MO 72 and go 4 miles to MO Route D. This road leads to **Silver Mines Recreation Area,** a U.S.D.A. Forest Service campground. A self guiding brochure leads you to interesting geologic formations, scenic views, and an abandoned silver mine.

The St. Francis River cascades over granite boulders at Millstream Gardens Conservation Area.

Once back on MO 72, go 4 miles and look for a wooden sign indicating **Millstream Gardens Conservation Area** to the left. Turn on the gravel road, which leads to a parking lot and trailhead. The half-mile, paved Turkey Creek Trail leads to spectacular views of the St. Francis River Natural Area. Here the river has cut through the igneous St. Francois Mountains, forming a gorge, or "shut-in," that extends over 2 miles downstream into Silver Mines Recreation Area. In the spring, white-water boating is popular in the shut-ins when the water is high and reaches Class IV in difficulty. The area is not suitable for large boats. There is a 2.5-mile hiking trail along the river from Millstream Gardens to Silver Mines that is especially rewarding in the spring and fall.

Ancient Rocks

POTOSI TO TAUM SAUK MOUNTAIN, MISSOURI

GENERAL DESCRIPTION: A 40-mile drive that begins at Potosi, heads south into the St. Francois Mountains, and ends at Taum Sauk Mountain, the highest point in Missouri.

SPECIAL ATTRACTIONS: Big River; Hughes Mountain Natural Area; Arcadia and Belleview valleys; Buford Mountain Conservation Area; Elephant Rocks, Johnson's Shut-Ins, and Taum Sauk Mountain state parks; Fort Davidson State Historic Site; and the Ozark Trail; scenic views, hiking, camping, fishing, hunting, canoeing, and geology.

LOCATION: Northeastern Ozarks. The drive begins at the junction of Missouri Highways 21 and 8 on the east side of Potosi.

DRIVE ROUTE NUMBERS: Missouri Highways 8, 21, U, MA, N, V, and CC.

CAMPING: Taum Sauk Mountain State Park is a new park with 8 primitive campsites, pit toilets, and water. Johnson's Shut-Ins State Park has 52 campsites, half of which have electrical hookups. Facilities include modern rest rooms that are wheelchair accessible, hot showers, a dumping station, and a coin-operated laundry. A daily fee is charged for camping at both state parks. Mark Twain National Forest has campgrounds nearby. Check at the Potosi Ranger District office or the forest headquarters in Rolla for more information. Primitive camping is allowed at Buford Mountain and Ketcherside Mountain conservation areas.

SERVICES: All services at Potosi, Pilot Knob, and Ironton.

NEARBY ATTRACTIONS: Washington, St. Francois, and St. Joe state parks; Mineral Mines State Historic Site; Royal Gorge Natural Area, Ketcherside Mountain, and Bismarck Lake conservation areas (Missouri Department of Conservation); Bell Mountain Wilderness Area and Council Bluff Lake Recreation Area (Mark Twain National Forest); and exhibits at Union Electric Hydroelectric Power Plant.

THE DRIVE

This drive leads through the heart of the St. Francois Mountains to Taum Sauk Mountain, the highest point in Missouri. This region was formed by ancient volcanoes more than 1.5 billion years ago, making it the oldest landform in the midcontinent.

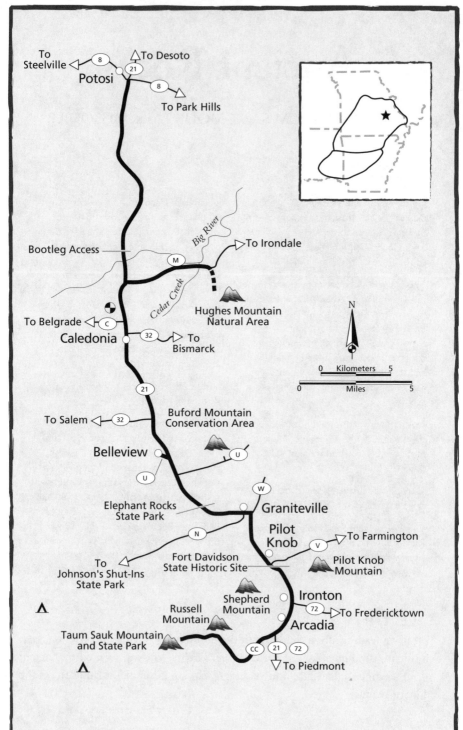

POTOSI TO GRANITEVILLE

The drive begins on the eastern side of **Potosi** at the intersection of MO 8 and 21. (For information on maps, hiking, camping, and points of interest in the Mark Twain National Forest, go west through Potosi on MO 8 for 1.5 miles to the Potosi Ranger Station.) Potosi, with a population of 2,683, is the seat of Washington County and a former lead-mining and smelting town. It was once an important shipping point for railroad ties, and it had one of the largest sawmills of the era located nearby. The lead deposits were discovered in 1773, and Mine Au Breton (later Potosi) became one of the first settlements in the Ozarks. In 1797 Moses Austin, an experienced metallurgist, opened several mines and built furnaces at Potosi to smelt the ore. He soon became wealthy but went bankrupt in 1818, following the collapse of the Bank of Saint Louis and the worldwide depression caused by the Napoleonic Wars. The following year he went to Texas to form a colony, which he passed on to his son Stephen A. Austin, who later became the "Father of Texas." Moses Austin died in 1821 when his health failed during one of his trips to Texas. Austin is buried in the cemetery 1 block northwest of the courthouse.

Most of the hills around Potosi are pockmarked with numerous shallow pits dug with only a pickax and a wooden shovel. Early prospecting amounted to digging 4-foot-deep test holes with which to judge the quantity of ore each hole might produce. Ore prospecting continued until the 1850s, when tiff (barite) mining became important. This resulted in more shallow holes being dug. Tiff is a relatively soft, white-to-gray mineral used in oil drilling to contain gas pressure. It is also used as a filler in paint, ink, paper, textiles, and asbestos products.

Beginning the drive on MO 21, notice the first of several TRAIL OF TEARS AUTO ROUTE signs along this highway. An explanation of this historic designation is provided in Drive 5. Proceed south on MO 21 for 8 miles to the **Big River.** Just before the bridge, a road to the left takes you to **Bootleg Access.** There is a developed trail in the hills above the river valley. The river, which stretches a permanent distance of 117 miles, is shallow along this section and offers opportunities to explore the gravel bars and view small fish. Although it suffers from agricultural runoff and heavy loads of gravel from erosion in the watershed, it is better off here than farther downstream. Lead mine tailings around Deslodge and Bonne Terre sometimes drain into the Big River. Toxic heavy metals accumulate in aquatic animals, resulting in unsafe levels in the bodies of fish. Nevertheless, the Big River remains a popular float downstream from here, and canoes are available for rent near the deeper water at Washington State Park.

Of geologic interest at this stop is the **Palmer Fault Zone.** Notice the rugged hills to the north and their cherty soil covered with trees. To the south of the Big River, the landscape is open, rolling, and suitable for farming. The contrast in the two areas is the result of a massive, 1000-foot vertical uplift on the south side and its subsequent erosion down to the present level. The south side's older bedrock of sandstone and dolomite was exposed and weathered, producing a richer soil. This fault zone extends more than 45 miles trending east and west; it is thought to have been formed along the northern boundary of the St. Francois Mountains as they were uplifted.

Return to MO 21 and drive 8 miles south to MO M. Turn left, and after 2 miles notice the prominent mountain to the southeast. That is **Hughes Mountain,** one of the premier natural areas in Missouri. Proceed 3 more miles, cross over Cedar Creek, and turn right onto the first gravel road. Drive to the crest of a small hill, then turn left and park in the lot. Follow the slightly strenuous trail less than half a mile to a large opening. This is an igneous glade ("igneous" describes a rock of molten origin) and is covered with various lichens, mosses, wildflowers, and grasses. Continue to the top and notice that the rocks resemble columns or fence posts. This formation is called **Devils Honeycomb** and was formed when molten rock cooled and contracted into vertical polygonal

At Hughes Mountain Natural Area, unique weathered rocks resembling fence posts comprise the core of an ancient volcano.

joints. These formations are much like those found at Devils Tower National Monument in Wyoming and Devils Postpile National Monument in California, though on a much smaller scale. Be sure to take the time to enjoy one of the few panoramic views in the Ozarks.

Return to MO 21 and proceed south, passing the Caledonia Methodist Cemetery established in 1834. Notice the colorful red granite tombstones that were quarried just a few miles south of here. There is also a historical marker worth reading. Travel another half mile to **Caledonia,** which was founded in 1819 and named for New Caledonia in Scotland. The town has several pre–Civil War houses located in a seventeen-acre historic district along Main and Central Streets. The area is on the National Register of Historic Places.

Continuing on MO 21 south of Caledonia and half a mile beyond the intersection of MO 21 and MO 32, notice the roadside pullover on the east of the road. The prominent landform to the east that extends for miles in either direction is **Buford Mountain.** It is perhaps the most scenic "mountain" in Missouri and only 32 feet shy of being the tallest point in the state. Buford Mountain is accessible by taking MO U east, a little over 1.5 miles south of here. The road leads to a parking lot where a primitive trail winds up and along the top of the mountain. Most of Buford Mountain is owned by the Missouri Department of Conservation.

From the scenic view, continue about another 1.5 miles passing MO U west, which leads to Belleview. Historic **Belleview Valley** and **Arcadia Valley** (to the south) are known as one of the most scenic cultural landscapes in the Ozarks. In the 1880s the area was "discovered" by wealthy families from St. Louis, and it became popular with vacationers after the Civil War. Today many of the farmhouses have been remodeled to serve as country retirement homes.

About 3 miles beyond MO U west, MO 21 leads to **Elephant Rocks State Park.** At the north end of the large parking lot, a trail weaves through large, rounded granite boulders that resemble elephants. These extraordinary rocks were formed more than a billion years ago when subterranean molten rock (magma) pushed upward to just below Earth's surface and slowly cooled to form granite. As it cooled, nearly vertical cracks (joints) developed, and these were strained further by the uplift that formed the Ozarks. Over time, natural weathering (freezing and thawing) has widened the cracks and rounded off the corners to produce elephant-shaped boulders. Although there are other locations in the St. Francois Mountains where ancient granite has been exposed, Elephant Rocks is the only place where the huge, oblong granite boulders can be found. It was designated in 1978 as a state natural area.

A combination of special fracturing and weathering has sculpted these huge granite boulders at Elephant Rocks State Park.

Return to MO 21 and drive east, immediately passing **Graniteville.** Graniteville is home to the "World's Finest Red Granite," as the quarry company sign proclaims on the north side of the community. The attractive red granite, adorning several of the buildings, has been quarried here since 1869. The stone was also used for the piers on historic Eads Bridge and many other structures in early St. Louis, as well as for cobbles in that city's streets.

About 1 mile beyond Graniteville on MO 21, MO N on the right leads to **Johnson's Shut-Ins State Park,** which is well worth the visit. Here the swift waters of the East Fork Black River flow through a canyonlike gorge called a "shut-in," which can be seen by taking a 0.4-mile walkway to an observation deck overlooking the shut-ins. The park also has several scenic hiking trails, one of which is the Ozark Trail that goes to the top of Taum Sauk Mountain.

PILOT KNOB, IRONTON, AND ARCADIA

Back on MO 21, the next stop is Arcadia Valley. Here the towns of Pilot Knob, Ironton, and Arcadia flank the historic railroad line that once transported hematite, a type of iron ore, out of the mining towns. In Pilot Knob, turn left on MO V and proceed half a mile to **Fort Davidson State Historic Site.** The prominent mountain to the east of the visitor center is Pilot Knob Mountain, for which the town is named. In the mid-1800s iron-ore mining began on the north part of the mountain and continued until the 1930s. Then, from the 1950s to 1980, shafts were driven into the base of the mountain to extract more iron ore, but low ore prices eventually caused the mine to shut down. A chain-link fence now surrounds the mountain to keep the public from entering the extremely dangerous mine openings. More than a century of weathering has caused numerous breakdowns, which are sometimes triggered by would-be explorers. A major rescue effort in the mid-1980s to free a trapped young man convinced the mining company to give up its claim on the mountain. It was then donated to the U.S. Fish and Wildlife Service to manage for the thousands of federally endangered Indiana bats that live in the numerous passageways. A census conducted in 1978 estimated that 139,000 Indiana bats—or one-third of the world's population of this species—call Pilot Knob Mountain their home.

The new visitor center at Fort Davidson State Historic Site contains exhibits that interpret the Civil War battle that was fought here. Plan to spend some time visiting the displays and walking over the grounds, which still resemble a small earthen fort.

TAUM SAUK MOUNTAIN

Return to MO 21 and proceed through Ironton. As you leave town, the road begins climbing up the flanks of **Taum Sauk Mountain.** In a couple of miles, turn right onto MO CC and begin the 3-mile climb to the top. Halfway up, you will notice a pullout and a sign on the left. This is the entrance to the Russell Mountain Trail, a section of the **Ozark Trail.** The trail leaves Russell Mountain, heads south through a part of Ketcherside Mountain Conservation Area, and ends at a parking lot off MO 21 near Royal Gorge. This 2-mile trail is maintained by the Missouri Department of Conservation.

As MO CC nears the top of the mountain, there is a choice of stops. To the left, you can enjoy a 360-degree view of the surrounding countryside from the Taum Sauk Mountain Lookout Tower; to the right, you can enter **Taum Sauk Mountain State Park.** Both stops are recommended. The newly designated state park has camping facilities and a short trail that takes you to the highest point in Missouri, which is 1,772 feet above sea level. Another trail goes to **Mina Sauk Falls,** which is the highest waterfall in Missouri. It falls a total of 132 feet in cascades, with the main cascade falling a distance of nearly 105 feet. The waterfall does not flow the year around and is best seen in the spring or after a good thunderstorm. The trail is 3 miles round-trip.

One mile beyond Mina Sauk Falls, the trail passes through **Devil's Toll Gate.** This is an 8-foot-wide gap in a 50-foot-long, 30-foot-high ridge of orange and red igneous rock. The gap probably began as a vertical rock frac-

Mina Sauk Falls plunges 132 feet over several cascades at Taum Sauk Mountain State Park.

ture that was enlarged by weathering. The trail passing through this gate is a historic military road leading to the Southwest Territory and, according to some, is also a portion of the infamous Trail of Tears endured by the Cherokee Indians during their forced relocation of 1838–39. The Devil's Toll Gate was aptly named because it was as if the Devil was collecting his toll by forcing the unloading of long wagon trains, unhitching the horses, and swinging the wagons around a sharp turn by hand to penetrate the narrow passage.

The trail through the Devil's Toll Gate is now a part of the Taum Sauk section of the Ozark Trail. The Ozark Trail, although not yet complete, will someday extend from St. Louis through western Arkansas, a distance of more than 500 miles. This section of the trail extends to Johnson's Shut-Ins State Park, a hiking distance of 12.8 miles. The state park office can provide you with more information on the various sections of the Ozark Trail that are available to hikers.

Meramec Hills

ST. JAMES TO ONONDAGA CAVE, MISSOURI

GENERAL DESCRIPTION: A 44-mile drive that begins at St. James and winds through the scenic wooded hills of the Meramec River valley to Onondaga Cave State Park.

SPECIAL ATTRACTIONS: St. James, Maramec Spring Park, Meramec River, Route 66, Onondaga Cave State Park, and Vilander Bluff and Spring's End natural areas; wineries, canoeing, hiking, auto tour, camping, trout fishing, and hunting.

LOCATION: Northeastern Ozarks. The drive begins at the junction of U.S. Interstate 44 and Missouri Highway 8 at the St. James exit.

DRIVE ROUTE NUMBERS: U.S. Interstate 44 and Missouri Highways 8, 19, and H.

CAMPING: Private and public land is available for camping along the drive. Maramec Spring Park offers 58 campsites between March 1 and October 31. Each campsite in

the campground is furnished with a picnic table, grill, fire ring, and lantern stand. Water is available at the modern shower house. Recreational vehicles are welcome, but generators are not allowed. Reservations can be made by calling the privately owned park anytime between March 1 and October 31. Onondaga Cave State Park has 72 campsites, 17 of which have electrical hookups. The campground area includes modern rest rooms with hot showers and a dumping station. Nearby Huzzah Conservation Area offers primitive camping at designated sites.

SERVICES: All services at St. James, Steelville, and Cuba.

NEARBY ATTRACTIONS: Meramec State Park, Dillard Mill State Historic Site; Meramec and Indian Trail conservation areas; Meramec Caverns (commercial); and Berryman Trail and Red Bluff recreation areas (Mark Twain National Forest).

THE DRIVE

This drive begins on the eastern edge of the narrow plateau that separates the Gasconade River drainage (15 miles to the west) from the Meramec River hills (just to the east). Small patches of prairie once grew on this more level, open plateau, but the grasses quickly gave way to forest on the steep hills leading down to the Meramec River, a drop of about 300 feet in elevation. Very little erosion occurs in these densely wooded hills, resulting in clear-flowing streams and springs.

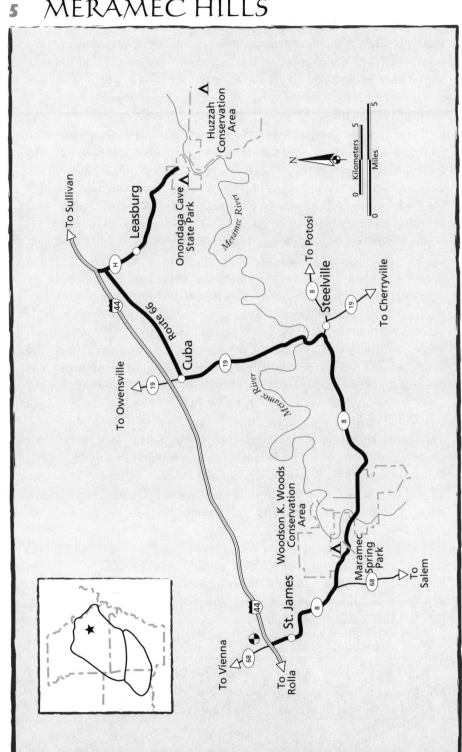

ST. JAMES TO STEELVILLE

Begin the drive at the intersection of I–44 and MO 8 at **St. James.** On the northwest side of the intersection, the St. James Tourist Information Center is a good place to obtain brochures and learn about area attractions and services. There are several local wineries that offer tours, wine tasting, and a variety of German foods.

Proceed on the overpass above the interstate (formerly Route 66) to St. James. The town was settled in the early 1800s as a trading post on Big Prairie. Indians of the Shawnee and Osage tribes bartered their pelts at the post, and the pioneers replenished their supplies there. Legend has it that a local band of Shawnee Indians once traveled to Washington, D.C., to visit the "great white father," President John Quincy Adams. One day in 1825, these journeyers camped on the grounds of Thomas James, a banker and merchant from Chillicothe, Ohio. He noticed their decorative red paint, which he recognized as hematite, an agent of iron ore. His interest was piqued when they told of the red earth beside a huge spring in the West. Upon their return trip, James's business partner accompanied the Shawnee group to inspect the enormous spring and red earth. A favorable report led to construction of the Maramec Iron Works in 1826. Six miles north of the works, a town was founded on Big Prairie to serve as a source for grain and cattle to be used at the works. The James family proposed the town to be "Jamestown." When the post office notified them that name was already in use elsewhere, they followed a custom prevalent at the time by prefixing "James" with "Saint."

St. James, known for its trees, is called the "Forest City of the Ozarks." *Time* magazine called St. James "the most handsomely wooded town in the nation" in an article in 1967. The trees were planted as a project started in the late 1950s. Each autumn, residents enjoy the brilliant reds of the planted sweet gum trees, which are actually native to southeastern Missouri and states further south.

A descendant of the early Iron Works family, Lucy Wortham James, inherited the land surrounding the old Iron Works. Upon her death in 1938, she willed her estate as part of a trust that was later known as The James Foundation. The foundation has provided many gifts to the city of St. James including the city hall, the fire station, the library, and a city park. Most noteworthy of all was its establishment of Maramec Spring Park, where the old Iron Works had been.

Proceed 6 miles east on MO 8 to **Maramec Spring Park.** As you leave St. James, notice the transition from level terrain to the rugged, forested hills leading to the Meramec River valley. Also along this route notice the TRAIL OF

TEARS AUTO TOUR ROUTE highway signs. These markers designate one of three nationally recognized routes across southern Missouri in which the Cherokee Indians were force marched to their final destination in Oklahoma. In the late 1830s the Cherokee Nation was removed by the military, under the 1830 Indian Removal Act, and force marched from the southeastern United States to Indian Territory. This relocation event was called the "Trail of Tears" because of the huge loss of Cherokee lives due to harsh winter travel conditions, disease, and starvation. Approximately 4,000 of the 16,000 tribal members died along the route. The highway markers encountered along several scenic drives in this book identify designated highways that closely parallel the actual Trail of Tears routes. More information about the Cherokee Nation is found in Drive 32.

Continuing on MO 8 and at the bottom of a steep hill, turn left and enter the park. A nominal fee is charged. Before entering the park, note the building to the right, which is an office of the Missouri Department of Conservation. Here information is available on public lands in the region.

Maramec Spring Park and the once-active Maramec Iron Works were named for the nearby river, using the river's spelling of the time. Later, maps showed the river as *Meramec*. In 1971 Maramec Spring Park was designated as the first Registered Natural Landmark in the State of Missouri by the National

*Five iron refinery forges are among the historical structures
that can be viewed at Maramec Spring Park.*

Park Service. The 1,856-acre park contains a small restaurant, picnic and camping facilities, comfort stations, sports fields, an auto trail and observation tower, a historical museum, an agriculture museum, a nature center, the ruins of the Maramec Iron Works, trout-rearing pools, and trout fishing. The best place to start is the **Maramec Museum,** where exhibits re-create the days from 1826 to 1876 when the Maramec Iron Works produced iron. The museum contains exhibits, dioramas, and working models that trace the origin of the works, the iron manufacturing process, the life of the miners and their families, and life of the Shawnee Indians.

Leaving the Maramec Museum, you can walk through Maramec Village as it was in the 1870s. The trail passes through what was a company town that once supported a community of 500 residents. Interpretive signs illustrate where buildings once stood. Remnants of the cold blast furnace and the five refinery forges have been preserved and restored in their original locations. Also be sure to tour the nature center and agriculture museum.

A visit to **Maramec Spring,** the seventh-largest spring in Missouri, is a must. A rustic path leads around the spring opening, which issues an average of ninety-six million gallons of water a day. The water rises almost vertically from a depth of 190 feet into a pool, which was formed when the original channel was dammed during construction of the Iron Works. The water source is from a drainage basin approximately 15 to 20 miles south and southwest of the park. The water courses through porous dolomite rock and joins into one main artery that feeds the spring. Below the spring pool, notice the trout-rearing raceways. More than 180,000 trout are released annually into the spring branch after they attain a length of 10 inches. The Missouri Department of Conservation stocks 2.25 trout for each fisherman it anticipates will be fishing the next day. Trout-fishing season occurs between March 1 and October 31; a daily trout tag can be purchased at the park office along with a state fishing license.

An **auto tour road** within the park leads to the Maramec Iron Works Cemetery, the Maramec Iron Works Mine, and the old Stringtown Road. This road once connected the industrial area of the ironworks with the mine; it was the first road in this area between Ste. Genevieve and Springfield, Missouri. The area was called "Stringtown" because of the string of homes that bordered the winding, busy mine road. In 1982 four large murals depicting different types of homes were erected along the road. These murals also give some insight into the lives of these early pioneers.

There are more than 4.5 miles of hiking trails throughout the park. A map is available at the office. A short distance off of trail #5, which follows along the Maramec Spring Branch, is **Spring's End Natural Area.** This state-

Trout anglers edge the cold spring waters at Maramec Spring Park.

designated natural area is part of the Woodson K. Woods Conservation Area and features a fourteen-acre old-growth bottomland forest. Here large, towering trees more than 150 years old dominate the canopy. Species include bur oak, bitternut hickory, white oak, sycamore, butternut, and northern red oak, and an understory of spicebush, elderberry, and a variety of wildflowers. To reach the natural area, follow the Spring Branch Trail to the suspension bridge over Spring Branch. There is a fisherman's trail at the base of a hill. Follow it, going downstream, past the point where Spring Branch joins the Meramec River. Continue along the trail about 100 yards to a gravel road, which leads through the natural area. A short walk brings you to one of the best examples of an old growth bottomland forest in the Ozarks.

Leave the main part of Maramec Spring Park and continue east on MO 8 toward Steelville. After a mile, the road crosses the **Meramec River;** an access road to the left leads to a popular public canoe-launching site. A good view of the river is available just beyond the parking lot. There are several canoe and raft rental operators in the area that can provide all the equipment you need (even a put-in and take-out service) for single-day or overnight floats down the Meramec River. Ask for information about local canoe outfitters at the St. James Tourist Information Center.

The Meramec River, which empties into the Mississippi River just below St. Louis, is classified as an easy floating stream with a permanent flow distance of more than 201 miles. It is also one of the most popular recreational streams in Missouri. Numerous caves, scenic bluffs, and a diversity of wildlife can be seen along the river. Just past the river access road to the left stands the Brinker House, a historic site, which is part of Maramec Spring Park.

Continue on MO 8 to **Steelville,** which has a population of 1,465. A welcome sign proclaims Steelville as the "population center of the U.S.A." and the "floating capital of Missouri." Steelville was founded in 1835 when James Steel sold forty acres of land to the Crawford County Court for fifty dollars. The court named the little settlement in honor of Mr. Steel. A tourist information center is located on the east side of town along MO 8.

CUBA TO ONONDAGA CAVE STATE PARK

Leave Steelville on MO 19 and head north to **Cuba,** a distance of 8 miles. Along the way you will cross over the Meramec River again as it flows northeast. Cuba advertises itself as the "Gateway to the Ozarks," a common claim made by several towns along the border of the Ozarks. Local history claims that the town's name was derived from two former California gold miners who wanted to perpetuate the memory of a vacation spent on the island of Cuba. About halfway through town, you cross under a Burlington Northern railroad bridge. At the first traffic light, turn right onto Washington Street. Follow this street, which is part of historic **Route 66,** north for about 6.3 miles.

Begun in 1926, this famous federal highway stretched about 2,200 miles from Chicago to Los Angeles. Although I–44 now replaces the 300-mile stretch through the Missouri Ozarks, there are segments that are still driveable. Route 66's legendary appeal has been captured through the years in John Steinbeck's immortalization of the route as the "Mother Road" in the 1939 novel *Grapes of Wrath;* in the dramatic 1960s television show; and in a Top-40 instrumental hit of the show's TV theme song for the Nelson Riddle Orchestra in 1962. Bobby Troup wrote the highway's original theme song, "Get Your Kicks on Route 66," in 1946. Since then everyone from Nat King Cole to the Rolling Stones has recorded a version. In September 1990 the U.S. Congress recognized the route's cultural, natural, and historic impact when it passed the Route 66 Study Act of 1990. The act recognized that Route 66 "has become a symbol of the American people's heritage of travel and their legacy of seeking a better life."

Just before approaching MO H, on the west side of the road, the Oak Grove Roadside Park offers a brief respite. A nearby historical marker explains the history of Crawford County. Turn right onto MO H for 2 miles to Leasburg. A historical marker in town details the Battle of "Leesburg," a Civil War battle fought September 29 and 30, 1864. Continue another 5 miles to **Onondaga Cave State Park.** Follow the signs to the new visitor center; plan to spend some time exploring its interesting exhibits and be sure to take the Onondaga Cave tour.

Missouri, which has more than 5,000 caves, is known as the "Cave State"; however, a detailed inventory of Tennessee has revealed more than 6,000 caves there! Arkansas is third, with more than 2,000 caves. Of course, these numbers are subject to change as new caves are discovered each year.

Onondaga Cave was discovered in 1866 by two young explorers who entered the cave by navigating their johnboat into a spring outlet. Onondaga Cave became the official name in 1904 following a name-the-cave contest. Onondaga means "Spirit of the Mountains" and is the name of a northeastern

Massive flowstone provides a backdrop for unusual rimstone features in Onondaga Cave.

Iroquois tribe. The tribe, and therefore the name, have little to do with local history. The cave was one of the feature attractions during the 1904 St. Louis World's Fair. As a commercial enterprise, Onondaga Cave gained national recognition in the 1950s and 1960s when it was owned by Lester B. Dill, who was often called "America's Number One Caveman."

Onondaga Cave and the surrounding region were threatened in 1967, when the U.S. Congress authorized the U.S. Army Corps of Engineers to construct a dam across the Meramec River for flood control and recreation. In 1973, when Mr. Dill learned that the proposed lake would flood up to 80 percent of Onondaga Cave, he joined the farmers, environmentalists, and conservationists opposing the dam. Because of their letters, petitions, hearings, and other efforts, a nonbinding vote of 64 percent against the dam convinced political leaders to deauthorize the dam in 1981. Prior to his death in 1979, Mr. Dill approached the Missouri Department of Natural Resources with the idea of making Onondaga Cave a state park. With the help of The Nature Conservancy, this became a reality in 1982. The cave is also a National Natural Landmark. The seventy-five-minute tours are almost a mile long, and visitors can experience the cave from lighted concrete walkways with handrails. The temperature of the cave is 57 degrees Fahrenheit year-round. Visitors see spectacular cave formations including soda straws, stalactites, stalagmites, and columns; flowing water has created rimstone dams and massive flowstones.

While in the area, ask at the park office about access to **Vilander Bluff Natural Area,** which is 10 miles from the park. Although no trail is currently available, the hike up to one of the highest and most spectacular bluffs along the Meramec River is well worth the effort. Eastern red cedars up to 500 years old cling to a ledge on a sheer, 200-foot cliff. An excellent view of the bluff is also available when floating the river.

Another recommended stop is **Meramec State Park,** which is located north of Onondaga Cave State Park and east of Sullivan on MO 185. The park offers many interesting sites, including a new visitor center with excellent exhibits, tours of Fisher Cave, scenic views, and access to the Meramec River.

Missouri Rhineland

BUSCH CONSERVATION AREA TO HERMANN, MISSOURI

GENERAL DESCRIPTION: A 50-mile drive beginning at Busch Conservation Area and traveling through the German-settled Missouri River valley and hills to historic Hermann.

SPECIAL ATTRACTIONS: August A. Busch Memorial, Weldon Spring Site Interpretive Area, Grand Bluffs and Weldon Spring conservation areas, Katy Trail State Park, Missouri River, Judgement Tree Memorial, Daniel Boone Home and Monument, Augusta, Marthasville, and Hermann; German festivals, wineries, scenic views, hiking, biking, fall colors, fishing, hunting, and wildlife viewing.

LOCATION: Northeastern Ozarks. The drive begins at the junction of U.S. Highway 40 and Missouri Highway 94.

DRIVE ROUTE NUMBERS: Missouri Highways 94, 19, D, and F.

CAMPING: Primitive camping is permitted only in designated areas at Daniel Boone and Little Lost Creek conservation areas. No facilities are provided.

SERVICES: All services at Hermann, Washington, and nearby St. Charles and St. Peters. Gas and food at Marthasville. A bed-and-breakfast, food, and gas at Augusta.

NEARBY ATTRACTIONS: Babler State Park, Shaw Nature Reserve, Rockwoods Reservation and Howell Island conservation areas; and Powder Valley Conservation Nature Center.

THE DRIVE

The northern edge of the Ozarks extends just across the Missouri River into hills that barely escaped Missouri's last glacier more than 500,000 years ago. The Missouri River has been a major influence in this region of the Ozarks. Beginning as a coldwater trout stream in Montana, it flows 2,522 miles before joining the Mississippi River. The Missouri River, also known as the "Big Muddy," was a marvel to early explorers because of its natural resources. They reported fish large enough to capsize canoes and described extensive wetlands arranged along the river margins like pearls on a necklace.

The Missouri River was not always the single channel it is today. Called *Pekitanoui* by the Osage Indians, the river was a braided stream with many

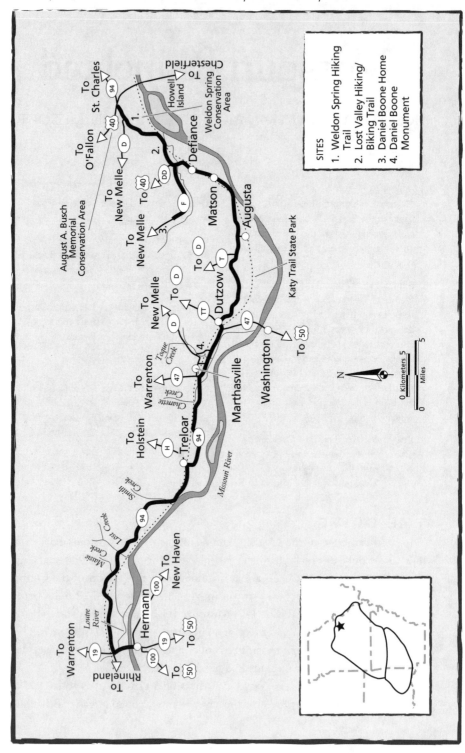

SITES
1. Weldon Spring Hiking Trail
2. Lost Valley Hiking/ Biking Trail
3. Daniel Boone Home
4. Daniel Boone Monument

chutes, sloughs, islands, and channels. Drastic channel modification began in the early 1900s, and by 1972 about 50 percent of the original surface of the river had been lost. Backwater habitat was eliminated and the main channel was deepened and narrowed for navigation. Most of the natural vegetation has now been replaced by agriculture. The Great Flood of 1993 awoke many to the consequences of river confinement when record-high waters broke through levees and flooded towns, farmland, and highways over a three-month period. A near repeat of this event occurred again in the spring of 1995. To help prevent major catastrophes like this, federal and state agencies are working together to try to partially restore natural floodways. This involves acquiring floodplains in critical areas and setting back levees to allow more room for the river to expand at high-water levels. These changes will also create more wetlands and bottomland forests in which fish and wildlife can thrive.

BUSCH MEMORIAL AND WELDON SPRING CONSERVATION AREAS

The drive begins at the junction of MO 94 and US 40. Proceed 1 mile west on MO 94 and turn onto MO D. Follow it for 1.8 miles and turn into the entrance of the **August A. Busch Memorial Conservation Area.** This 6,987-acre area was acquired by the Missouri Department of Conservation in 1947 from the federal government. A donation of $70,000 toward the purchase of the area was made by Mrs. August A. Busch as a memorial to her late husband, owner of Anheuser-Busch Brewing Company of St. Louis. Maps and information are available at the visitor center, which also contains exhibits and the Fallen Oak Nature Trail in the back of the building. You may also wish to pick up a map to Weldon Spring Conservation Area, which is the next stop on this drive.

The Busch conservation area provides opportunities for wildlife viewing, hiking, and fishing at its thirty-two lakes and ponds, and hunting during special seasons. At the headquarters you can pick up a brochure outlining an 8.7-mile auto tour of the area that begins and ends at the main parking lot. There are seven hiking trails varying from 0.2 to 3.0 miles in length at selected stops along the tour route. If you decide not to take the auto tour, at least visit the waterfowl refuge at the beginning of the route. Follow road "C," which is opposite the road to the visitor center, to the first parking lot on the right. The Ahden Knight Hampton Memorial Lake provides a boardwalk and viewing platform with opportunities to see giant Canada geese and other wildlife, including fish.

The return of giant Canada geese is a wildlife success story. Giant Canada geese look much like common Canada geese, except that they are up to one and one-half times larger than the latter and they do not migrate. Giant Canada geese originally nested over much of the Midwest. As settlement increased, these birds were practically eliminated. By the early 1900s there were no known nesting populations of giant Canadas in the entire country. It was later discovered that a few isolated populations were nesting along small ledges and depressions in cliffs above the Missouri River near here. The first efforts to restore nesting Canada geese were made at Busch in the late 1940s and early 1950s. As the population grew, the geese were moved to other areas to start new flocks. Giant Canada geese are now doing fine, and in some city parks and in yards around lake-edge homes, they have actually become pests. They are remarkable birds, however, and these resident giant geese would be sorely missed if they had been allowed to go extinct.

As you return the way you came on MO 94, the road enters **Weldon Spring Conservation Area.** This 7,356-acre area was purchased in 1978 from the University of Missouri, which had received it in 1948 from the federal government for use as an agricultural experiment station. Weldon Spring is named for the nearby town founded by John Weldon. He came to this area in 1796 with a Spanish land grant for 425 acres, including the spring. The conservation area has diverse natural features. In addition to the Missouri River, with its rugged limestone cliffs, the area contains seven ponds, Femme Osage Slough, and Prairie Lake. A unique 385-acre natural area contains examples of upland and bottomland forests and limestone cliffs that extend for a mile along the Missouri River.

Just down the road on the right, you will see the **Weldon Spring Site Interpretive Center.** This facility, completed in August 2002, contains numerous exhibits that explain the history of the nation's largest explosive manufacturing plant, which later became a uranium-ore processing plant. There is a viewing platform on top of the huge disposal cell that is covered with a mountain of limestone rock, and the newly constructed 10-mile Hamburg Trail runs along the site to the Katy Trail.

Beyond the Weldon Spring Site, the **Weldon Spring Hiking Trail** begins on the left at a parking area. Two trails, the 8.2-mile Lewis Trail and the 5.3-mile Clark Trail, begin and return here. A Weldon Spring Conservation Area map showing these trails and other features is available at the Busch Conservation Area headquarters. The trails enter the natural area and offer scenic views on bluffs overlooking the Missouri River.

After another 2.7 miles on MO 94, a road on the left leads to **Weldon Spring Public Fishing Access** and **Katy Trail State Park.** Formerly the old Missouri-Kansas-Texas (MKT) Railroad, which ceased operation in 1986, the right-of-way was purchased by the late Edward D. "Ted" Jones Jr. and donated to the State of Missouri for a state park. After its development as a hiking-biking trail, the MKT (nicknamed the "Katy" Trail) became the longest continuous trail in the United States, at 235 miles in length. Just after most of the trail was completed, it suffered a major setback during the Great Flood of 1993 and again in the spring of 1995. Major restoration efforts by the state of Missouri have it back in operation. This drive will encounter the trail at several crossings. The road beyond the state park leads to a fishing access and view of the Missouri River.

After another 0.7 mile on MO 94, the **Lost Valley Hiking-Biking Trail** begins beyond a parking area on the right. The 8-mile trail is more rigorous than the Katy Trail, following valleys and climbing up and over hills that provide challenges for mountain bikers.

In another 0.4 mile, a side trip on MO F on the right leads about 5 miles to the **Daniel Boone Home.** In 1766 the legendary Daniel Boone helped explore Kentucky and other areas west of the Appalachians. He was a trailblazer, Indian fighter, scout, trapper, surveyor, Virginia state legislator, and judge. In 1799, at the age of 66, Boone left Kentucky and came to Missouri when the region west of the Mississippi River was still ruled by Spain. While hunting along Femme Osage Creek, he came upon a spring flowing from a hillside near

A tour guide stands ready to greet visitors at the home of legendary Daniel Boone.

an enormous elm tree. It was here, in 1803, more than a day's ride from the nearest settlement, that he and his son Nathan began building the house their families would share. The Boones built a magnificent house entirely from materials found in the valley around them. Walls were constructed of quarried limestone. Floor timbers, beams, doorways, and fireplace mantels were made of black walnut. Even the primitive, wrinkled glass in the windows was made using valley limestone. When it was finished, the home was considered the finest house west of the Mississippi River. Daniel Boone lived out his final years in his rock mansion and died there in 1820, a year before Missouri became a state. His son Nathan continued to live in the house until 1837, when he sold it and moved his family to Ash Grove in southwest Missouri. Today the home is filled with furnishings of the era and interpreters in period costume describe life in the early 1800s.

A fee is charged to help maintain the historic buildings and grounds. Now operated by Lindenwood University, St. Charles, Missouri, the Museum Shop is open Monday through Saturday 9:00 A.M. to 6:00 P.M. and Sunday noon to 6:00 P.M. It closes at 4:00 P.M. during Standard Time. For more information call (636) 798-2005. There are daily tours of the Daniel Boone home and grounds.

DEFIANCE TO MARTHASVILLE

Return to MO 94 and after 1.5 miles enter the small community of **Defiance,** which earned its name in 1894 by building a depot that lured the railroad away from Augusta. From here to Hermann you are in wine country, and there are several vineyards along the route. Their exploration will be left to you.

Continue on MO 94 and just before **Matson** notice the sign on the south side of the road for **The Judgement Tree Memorial.** This recently built exhibit describes the place where Daniel Boone held court under a large tree from 1800 to 1804, when he was the Spanish Syndic (a civil magistrate) for the Femme Osage District. Although the original judgement tree is gone, the panels explain the significance of the site, including: the first American trail west of the Mississippi River (the Boone Trace, 1800); the first major American settlement west of the Mississippi River (the Boone settlement, 1799); the Boone family Spanish land grants (1797–1804); and more. The American elm tree at the end of the exhibit area was planted from a cutting taken from the famous tree growing at Thomas Jefferson's Monticello estate.

Continue on MO 94 past Matson, and after 8 miles enter **Augusta,** which is on a side road heading south. The town is situated on the hills and bluffs overlooking the Missouri River valley. It was founded in 1836 by Leonard Harold, one of the settlers who followed Daniel Boone to this region. The town grew predominantly with German families who brought their wine-growing and agricultural expertise with them.

In the 1870s flooding caused the Missouri River to cut a new channel away from the town, depriving the town of its boat landing but providing several hundred new acres of fertile bottomland. Today Augusta is officially recognized as America's First Wine District. Much of the recent tourism interest in these old German towns has been spurred by the revival of the vineyards in the 1960s. In Augusta you will find specialty shops, wineries, bakeries, bed-and-breakfasts, restaurants, and access to the Katy Trail.

Return to MO 94 and proceed 7.7 miles to **Dutzow,** where Missouri's German heritage first took root. In the 1820s Gottfried Duden established a farm and sent enthusiastic accounts of his experiences back to Germany by way of a book he authored. The book was widely circulated and gave a glowing description of the climate and agricultural potential of the region. Because it described the region's similarity to Germany, Duden's book attracted thousands of Germans to this area. The settlement grew and was eventually established as a town by Baron Von Bock in 1832. Another Katy Trail State Park access is located on the west side of town.

Continue on MO 94 to the junction of MO 47. A side trip south for 4 miles takes you to **Washington.** Founded in 1839, this town also drew German families that would shape the area's economy, arts, architecture, and culture. The city has two registered historic districts, along Main Street and Front Street.

Continuing on MO 94, in about a mile you'll see the sign for the **Daniel Boone Memorial Site** and another for the **Daniel Boone Monument,** which is about half a mile away. Turn right and proceed north, turn left (west) at the "T" intersection, and drive to a cemetery with a parking lot on the left side of the road. Daniel Boone was familiar with the Marthasville area and selected a site on a tree-covered knoll overlooking Toque Creek to be his final resting place. Steps lead up a small knob to the monument, which still stands as a tribute to the old fighting Quaker. In 1845 a group of developers persuaded the surviving Boone relatives to move the remains of Daniel and his wife back to Kentucky, where they were reburied in a Frankfort cemetery. There is some skepticism that the remains are actually that of Daniel Boone; however, for now, exhuming the graves for possible identification has been ruled out.

Return to MO 94, and after another 2 miles, the town of **Marthasville** provides a popular access point for the Katy Trail and a variety of services. Founded in 1766, the town was originally a French village called La Charrette.

Massive dolomite cliffs provide an impressive backdrop to the colorful sugar maple trees in autumn.

Located at the mouth of Charrette Creek, it was a convenient place for hunting, trapping, and trading with the Indians. The village was the westernmost settlement of white men when the Lewis and Clark Expedition went up the Missouri River in 1804 and when it returned in 1806. After the purchase of the Louisiana Territory in 1803, the French villagers of Charrette began selling their land claims to Americans. The French settlement had become an American one when Dr. John Young refounded the town, named it for his wife, Martha, and advertised its founding in the *Missouri Gazette* of St. Louis on June 21, 1817.

Continue on MO 94 another 10.5 miles to a parking area on the left. This stop is the only roadside view of the Missouri River other than that in the town of Hermann. With its confined, single channel, the river is traveling faster now than in the days of Lewis and Clark. In the cold of winter, when the temperature remains below freezing for several days, ice floes form on the river. Although too small to support anything but a bird, their circular shapes are interesting to watch as they go floating by.

Travel another 15 miles on MO 94 to the junction with MO 19. A 7-mile side trip west on MO 94 leads to the most dramatic stretch of bluffs along the Missouri River in Missouri. Towering dolomite cliffs rise over the Missouri

River valley and parallel the highway for 3 miles. The Missouri Department of Conservation has purchased a section of this impressive feature, now called **Grand Bluffs Conservation Area.** Access to the area is reached by following the entrance sign at the west end of the bluff and turning north on Bluffton Road and proceeding 0.2 mile to a parking lot on the right. A 1-mile trail, somewhat strenuous at first, has been developed that takes you up to the top of the bluff where a wooden deck provides a spectacular view of the Missouri River bottoms. October is a particularly rewarding time, when the sugar maples turn crimson red against the white cliffs. Returning to MO 19, you again pass through the town of Rhineland, which after the devastation of the 1993 flood, was moved into the hills. Access to Katy Trail State Park is also provided in Rhineland.

HERMANN

At the junction of MO 94 and 19, turn south and proceed to **Hermann.** As you cross the Missouri River valley, notice the deep scours on both sides of the highway. During the Great Flood of 1993, the river broke through a levee upstream and for a period of several weeks reclaimed some of its historic course, taking out the highway in the process.

Hermann's Octoberfest is a popular attraction complete with parades, pageants, foods, and music celebrating the town's German ancestry.

In 1837 a group of German immigrants landed on the rugged south shore of the Missouri River to establish Hermann. The town was named to honor a Germanic hero (called Arminius by the Romans, but Hermann in modern German) who in A.D. 9 gathered a force of Germans and crushed an army of 15,000 to 18,000 veteran Roman soldiers. The victory saved the Germans from being enslaved by the Romans.

Soon after their arrival on the south shore, the immigrants cleared the steep wooded hills of the northern Ozark settlement and established vineyards. By 1870 Hermann had become the second-largest wine-producing region in the United States. The community endeavored to preserve its ancestry and culture by building homes, churches, schools, and wineries in traditional German-style architecture; many of these structures still stand today.

Each spring and fall the streets are crowded with visitors during Maifest and Octoberfest, when many of the old houses are opened for tours. There are also pageants and parades with German bands and folk dancing. The historic wineries of Hermannhof, Stone Hill, Bias, and Adam Puchta display their products and serve them with traditional German foods. In addition to the popular festivals in May and October, various gift shops, restaurants, and historic sites are open year-round, which offers an alternative for those who would rather visit Hermann when it is less crowded.

For more information about things to do in Hermann, visit the Welcome Center at the Hermann Area Chamber of Commerce, which is open April through October 9:00 A.M. to 5:00 P.M., November through March 9:30 A.M. to 4:00 P.M., and Sunday year-round 11:00 A.M. to 4:00 P.M. Be sure to pick up a city map showing points of interest in Hermann.

Boonslick Country

COLUMBIA TO ARROW ROCK, MISSOURI

GENERAL DESCRIPTION: A 55-mile drive beginning in Columbia and heading west across the northern edge of the Ozarks through historic towns and trails.

SPECIAL ATTRACTIONS: Rock Bridge State Park, Eagle Bluffs Conservation Area, Columbia, Rocheport, Les Bourgeois Vineyards, Diana Bend, Overton Bottoms, Katy Trail State Park, Old Franklin State Historic Site, New Franklin, Boone's Lick State Historic Site, Missouri River, Santa Fe Trail, Boonville, and Arrow Rock; scenic views, hiking, camping, boating, fishing, hunting, fall colors, and wildlife viewing.

LOCATION: Northern Ozarks. The drive begins on Missouri Highway 163 at the junction of U.S. Highway 63 south of Columbia.

DRIVE ROUTE NUMBERS: U.S. Interstate 70; U.S. Highways 63 and 40; and Missouri Highways 5, 87, 41, 163, 187, 240, K, and BB.

CAMPING: Finger Lakes State Park has 35 campsites with modern showering facilities and water. Water is shut off from November 1 through March 31. Arrow Rock State Historic Site has 22 basic and 23 improved sites with a dump station and modern rest rooms. Pine Ridge Recreation Area has basic campsites and a pit toilet.

SERVICES: All services at Columbia and Boonville. Food and bed-and-breakfasts at Rocheport and Arrow Rock.

NEARBY ATTRACTIONS: Finger Lakes State Park; Rocky Fork Lakes and Three Creeks conservation areas; and State Capitol and Runge Conservation Nature Center (in Jefferson City).

THE DRIVE

This drive skirts along the northern edge of the Ozarks over a landscape that was once buried under a massive glacier. This is the only part of the Ozarks that was glaciated, and that occurred more than 950,000 years ago. Traditionally this has been called the Kansan glacial period, the second in a series of four major ice advances over the three-million-year period called the Ice Age. Each period was named after the present-day states where these glacial fronts pretty much ended. The first was the Nebraskan, then the Kansan, next the Illinoisan,

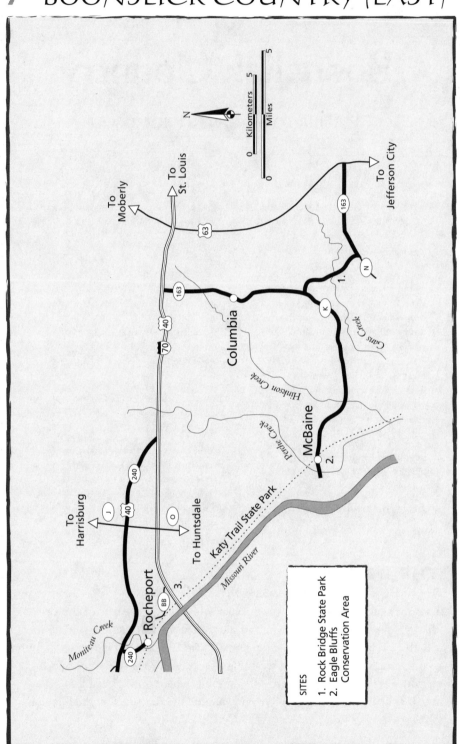

SITES
1. Rock Bridge State Park
2. Eagle Bluffs
   Conservation Area

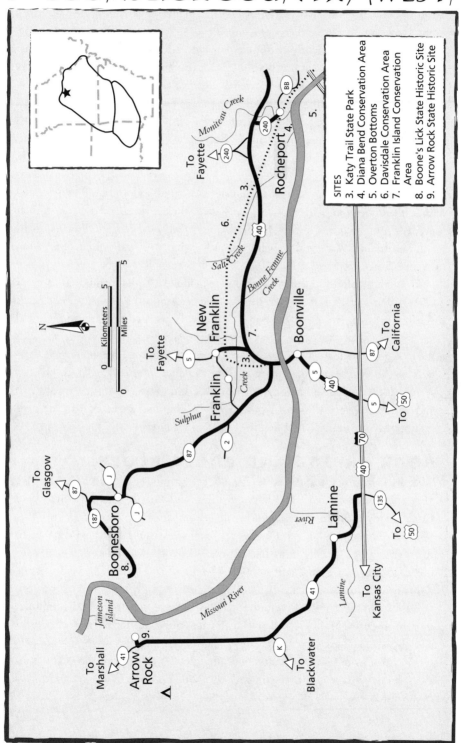

SITES
3. Katy Trail State Park
4. Diana Bend Conservation Area
5. Overton Bottoms
6. Davisdale Conservation Area
7. Franklin Island Conservation Area
8. Boone's Lick State Historic Site
9. Arrow Rock State Historic Site

and last the Wisconsinan glaciation, which melted away about 10,000 years ago. However, recent studies cast doubt on the idea that there were only four major glaciations; currently textbooks refer to early glaciers as "pre-Illinoisan."

Imagine a wall of ice up to a mile thick leveling everything in its path. As the massive ice flowed along, it carried silt, clay, sand, gravel, and a few boulders (collectively called glacial till), leaving them behind as the climate warmed and the glacier receded. Some rocks found in this area can be traced back to what is now Minnesota and Canada. Some car-sized boulders were ground smooth by the tremendous pressure and friction of transport.

Ahead of these glacial advances, the landscape was much different than it is today. Immediately south of the glacier was tundra, dominated by ground-hugging lichens and mosses; farther south were spruce and fir forests that graded into birch and pine. The gradations continued even farther south to oak and hickory forests that were found in what is now Louisiana and Mississippi.

Animals that lived in this colder climate included 20-foot ground sloths, giant beavers that were 4 feet high at the shoulder, mastodons and mammoths, huge versions of bison and musk ox, horses and camels, and giant American lions and saber-toothed cats, to name a few. These unusual animals became extinct with the changes in climate and habitat and early man's hunting pressure.

Today it may seem that there is little evidence of past glacial events; but search along eroded soil banks, plowed fields, and gravel-bottomed streambeds and you may just find one of those smooth, rounded rocks of pink or grey granite that was transported here by a glacier more than 950,000 years ago.

ROCK BRIDGE AND EAGLE BLUFFS

The drive begins southeast of Columbia at the junction of US 63 and MO 163. Head west on MO 163 about 5 miles and turn left at the entrance of **Rock Bridge State Park.** Follow the short drive to a parking area that accesses the rock bridge and Devil's Icebox. Follow the trail a short distance to the rock bridge. Actually more like a tunnel, the rock bridge has a 15-foot ceiling, is 150 feet long, and is from 50 to 75 feet wide. This natural bridge is the remnant of a limestone cave that collapsed, leaving only a section of the ceiling still standing. The trail continues to Devil's Icebox, a sinkhole that empties into an underground cave system. Devil's Icebox has so far been explored for a total passage length of 6 miles. Only experienced spelunkers who obtain permission from the park superintendent are allowed to explore the cave's interior. The western part of this state park also contains three trails covering a total of 4.5 miles.

A family explores Devil's Icebox, a sinkhole whose roof has collapsed.

Return to MO 163 and continue west to MO K. A side trip of about 7 miles leads to **Eagle Bluffs Conservation Area.** This is a relatively new acquisition by the Missouri Department of Conservation. It is the largest wetland area in the United States that uses treated municipal wastewater (from Columbia) to supplement its water needs. The area was nearly completed and operational when it was devastated by the Great Flood of 1993. Sections of newly built levees, designed to hold water in pools for waterfowl use, were overtopped and washed away. As of this writing, the 4,156-acre complex is almost totally repaired. In addition to providing feeding and resting areas for migrating ducks and geese, the area will eventually have hiking trails and viewing blinds along the levees and in a marsh, allowing visitors to observe wildlife firsthand. A short auto tour route offers good viewing as more wildlife become accustomed to seeing vehicles. Whether planned or by coincidence, a pair of American bald eagles have recently adopted Eagle Bluffs Conservation Area. They raised their first young in 1999! The area is used for outdoor classroom studies by nearby schools. Above the prominent cliff and upland overlooking the vast wetland development, the Missouri Department of Conservation plans to develop a loop hiking trail with observation decks that will provide sweeping views of the Missouri River valley.

Before entering Eagle Bluffs, the road crosses over **Katy Trail State Park.** Beginning in St. Charles, this state park is 235 miles long and 60 feet wide, making it the longest, narrowest state park in the United States. This reconditioned bed of the old Missouri-Kansas-Texas Railroad (MKT) was purchased by the late Edward D. "Ted" Jones Jr. and donated to the State of Missouri for a state park. The MKT, nicknamed "Katy" Trail, is now a popular hiking-biking trail extending from St. Charles to Boonville and southwest to Sedalia. An abandoned railroad spur from Columbia to the Katy Trail is being developed by the city as a hiking-biking route to the main trail.

COLUMBIA TO ROCHEPORT

Return to MO 163 and proceed northwards into **Columbia.** Settlers began to arrive here as far back as 1819, but it was not until 1836 that the settlement really began to grow. New arrivals came largely from Kentucky, attracted by the area's similarity in soils and landscape to their Madison County, Kentucky, homeland. Columbia is the seat of Boone County, which was formed in 1820. This was almost nine months before Missouri's official entrance into the union on August 10, 1821, making the county older than the state. At the time Boone County was formed, members of the legislature were wearing black arm bands to mourn the death of Daniel Boone on September 26, 1820; naming the county in his honor seemed a fitting tribute.

A biker exits the only tunnel along the 225-mile Katy Trail State Park.

It is said that Columbia was probably named after the county seat of Adair County, Kentucky, in the hope that it, too, would be a county seat. One of the most popular names in the United States, "Columbia" has been used in some thirty-two of the fifty states. By the 1840s Columbia was steadily growing into a prosperous town, serving as a retail center for a wide area. It was also in the 1840s that the most influential event in all of Columbia's history came about—the acquisition and organization of the University of Missouri. This established Columbia as a center of education. Today the university's Columbia campus enrolls more than 22,000 students and specializes in teaching, research, and extension services. Two other colleges, Stephens College and Columbia College, help to make Columbia worthy of its nickname, "College Town, U.S.A." To obtain information about events and points of interest in Columbia, visit the City of Columbia Convention and Visitor Bureau (see Appendix A for address and phone number).

The next stop is **Rocheport.** Continue on MO 163 to I–70 and travel west on the interstate for about 2 miles until it intersects US 40 at exit 121. (An alternative is to continue on the interstate to exit 115 and follow MO BB into Rocheport.) US 40 was America's first highway west and begins at the docks in Baltimore, Maryland. Travel west on US 40 for 8 miles to MO Spur 240 and proceed south for a mile to Rocheport. Founded in 1825, the settlement was first intended to be called "Rockport," but the name was changed to "Rocheport" at the insistence of a French missionary who happened to be in the area. The name refers to a large rock outcrop just west of the town. The Missouri River once flowed against this rocky point, creating a safe harbor just below it. Moniteau Creek, or "Creek of the Great Spirit," still flows by this rocky point today.

During their expedition up the Missouri River, Lewis and Clark landed here in June 1804 and explored the surrounding countryside. They noted the "painted rocks" in their journal as being "very remarkable. They are covered with strange and uncouth hieroglyphics and representations. We were prevented from making a careful inspection by reason of the presence of so many ferocious rattlesnakes, which are very venomous at this season of the year, and which were crawling among the rocks in great numbers."

After settlement, the town grew along with the steamboat transportation on the river. Nothing remains of the large tobacco and lumber warehouses that once occupied the busy dock area. During the Civil War, Rocheport was raided by both Confederate and Union troops. The town was also the site of important Underground Railroad efforts to aid runaway slaves in their escape northward. The popular harbor is now gone because the Missouri

River, having shifted about a quarter of a mile south, no longer flows against the rocky point.

Today Rocheport is an attractive historic site with restored nineteenth-century homes and buildings. Restaurants, a bookstore, and shops are found about town, and a winery is perched nearby on the high bluffs overlooking the river valley. The popular Katy Trail State Park occupies the old Missouri-Kansas-Texas Railroad bed along the south side of town. Bike rentals, refreshments, a rest room, and parking are found along the trail. Be sure to take the short walk west to see Moniteau Creek and the only tunnel along the Katy Trail. The tunnel is an impressive 243 feet in length. Just before the tunnel, a trail to the left leads to the Diana Bend Overlook. A boardwalk leads to a deck at the edge of a marsh-viewing area. There is also a trail straight up a very steep hill to an overlook deck with a nice view of Diana Bend Conservation Area. If you feel comfortable climbing a series of stairs, this trail is for you.

While in Rocheport, a visit to **Les Bourgeois Vineyards** offers visitors a taste of some of the Show-Me State's finest award-winning wines, excellent bistro cuisine, and beautiful scenery. At the stop sign in Rocheport, turn left and follow MO BB toward I–70. In a short distance, Les Bourgeois Vineyards appears on the right. A recently completed restaurant offers a great view of the Missouri River and surrounding landscape. The wetlands across the river is called Overton Bottoms and is jointly owned by the U.S. Fish and Wildlife Service and the U.S. Army Corps of Engineers. **Diana Bend Conservation Area** is one of the tracts purchased after the Great Flood of 1993. As part of the Big Muddy National Fish and Wildlife Refuge system, the goal is to eventually acquire tracts from Kansas City to St. Louis totaling 60,000 acres. This floodprone farmland will be returned to wetlands and bottomland forests to provide habitat for wildlife and recreational opportunities such as hunting, fishing, bird-watching, and hiking.

NEW FRANKLIN AND BOONESBORO

Return to US 40 and continue west, passing the 1,100-acre Diana Bend Conservation Area and 2,521-acre **Davisdale Conservation Area,** which features opportunities for hunting and fishing. In another 4 miles, the 1,517-acre **Franklin Island Conservation Area** lies to the south. The Missouri River once cut a channel on the area's north boundary and the land was surrounded by water. In 1952 the remnant chute was permanently closed by a flood-control levee. The conservation department purchased the land in 1978. The area offers fishing along streams and the Missouri River, plus deer and turkey hunting.

A side trip on MO 5 north to **New Franklin** provides an opportunity to visit numerous pre–Civil War homes. A self-guided tour brochure is available at the information center on the north side of the main street. The town was established in 1828 in the hills above the Missouri River valley after the original Franklin was destroyed by floodwaters.

As you continue on US 40/MO 5, a side trip on MO 87 goes to **Boone's Lick State Historic Site.** Just as you begin MO 87, a parking lot on the right contains a historical marker that describes the beginnings of the historic **Santa Fe Trail,** along with information about the Katy Trail.

Santa Fe Trail auto tour signs along the road mark the 900-mile route to Santa Fe, New Mexico. Its first travelers left Franklin in 1821. Just beyond this marker, a sign and flagpole marks the Old Franklin State Historic Site. The original town was established in 1816. Across the highway, notice the "blew hole." This 40-foot deep pond developed when surging flood waters "blew" out the levee and scoured this hole outside the Missouri River channel. Many such blew holes were created during the Great Flood of 1993. Follow MO 87 across the Missouri River valley 8.5 miles to Boonesboro. Notice the sand deposits and scour holes that resulted from the Great Flood of 1993.

Pass the town of **Boonesboro,** and after 1.2 miles, turn left on MO 187 and follow it for 2.5 miles to Boone's Lick State Historic Site. An interpretive center and short trail are provided. The site contains a natural saltwater spring—a salt lick—that was named for Nathan and Daniel M. Boone, sons of famed pioneer Daniel Boone. In the early 1800s the brothers processed salt here for other early settlements along the Missouri River. As a measure of the salt lick's importance, communities in, and indeed the region itself, were named for the family's and the lick's legendary status. Boone's Lick Road became an important thoroughfare for westward expansion in the Missouri Territory.

BOONVILLE TO ARROW ROCK

Return to US 40/MO 5 and enter **Boonville** by way of the Boonslick Bridge. A walkway on the bridge connects the Katy Trail as it heads south to Sedalia. Boonville was established in 1817 as a river port and its merchants, along with fur trappers and traders, explorers, soldiers, and educators, contributed to the opening of western lands for settlement. An important battle in the western campaign of the Civil War was fought just 4 miles downstream on June 7, 1861. Confederate soldiers were defeated by Union forces at the battle of Boonville, and Missouri was preserved for the Union. A well-known Boonville landmark, the now closed Kemper Military School and College, is located at

Arrow Rock's historic Lyceum Theatre provides summer plays performed by nationally known professional actors.

Center Avenue and Third Street. Founded in 1844 by Federick Kemper, it was the oldest boys' school and military academy west of the Mississippi River.

Continue on US 40/MO 5 through Boonville to I–70 and follow the interstate west for 5 miles to exit 98 and MO 41. Once on MO 41, follow the signs 13 miles to **Arrow Rock. Arrow Rock State Historic Site** is located on the right just before you enter the town. A visitor center interprets Boonslick country in the early nineteenth century. The nearby Arrow Rock bluff was a significant landmark and a crossing place on the Missouri River for Indians, explorers, and early westward travelers. The town's name first appeared in 1732 on a French map drawn by D'Anville, who called it **Pierre a Fleche,** or "Rock of Arrows." Lewis and Clark passed through this area on June 9, 1804. Clark recorded in his journal, "We set out early, and reached a cliff called Arrow Rock, near to which is a prairie called the Prairie of Arrows and Arrow Creek . . . " In 1819 the explorer Stephen Long reported that the bluff was so named because the Indians gathered flint from the bluff for arrowheads.

Located above the Missouri River and across from Boone's Lick, Arrow Rock became an important trading center for area farmers and, as an outfitting town, provided supplies for westward expeditions on the Santa Fe Trail. By the mid-1800s, Arrow Rock's population had grown to more than 1,000. By the late nineteenth century, more modern means of transportation had replaced river travel, and Arrow Rock declined in importance. Fires devastated the business district in 1873 and again in 1901, hastening the decline. Today Arrow

Rock is a quiet village where visitors to the site often outnumber the town's population of seventy.

Many of the buildings have been restored in Arrow Rock, and walking tours are offered from Memorial Day through Labor Day, as well as by special arrangement during the rest of the year. Special events and historical reenactments are held at different times throughout the year. Of particular note is the Baptist Church, which was built in 1872 and has since been converted into a summer theater. Now called the Lyceum Theatre, it houses Broadway-caliber shows featuring professional actors from around the country.

Lake of the Ozarks

BAGNELL DAM TO HA HA TONKA, MISSOURI

GENERAL DESCRIPTION: A 22-mile drive starting at Bagnell Dam and the Lake of the Ozarks. Attractive features along the way include picturesque hills, bluffs, glades, caves, and springs.

SPECIAL ATTRACTIONS: Osage River, Bagnell Dam, Lake of the Ozarks, Ha Ha Tonka and Lake of the Ozarks state parks, Castle Ruins, Ozark Caverns, and Grand Glaize Recreation Area; Dogwood Festival; wildlife viewing, camping, hiking, wildflower displays, fall colors, scenic views, fishing, hunting, boating, horseback riding, and swimming.

LOCATION: Northern Ozarks. The drive begins at the junction of U.S. Highway 54 and Missouri Highway W.

DRIVE ROUTE NUMBERS: U.S. Highway 54 and Missouri Highways 42, 134, A, D, and W.

CAMPING: Lake of the Ozarks State Park has 230 tent and trailer campsites, both basic and improved. Facilities include a dumping station, modern rest rooms, a laundry, and a store. Four group camps are available for use by nonprofit organizations. Reservations must be made in advance with the park superintendent. Each group camp accommodates from 40 to 200 campers and includes sleeping cabins, rest rooms with showers, a dining lodge with kitchen, a playing field, and swimming facilities. Ha Ha Tonka State Park offers picnicking only.

SERVICES: All services at Osage Beach and Camdenton.

NEARBY ATTRACTIONS: Bennett Spring State Park, Fiery Forks Conservation Area, Bridal Cave (commercial), and State Capitol and Runge Conservation Nature Center (in Jefferson City).

THE DRIVE

The **Lake of the Ozarks** is a resort-based destination for water recreation, restaurants, roadside gift shops, shopping malls, family rides, and country music halls. The lake also draws people looking for second homes and retirement homes. Amidst all of this development remain special areas where one can experience and enjoy what the rugged Osage River Hills have to offer.

The Osage Indians were the first inhabitants of this region. East of here, a village site remained as late as 1822. The first white man to record his visits to

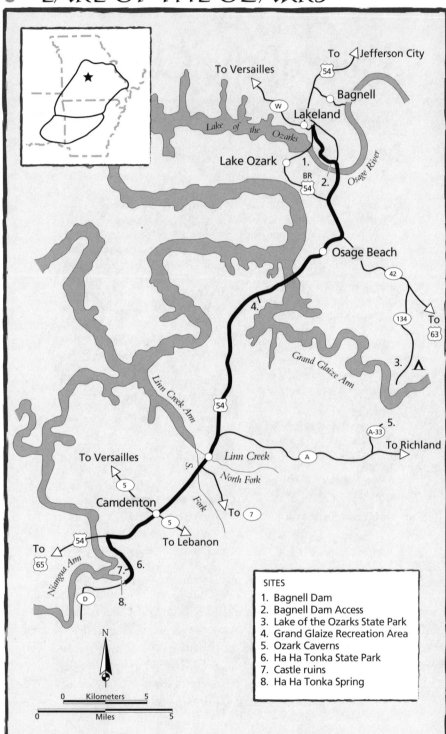

SITES

1. Bagnell Dam
2. Bagnell Dam Access
3. Lake of the Ozarks State Park
4. Grand Glaize Recreation Area
5. Ozark Caverns
6. Ha Ha Tonka State Park
7. Castle ruins
8. Ha Ha Tonka Spring

this area was Zebulon M. Pike, who with a group of Osageans, traveled up the Osage River in 1806. Like the other large rivers in the Ozarks, the Osage served as a highway for settlers into the roadless interior. Special steamboats that required only about a foot of water in which to float were built for the Ozark rivers in the mid-1800s. The boats were also built shorter than their big river counterparts to navigate the many sharp bends. These paddle wheelers traveled as far upriver on the Osage as Warsaw, Missouri. The Osage River remained important for river traffic well into the twentieth century.

The main industry in the early years was cutting timber and making railroad ties. The ties were made along the Osage and adjacent rivers and then floated down to the city of Bagnell, the site of the closest railroad spur, for shipment.

In 1923 a study was conducted on damming the Osage, Niangua, and Glaize Rivers. Six years later, Union Electric Company began to build Bagnell Dam across the Osage River. Four months into construction, the stock market crashed, initiating the Great Depression. Because this was just about the only major construction project going on in the country, it drew some 4,600 workers to the area. Many earned only a dollar a day working on the dam, which took only two years to complete. When the dam was finished in 1931, the water backed up and formed a channel 92 miles long, ranging from 0.5 to 2 miles wide, and creating over 1,370 miles of shoreline, more than the state of California. The lake covered 58,500 acres, forming the shape of a ragged-looking dragon, a symbol promoted by businesses in the area.

BAGNELL DAM

The drive begins at the junction of US 54 and MO W at Lakeland. Turn onto MO W and proceed only 0.3 miles. The turn to **Bagnell Dam** is on the left. For a scenic view of the Lake of the Ozarks, bypass the turn and continue on US 54 to a pullout on the right side of the road. Continuing down the hill, the highway crosses over Bagnell Dam and into the town of **Lake Ozark,** the "Miracle Mile" of amusement, antique, and bric-a-brac, the oldest commercial development in the area to accommodate tourists.

Return to the side road that is highlighted by the sign UNION ELECTRIC DAM TOURS and follow it to the dam. In 0.6 mile, a picnic area overlooking the lake is provided by Union Electric. After another half a mile the road descends, with some sharp turns, to the bottom of the hill at the Osage River floodplain. Turn right and proceed to Bagnell Dam. There are overlooks near the dam, and tours show the inner workings of the hydroelectric power plant. When the spillway gates are open, there is sometimes a frenzy of avian activity as gulls, terns, and great blue herons dive at injured or stunned fish that have been swept through the rushing waters.

Below the dam, snagging for paddlefish is a popular event in the spring. Since paddlefish feed only on microscopic plankton, they will not take baited hooks. Fisherman, using special hooks, snag the fish bodies, which can weigh more than a hundred pounds and can be up to 7 feet long. The paddlefish has declined drastically from its former nationwide range due to destruction of its habitat and overfishing. The impoundments of the Osage River at the Lake of the Ozarks and upstream at Truman Lake eliminated many of the paddlefish's spawning areas, which were the gravel bars along the river and its bordering streams. Fortunately, the Missouri Department of Conservation has been successful in its efforts to spawn and raise paddlefish for release into their historic waters.

Commonly seen along the shore below Bagnell Dam, great blue herons feed and search for nesting materials.

In the winter another type of "angler" can be seen patrolling the waters below the dam—the bald eagle. Eagles fly all around the lake, but when the surface water freezes, they concentrate below the dam where the water remains open. Eagles perch in trees along the river and occasionally swoop down to snatch a stunned fish that has gone through one of the power plant's turbines. A majority of these eagles only winter here and spend their summers in Minnesota, Wisconsin, and Canada. Eagles had not nested in Missouri or most of the other lower forty-eight states since the 1950s, due to habitat destruction and the widespread use of DDT. DDT, a long-lived insecticide, was washed by rainfall from cropland into lakes and streams, where it entered the food chain and grew increasingly concentrated as it passed from plankton to aquatic insects to fish to eagles. DDT in birds was discovered to reduce the amount of calcium in egg shells, allowing the eggs to be crushed by the birds' own weight during incubation. After the banning of DDT use in the United States, meat-eating birds started making a comeback. Now with an annual winter count of more than 2,000 eagles, Missouri ranks second only to the state of Washington with the most eagles in the lower forty-eight. Thanks to a ten-year release program of young eagles into Missouri by the conservation department, by 1995 there were twenty-three active bald eagle nests, and their number promises to grow. The bald eagle has returned to nest in the Ozarks.

Continue down the river road to **Bagnell Dam Access,** where boats may be launched into the Osage River. The access also provides an opportunity to see wildlife feeding along the river. After half a mile the road meets US 54; turn right onto the highway and cross the Osage River Bridge. After climbing a long, steep hill, the highway follows a ridge bordered with an 8-mile-long development of tourist attractions.

In a mile, a sidetrip on MO 42 leads to **Lake of the Ozarks State Park.** In 3.3 miles MO 134, on the right, enters the 17,087-acre state park, the largest in Missouri. The park was originally established by the National Park Service in the mid-1930s, following the damming of the Osage River and the creation of the lake. The recreational area was turned over to the state in 1946. Lake of the Ozarks State Park has ten hiking trails that lead through dense oak-hickory forests and lush ravines, across open glades with showy wildflowers, and along towering bluffs overlooking the lake. There are also two equestrian trails and trail rides are available at the park stables for a nominal fee. A rental service provides boats for fishing, skiing, and taking a self-guided aquatic trail, marked by buoys, which has been developed on the Grand Glaize arm of the lake. Ask for brochures at the park office upon entering the park.

OSAGE BEACH TO CAMDENTON

Return to US 54 and continue west through **Osage Beach.** This 8-mile-long community has become the shopping destination for tourists from as far away as Chicago and Indianapolis. Cross the Grand Glaize Bridge and continue about 3 miles to the **Grand Glaize Recreation Area** on the left. It provides swimming, picnicking, rest rooms, and the Rocky Top Trail with two 1.5-mile loops.

The south end of Lake of the Ozarks State Park is reached from MO A. Continue on US 54 to the junction of MO A. A side trip leads to **Ozark Caverns,** which is part of the park. You can reach it by traveling 6.5 miles to MO A-33 and following the signs another 2 miles to the caverns. A small parking lot is next to the visitor center. A naturalist is on duty to lead daily cave tours throughout the summer months and at varying times the rest of the year. This cave tour is unique in that visitors are given their own lights to carry. You feel like an explorer entering the cave for the first time.

The Coakley Hollow Self-Guiding Trail interprets a variety of habitats including a rare Ozark fen. Fens are open areas that resemble meadows but are fed year-round by seep water percolating down through the hills and emerging at their base. Special plants grow in these fens and nowhere else. If you do not have time to walk the mile-long trail, be sure to at least see the fen. Walk behind the visitor center and follow the path to a boardwalk overlooking the fen.

Return to US 54 and continue west. You will pass through what is left of **Linn Creek.** Once the seat of Camden County, the townsite that once supported 500 residents was inundated when the water rose to form the Lake of the Ozarks. The residents of Linn Creek fought the lake project in court, but lost. The town was moved up the hill 3 miles west to the newly formed town of Camdenton, which became the new county seat. Thirty-two cemeteries and seventy-four scattered graves were also relocated. **Camdenton,** often called the hub city of the lake area, is home to the Dogwood Festival. This event, which is timed to coincide with the blooming of the flowering dogwood, was started in 1950. Around the third weekend in April, the white-bracted flowers of the dogwood are at their peak. They are particularly visible in the understory of the tall oaks and hickories because the hardwoods are then only just beginning to leaf out. Of course, nature does not always cooperate, and an early spring sometimes causes the festival's main attraction to look a bit faded. This does not dampen spirits, however, as there are plenty of activities for all ages.

MO 5 heads north from the center of Camdenton and in about 2 miles passes the Camdenton Office of the Missouri Department of Conservation, located off Lake Road 5-88 on the left. Maps and information about recreational opportunities on public lands are provided. The lake road continues to Bridal Cave, a commercial cave that offers tours and is also a popular location for wedding ceremonies.

HA HA TONKA STATE PARK

Proceed west out of Camdenton on US 54 for 2 miles to MO D and follow the signs to **Ha Ha Tonka State Park.** The name is said to be an Osage Indian phrase, meaning "Laughing Water." This probably referred to the sound made by Ha Ha Tonka Spring as it once cascaded over rocks on its course to the Niangua River. With the establishment of the lake, the spring now forms a pool, and the rocks are silent. The spring issues an average of forty-eight million gallons of water a day, making it the twelfth-largest spring in Missouri. The Spring Trail has a barrier-free section that goes to a viewing platform overlooking the spring branch. A boardwalk extends beyond this point to the spring.

Ha Ha Tonka is considered to be one of the most outstanding combinations of geologic and human history in the Ozarks, with both in an area of less than 1 square mile. Geologically, the Ha Ha Tonka area is a classic example of collapsed structures in a karst landscape. *Karst* is a term taken from an area in the former Yugoslavia that is known for its solution features of sinks, caves, under-

Visitors stand at the doorway to the ruins of a European-style castle at Ha Ha Tonka State Park.

ground streams, and large springs. The Missouri Ozarks, because of its large areas of dolomite and limestone, are also known for its numerous karst features. They include: Counterfeiters', Robbers', and River Caves; Dry Hollow; Natural Bridge; Devil's Promenade; Devil's Kitchen; and Red and Black sinks. Pick up a trail map at the park office or at the Castle parking lot for directions to these fascinating features.

Ha Ha Tonka Spring was one of the first features to lure humans to the area. The Osage Indians used the large sinkhole southwest of the natural bridge for tribal powwows. Indians from Minnesota prairies and the Teton Indians were known to winter here by the "Great Spring." Daniel Boone and his son Nathan visited the area in 1801, when they followed the Niangua drainage to the spring. Reportedly their first winter's catch of pelts was confiscated by the Osages; the Boones returned the following year and kept their pelts by hiding them in nearby caves.

Counterfeiters' and Robbers' Caves were named for a local group of counterfeiters and robbers operating here in the 1830s. In 1903 Robert M. Snyder, a wealthy Kansas City businessman, visited the area on a fishing expedition and conceived of a private retreat having as its centerpiece a magnificent European-style mansion or castle. In 1905 stonemasons from Scotland began construction with stone quarried from about a quarter of a mile away. Snyder did not live to see the completion of the castle, for on October 27 of that year he was killed in an automobile accident near his Kansas City home. The castle stood unfinished until his son completed it in 1922. In 1942, however, sparks from a fireplace caught the roof's wooden shingles on fire and the building was gutted. Then, after many years of semicommercialization and general neglect, the castle ruins were acquired by The Nature Conservancy and sold to the state to become Ha Ha Tonka State Park. The impressive karst features of the park have been designated a state natural area.

With a self-guided tour brochure in hand, be sure to hike the three-quarter-mile Turkey Pen Hollow Trail off MO D in the park. The trail passes through a savanna, which is a scattering of open-grown trees with a grassy understory, and crosses interesting glades with weather-worn rocks. The glades are rich in showy wildflowers from April through October. In the spring look for Indian paintbrush, yellow star grass, downy phlox, and wild indigo. Early summer is ablaze with large stands of yellow coneflower, butterfly weed, and Missouri primrose.

9

Two Rivers

SALEM TO BLUE SPRING, MISSOURI

GENERAL DESCRIPTION: A 64-mile drive that starts at Salem and travels south into the scenic river hills of the Current and Jacks Fork Rivers.

SPECIAL ATTRACTIONS: Alley and Round Springs, Current and Jacks Fork Rivers, Devils Well, Akers Ferry, Blue Spring Natural Area, Rocky Falls, Ozark Trail, and Virgin Pine Forest; scenic views, fall and spring colors, hiking, canoeing, swimming, camping, fishing, hunting, and large springs. (Exceptional drive for fall colors in October and white-flowering dogwoods in April.)

LOCATION: Central Ozarks. The drive begins at the junction of Missouri Highways 19, 32, and 72 on the south side of Salem.

DRIVE ROUTE NUMBERS: Missouri Highways 19, 106, KK, H, Y, and NN.

CAMPING: Akers (81 campsites), Round Spring (60 campsites), Alley Spring (187 campsites), Pultite (55 campsites), Two

Rivers (10 campsites), and Powder Mill (10 campsites) all have rest rooms and water and are maintained by the National Park Service. Other possibilities include Little Scotia Pond Campground and Picnic Area (14 campsites) and Loggers Lake Recreation Area (41 campsites) in the Mark Twain National Forest. Primitive camping is allowed in the Missouri Department of Conservation's Sunklands, Angeline, Rocky Creek, and Current River conservation areas.

SERVICES: All services at Salem and Eminence.

NEARBY ATTRACTIONS: Montauk State Park (trout fishing); Peck Ranch Conservation Area (includes five natural areas); Sunklands, Burr Oak Basin, Mill Mountain, and Cardareva Bluff natural areas (Missouri Department of Conservation); Jam Up Cave and Prairie Hollow Gorge natural areas; and Klepzig Mill (National Park Service).

THE DRIVE

The highway travels across a broad, gently rolling upland plains that is part of the Salem Plateau. As you head south, the plateau is deeply dissected by rugged hills whose steep slopes drain into spring-fed streams. Some of the largest springs in the United States—even in the world—are within this region.

75

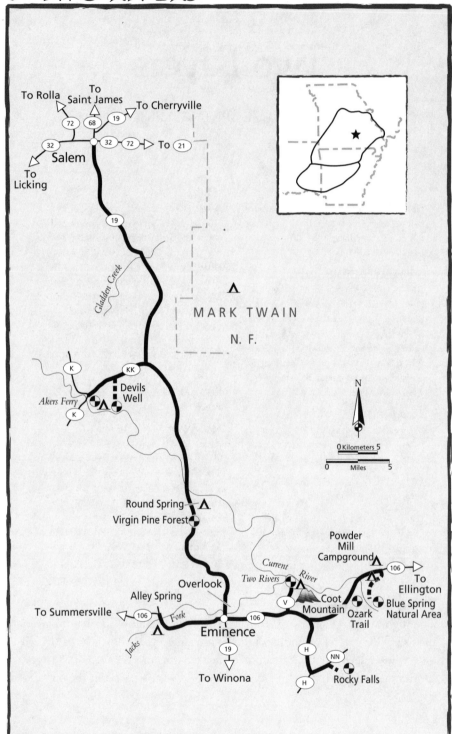

SALEM TO THE VIRGIN PINE FOREST

Begin the drive on the south side of Salem at the intersection of MO 19, 72, and 32. To the south, just beyond the intersection on the right is the Salem Ranger Station of the Mark Twain National Forest. It has information on nearby recreational opportunities in the national forest. **Salem,** with a population of about 5,000, is the northern gateway to the scenic riverways and the big springs country. Founded in 1851, Salem has had a long and steady growth as a mining and shopping center. The Tower Inn, a ten-story motel and shopping center, is a dominating landmark that can be seen for several miles.

About 7 miles south of Salem, as the road begins to curve along narrow ridges, notice the broad upland plains giving way to hill country. Shortleaf pine trees become more prominent, favoring the thin, cherty soils on south and west slopes. After 9 miles the road descends to **Gladden Creek.** Notice the prominent rock outcrop in the creek to the right of the bridge. Called Standing Rock, it is composed of sandstone that is so thoroughly cemented it is quartzlike, making it resistent to erosion. Gladden Creek is typical of many modern Ozark streams; it is gravel-choked and has a less-than-permanent flow. Longtime residents can recall that these smaller streams once contained deep pools for fishing and swimming; however, extensive logging and open-range grazing early in the 1900s caused considerable erosion of the hillsides. Heavy rains carried loads of chert gravel down the slopes and into the streams. Today there is less erosion, but it will take centuries for some of these streams to reclaim some semblance of their original character.

After another 9 miles, MO KK appears on the right. A side trip to see Devils Well and Akers Ferry is recommended. Just 2 miles down MO KK is a sign and entrance road on the left. The gravel road goes 2 miles to **Devils Well,** which is on the Ozarks Riverways. You can see the well by peering through a 2-foot-wide sinkhole opening to the underground lake 100 feet below. The lake is more than 400 feet wide and 100 feet deep and emerges a mile south at Cave Spring on the Current River. An estimated twenty-two million gallons of water per day flows through the sinkhole.

Return to MO KK and proceed almost 4 miles to **Akers Ferry.** The National Park Service provides a campground and access to the Current River. Akers Ferry, a commercial outfitter, rents canoes and sells supplies for float trips. Akers Ferry also operates a ferry crossing over the Current River for those traveling on MO K. The ferry has been in operation since the mid-1800s.

The **Current River** flows through the heart of the Missouri Ozarks for 133 miles to its confluence with the Black River in Arkansas. The Current River is fed by more springs than any other river in the Ozarks; this is evident in its

Onlookers watch Akers Ferry transporting vehicles across the Current River.

water quality. The Current, along with its tributary, the Jacks Fork, was protected by the establishment of the Ozark National Scenic Riverways Act on August 27, 1964, and is managed by the National Park Service. The Current River is rated the most popular river for recreational value in Missouri. Unfortunately, the summer months are crowded with canoes, kayaks, float tubes, and, farther down river, jet skis and johnboats. Increased regulations may be implemented to maintain a quality experience for all who enjoy the river. Because springs maintain the river's flow year-round, fall, winter, and spring can provide more solitude on the river. This particular stretch of the Current River is the most popular; a one-day float trip (lasting six to seven hours) from Baptist Camp near Montauk State Park to Akers Ferry can be arranged through several commercial operators in the area. Shorter or longer floats are also possible.

Back on MO 19, proceed another 11 miles to where the highway crosses the Current River. A bridge for pedestrians parallels the highway bridge; you can get to it by turning onto a campground road on the left, parking, and walking over to the bridge. The **Round Spring** entrance is just down the highway. Besides providing camping and a river access, a short trail with interpretive signs leads to the fourteenth-largest spring in Missouri. A daily flow of twenty-six million gallons emerges through a collapsed cave roof. Part of the roof remains intact as a natural bridge, beneath which the waters of the spring flow toward the nearby Current River. Round Spring Cave is located on the west side of the highway; guided tours are offered during the summer for a small fee.

The road climbs a steep hill after leaving Round Spring. A pullout on the right offers a dramatic view of the rugged wooded hills and narrow valleys of the Current River country. After 2 miles, you enter an area of old growth shortleaf pine trees known as **Virgin Pine Forest.** This native stand of towering pines, many more than 200 years old, extends for a mile along the highway and for 200 feet on either side of the center line. It was donated to the State Highway Department by Leo A. Drey, owner of Pioneer Forest and the largest private landowner in the state. Pine forests were once common in this part of the Ozarks, but extensive logging and fire suppression have eliminated most of them. Several public agencies are now working to manage some areas for native pine as a natural component of the Ozark forest. On the south boundary of the Virgin Pine Forest, an interpretive auto drive of 2 miles leads through part of the Pioneer Forest, a private, conservatively managed forest of about 160,000 acres. A self-guided tour brochure is available at an information box along the drive. A "Virgin Pine Walk" of approximately fifteen to twenty minutes provides close-up views of the towering pines.

After 8 miles, watch for a scenic overlook and parking lot on the left. On the eastern horizon, a fire tower marks the summit of Coot Mountain. This prominent hill and the ones surrounding it are volcanic in origin and are considered an outlier of the St. Francois Mountains, which are more than 50 miles to the northeast. One mile beyond this overlook, the Missouri Department of Conservation's Eminence Forest District office is located. It offers information describing recreational opportunities on M.D.C. lands in the area.

EMINENCE

Continue down the steep highway to the **Jacks Fork River** crossing, just north of Eminence. The Jacks Fork was named for John Jacks, a Shawnee Indian who settled near the headwaters of the river. The Jacks Fork has a permanent flow of 39 river miles, with much of it through dramatic steep-walled canyons. Beginning at the MO Y access, the river is most floatable during the higher water levels in spring. Just upstream from here, however, it can easily be floated from Alley Spring to where it joins the Current River, about 11 river miles below Eminence. Like the Current, the Jacks Fork is a river that is being loved to death, but by picking the right time of year, you can be rewarded with some very memorable experiences.

Eminence has a population of 582. Organized in 1841, it is the seat of Shannon County. The county was named after George "Pegleg" Shannon, who at age seventeen was the youngest member of the Lewis and Clark Expedition. He reportedly later lost a leg to an infection following a skirmish with Indians. Pioneers from Kentucky and Tennessee first settled this area in the 1820s. Missouri's first copper mine was opened near here by Joseph Slater in 1837. Eminence was first located farther north, along the Current River. The town was burned in the Civil War by guerrilla bands. After the war, Eminence was rebuilt at its present location by the Jacks Fork.

Proceed west on MO 106 through West Eminence, which was established by a lumber company in 1906. After 5 miles, the highway crosses the Jacks Fork and the **Alley Spring** section of the Ozark Riverways. An entrance on the right leads to a parking lot, picnic area, and path to Alley Spring and Mill. A turnoff just beyond this entrance allows easy access to the mill for elderly and disabled visitors. Alley Spring is the seventh-largest spring in Missouri, with an average of eighty-one million gallons passing through the millrace each day. In 1894 a three-story mill was completed with a steel turbine to drive the roller mill rather than the commonly seen waterwheel. The mill originally provided finely ground wheat flour for local farmers. Later its services expanded to include corn grinding, a sawmill, and an electrical generator for the community. A small museum in the mill house is open to visitors during the summer.

The ever-flowing Alley Spring discharges through a gate adjoining Alley Mill.

There are two hiking trails (1.5 and 0.3 miles) located near Alley Spring. Camping and access to the river is available on the other side of the highway.

Return to Eminence and continue on MO 106 east for 5 miles. A 3-mile side trip on MO V goes to **Two Rivers,** an Ozark Riverways campground and access to the Current River. While traveling to Two Rivers, watch for a large hill with a fire tower on top. This is Coot Mountain, which could be seen from the scenic overlook above Eminence. The fire tower is closed to visitors.

The highway ends at the base of a steep hill. It is here that the Jacks Fork flows into the Current River. An excellent view of this convergence is from the deck of the Two Rivers Store.

ROCKY FALLS, OZARK TRAIL, POWDER MILL, AND BLUE SPRING

Back on MO 106, proceed east another 2 miles and turn right onto MO H, and travel almost 4 miles to MO NN. Turn left and go another 2 miles, then turn right onto the gravel road for 0.3 mile to the entrance to the **Rocky Falls** parking lot. Follow the short trail down to the falls. Although best seen in the spring and after heavy rains, Rocky Falls Shut-Ins is impressive year-round. Here the waters of Rocky Creek tumble in a 40-foot cascade down a steep slope of pink to purple igneous rock. The large plunge pool at the base of the falls is a popular swimming hole during the hot summer months. A path along the right side of the falls leads to the top. Autumn is also an excellent time to visit, because the site supports a variety of colorful vegetation.

Returning to MO 106, turn right and head east for 5 miles. The road enters the Current River valley and provides scenic views of the broad valley, hills, and cliffs that continue to be reshaped by the carving action of the river. The trailhead for the Current River section of the **Ozark Trail** begins in this valley and heads south. Contact the Mark Twain National Forest for a map and access information. Just after the bridge, a road to the right leads to **Powder Mill.** Although the visitor center is presently closed, picnicking, camping, and access to the Current River are possible. At the end of the campground road, a 1-mile trail leads to Blue Spring.

You can also reach **Blue Spring** by returning to MO 106 and driving east for about 2 miles, then turning right onto a gravel road. The first part of the 2.5-mile road is steep and not recommended for vehicles pulling trailers. The well-maintained road is accessible by two-wheel-drive vehicles and ends at a parking lot. From here a half-mile walk affords glimpses of the Current River and eventually skirts along a roaring spring branch leading to Blue Spring. The Indians called it "the Spring of the Summer Sky." Of all the springs in the

Ozarks, this is certainly the bluest. Ranked sixth in Missouri, with a daily flow of ninety million gallons per day, it is also the deepest known spring in the Ozark region, with an explored depth of 256 feet. The intense blue color is caused by the extreme depth and angle of the emerging water and the scattering of blue light by minute particles of mineral or organic matter suspended in the water.

Blue Spring is a state natural conservation area and is owned by the Missouri Department of Conservation. A deck along one edge of the spring pool affords a view into the depths of the spring orifice. A short path to the left leads to an observation deck overlooking the intensely blue waters below. Blue Spring has been a popular attraction for generations. However, heavy usage caused the banks to be worn bare and the vegetation trampled. The conservation department decided to "harden" the site by establishing walkways and viewing platforms a few years ago. Although some feel that this took away from the pristine look of Blue Spring, the vegetation has come back and the banks have healed, giving the area a more natural look.

10

Big Spring

VAN BUREN TO BIG SPRING, MISSOURI

GENERAL DESCRIPTION: A 7-mile drive beginning in Van Buren, crossing the Current River following the Forest Service's Skyline Drive, and ending at Big Spring.

SPECIAL ATTRACTIONS: Van Buren, Ozark National Scenic Riverways, Skyline Drive, Big Spring, Big Spring Museum, Big Spring Pines Natural Area, and Mark Twain National Forest; floating, swimming, fishing, camping, hiking, boating, hunting, fall colors, and spring wildflowers.

LOCATION: East-central Ozarks. The drive begins in Van Buren on U.S. Highway 60 and ends at Big Spring.

DRIVE ROUTE NUMBERS: U.S. Highway 60, Missouri Highways 103 and Z, and Forest Road 3280.

CAMPING: Big Spring Recreation Area has more than 100 campsites with rest rooms, showers, playgrounds, water, barrier-free campsites, and boat access. Rental cabins are available by calling the Big Spring Lodge. In Van Buren, Watercress Spring Recreation Site has 17 campsites, rest rooms, picnicking, and boat access. Primitive camping is allowed in the national forest.

SERVICES: All services at Van Buren.

NEARBY ATTRACTIONS: Peck Ranch and Current River conservation areas; Spring and Two Rivers scenic drives; the Ozark Trail; and Irish Wilderness Area (Forest Service).

THE DRIVE

Van Buren is the headquarters for the National Park Service's Ozark National Scenic Riverways. The riverways system includes both the Current and the Jacks Fork, a total of 134 miles of managed river. To help protect the river systems, 80,788 acres of land (61,374 of them federally owned) border the rivers. The riverways were officially established in 1964.

Controversy over what to do with the Current River country began early in the 1900s. Some wanted to protect it in its "natural state," while others wanted to dam the river for hydroelectric power. The region began to draw more visitors in the 1920s and 1930s when the state of Missouri developed state parks at Montauk Springs, Round Spring, Alley Spring, and Big Spring. Love and passion for the river rose to a new level in the mid-1930s, when the

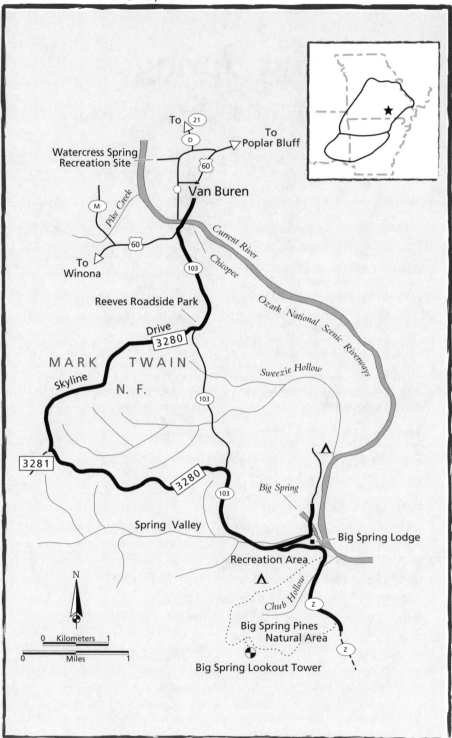

Big Spring

United States Corps of Engineers proposed damming the Current River. Editorials in the **St. Louis Post Dispatch** and **Kansas City Star** opposed the dam. The Missouri Conservation Commission and the Missouri Department of Conservation also opposed the dam and then-governor Forrest Smith announced there would be no dam, built on the Current River as long as he was in office.

Finally, on August 27, 1964, President Lyndon Johnson signed the act establishing the Ozark National Scenic Riverways. By mid-1966 the first tract was acquired. There was much bitterness and resentment among the local landowners who were against a national park. Missouri signed over the state parks at Round, Alley, and Big Springs in 1969, but kept Montauk. The national park was formally dedicated on June 10, 1972, when Tricia Nixon Cox "christened" the Ozark National Scenic Riverways by tossing a bouquet of flowers into the waters of Big Spring.

VAN BUREN TO THE SKYLINE DRIVE

The drive begins in **Van Buren,** a small town that serves as an outfitter for canoes, kayaks, float tubes, jet skis, and johnboats. Summer months often find the town and the river overcrowded with recreational users. Permanent springs maintain the river's flow year-round, so it is possible to enjoy the river in fall, spring, and winter when there is more solitude and space.

Probably the most historic building in Van Buren is the **Carter County Courthouse,** located on the square. The original building, built in 1837, was a two-story, wood-frame, four-room building held together with wooden pins. This early courthouse was located on the west bank of the Current River, half a mile west and across the river from the present county seat. It was used when Carter County was part of Ripley County, before the counties separated in 1859. A commission voted to retain Van Buren as the county seat. In 1871 court officials authorized a new courthouse to be built on the square. It was built with hand-planed pine lumber on a rock foundation.

Several proposals to build a new courthouse were defeated early in the twentieth century. Instead the 1871 building was remodeled, expanded, and covered with native cobblestones. It is the only courthouse in Missouri known to have been built with cobblestones. The building was last remodeled and expanded in 1936. Behind the courthouse is a log cabin that dates back to 1851. It was moved there in 1959 to commemorate the county's first one hundred years.

In 1994 a new bridge and a bypass around Van Buren were completed. A pedestrian/bicycle walkway is provided on the new bridge, affording a view of the Current River looking upstream. The Current River was once used to float

The unique Carter County Courthouse is built with cobblestones gathered from the surrounding area.

railroad ties and logs from a huge sawmill in West Eminence. The log rafts were collected just downstream from Van Buren at a place called Chicopee. From there the wood was transported to the west. Much of this wood was used in the railroads that crossed the Great Plains. The log drives were not popular with local residents because logjams often blocked the river for days, causing property to be flooded and barring passage across the river. The government imposed regulations in 1915 restricting the use of the Current River for floating ties and logs. The last recorded log drive on the Current was in 1935.

The National Park Service visitor center here is called the Watercress Headquarters. You can reach it by heading north along Main Street and turning left (west) on a road that leads to the visitor center, a Forest Service campground, and river access nearby at Watercress Park. Open from 8:00 A.M. to 4:30 P.M. Monday to Friday, the headquarters offers information on local natural, historic, and recreational sites along with a selection of books, tapes, and other items.

To continue on the drive, take US 60 south across the Current River and immediately turn left onto MO 103. The first mile is a steep climb up an unnamed Ozark mountain. On the right, Reeves Roadside Park, maintained by the Missouri Highway and Transportation Commission, provides a picnic area and a place to rest. Take FR 3280 on the right and begin the **Skyline Drive.** This 4-mile loop provides fifteen scenic vistas of the surrounding Ozark hills. About midway along the drive, FR 3281 heads southwest and in just over a mile, crosses the Ozark Trail. Just before joining MO 103, the last two vistas reveal Big Spring Lookout Tower on the horizon, 1.5 miles to the south.

BIG SPRING

At MO 103, turn right and follow the signs to **Big Spring.** There is ample parking with a short trail that leads to the mouth of the spring. The water roars from the base of a huge dolomite cliff. The rock is named Eminence dolomite after the town some 25 miles northwest of here. (After geologists discover and describe new bedrock, they name the rock after the nearest town.) This rock was deposited as sediment during the Cambrian Period, more than 600 million years ago. The land was covered by a shallow sea in which primitive marine life such as trilobites and brachiopods thrived. Today the compressed sediment that now forms this rock has a weathered face with nooks and crannies that harbor ferns, columbines, mosses, and other interesting plants.

Big Spring is appropriately named, for it is ranked as the largest spring in the United States and one of the largest in the world. The spring has an average daily flow of 276 million gallons. Water boils upward and out of the mouth of a cave, instantly forming a river that courses 1,000 feet downstream to enter the Current River. Dye tracings have shown the water to come from an area to the west of Big Spring, as far away as Willow Springs—an airline distance of more than 50 miles. Some of the water is even "pirated" from the watershed of the Eleven Point River to the southwest. It is thought that the area drained by Big Spring (the Big Spring Recharge Area) covers 967 square miles. It is estimated that Big Spring removes in solution each day about 175 tons of calcium and magnesium carbonate, the chemical component of limestone and dolomite. This means that in a year's time, enough bedrock (640,000 tons) is removed to form a cave passage 30 feet high by 50 feet wide and a mile long. It is interesting to note that the Big Spring system is now larger than it has ever been in the past and that the rate of growth is also greater than ever before. This is because each year the recharge system grows larger by the removal of rocks by groundwater solution, and, each year, more rock is exposed to the dissolving action of the groundwater.

Big Spring was a popular site long before the first European settlers set foot in the area. Today's campgrounds are filled with recreational vehicles and tents but were once also used as camps for prehistoric peoples. From about 10,000 years ago to 4,000 years ago, humans repeatedly camped in this area along the banks of the Current River. They hunted deer, turkey, elk, woods bison, and songbirds; caught fish; and collected plants from the surrounding forest. A

Canoeing and tube floating the Current River are popular activities during the hot summer months.

recent archaeological excavation in the park has unearthed knives, scrapers, drills, and projectile or spear points that had been buried over time, some 6 feet deep in the alluvial soil. These are significant finds that will add to our understanding of the early inhabitants of the region.

To the right of the walkway to Big Spring, a kiosk provides information on two trails. The mile-long Big Spring Slough Trail starts at the kiosk and leads to an archaeological exhibit where Native American camps more than 10,000 years old have been discovered. The trail also passes dikes built by the Civilian Conservation Corps to alter the Current River, thus protecting Big Spring from inundation. The second trail, Big Spring Chubb Hollow Trail, is a half-mile trail that begins at the Big Springs Lodge. It starts along the river bank and ascends to the bluff top offering great views of the Current River valley.

Returning to the main park road, MO Z passes the **Big Spring Lodge.** There is a display featuring the Civilian Conservation Corps (CCC) at that junction at a pullout. The Big Spring Lodge and cabins were built by the CCC in the late 1930s. President Roosevelt organized the CCC to create jobs and training for the unemployed during the Great Depression. Many structures built by the CCC can still be found throughout the Ozarks. The lodge is now open to dining, and the rustic cabins can be rented by calling (573) 323–8156 or by visiting "The Landing," a lodge located at the intersection of US 60 and MO 103.

Along the lane to Big Spring Lodge is a recently renovated CCC building that is now the **Big Spring Museum.** Here you will find exhibits about the CCC.

The **Big Spring Pines Natural Area** is located off MO Z, 1.1 miles from the junction of MO 103 and Z. There is a pulloff on the right and a service road leading to the Big Spring Lookout Tower. It is a comfortable half-hour walk through the natural area to the tower. The trail continues past the tower and ends in the vicinity of the rental cabins. The tower, by the way, is closed to the public. There are other trails at Big Spring, many of which were built by the CCC. A park official has explained that most trails have not been well-maintained, so they are not recommended at this time. The 345-acre natural area contains the largest, highest quality chert forest known in this region of the Ozarks. Old-growth oak and pine trees more than 120 years in age are common throughout this forest. Pine was once more common in this region and was often the dominant forest type. Early accounts by explorers describe this area as open and parklike, with abundant grasses and wildflowers in the understory. Because of past logging of the pines and fire suppression, the original forest type has changed dramatically. Plans for managing this natural area include the experimental use of controlled burnings to duplicate the open forest conditions that prevailed when Indians traveled the hills.

A view from Skyline Drive of Missouri Highway 103 as it winds its way to Big Spring.

Big Spring

11

Springs and Rivers

WINONA TO MAMMOTH SPRING, MISSOURI/ARKANSAS

GENERAL DESCRIPTION: A 57-mile drive traveling from Winona south through rugged hills with large springs and the Eleven Point River to Grand Gulf and Mammoth Spring.

SPECIAL ATTRACTIONS: Falling Spring, Turner Mill, McCormack Lake Recreation Area, Greer Spring, Eleven Point River, Grand Gulf and Mammoth Spring state parks, Mammoth Spring National Fish Hatchery, Spring River, Dam 3 Access, Mark Twain National Forest, and the Ozark Trail; canoeing, swimming, hiking, fall colors, spring flowers, fishing, camping, and hunting.

LOCATION: East-central Ozarks. The drive begins at the junction of U.S. Highway 60 and Missouri Highway 19 at Winona.

DRIVE ROUTE NUMBERS: U.S. Highways 60 and 63; Missouri Highways 19, AA, and W; and Forest Roads 3170, 3164, and 3155.

CAMPING: Greer Crossing Recreation Area provides 19 camping units with drinking water and pit toilets. McCormack Lake Recreation Area has 8 campsites with drinking water and pit toilets. Primitive camping is allowed in the national forest.

SERVICES: All services at Winona, Alton, Thayer, and Mammoth Spring.

NEARBY ATTRACTIONS: Irish Wilderness Area, Two Rivers Scenic Drive, and Peck Ranch Conservation Area.

THE DRIVE

When people first laid out MO 19, it seems as though they tried to connect the road "between the dots," which, in this case, are large springs. Beginning in the north and heading south, MO 19 goes by Montauk Spring, Welch Spring, Round Spring, Alley Spring, Blue Spring, Greer Spring, and Mammoth Spring, which are all within 10 miles of the highway. The only spring that did not fit into this scheme is Big Spring, which is near Van Buren, some 20 miles to the east. However, since it is the largest spring in the United States, maybe it should stand alone. These eight springs are among the fourteen highest-flowing springs in the Ozarks. The Missouri part of the Ozarks contains one of the nation's greatest concentrations of springs. In an average day, more than a billion gallons of water flow from Missouri's ten largest springs.

SITES
1. Falling Spring Recreation Area
2. McCormack Lake Recreation Area
3. Turner Mill Recreation Area
4. Turner Mill South Recreation Area
5. Greer Crossing River Access
6. Greer Spring
7. Cane Bluff Access
8. Grand Gulf State Park
9. Mammoth Spring State Park
10. Mammoth Spring National Fish Hatchery
11. Dam 3 Access

To Eminence

Winona

To Mountain View

To Van Buren

3164

3155

Ozark Trail

3170

3152

MARK TWAIN

3190

Eleven Point River

Greer

To 7.

To West Plains

Little Hurricane Creek

3153

Alton

N. F.

Tucker Creek

Piney

To Doniphan

Frederick

Creek

Creek

Warm Fork Spring River

To West Plains

Twomile Creek

Bussell Branch

MISSOURI

Thayer

To Doniphan

To Lanton

To Salem

Mammoth Spring

9,10

ARKANSAS

To Jonesboro

To

Spring River

N

0 Kilometers 5

0 Miles 5

All these springs are located in a part of the Ozarks called the Salem Plateau. This region, extending from the south-central part of Missouri to just into Arkansas, is composed largely of dolomitic rock. The soluble character of this rock makes possible the extensive cave and spring systems for which the Ozarks are noted. From 1,000 to 2,000 feet of dolomite rock is present in the Ozarks, and this mass has a tremendous volume for storing precipitation. Much rainwater is collected and transported through the connecting systems of conduits we call caves. You can gain a concept of the capacity of the dolomite aquifers by considering the number of caves in the region, many of which sustain large springs. Of a total of 5,000 caves in Missouri, more than 3,500 are in the Missouri Ozarks.

WINONA TO THE TURNER MILL

The drive begins at the junction of US 60 and MO 19, just outside of **Winona.** In the 1890s this town was the home of the Ozark Land and Lumber Company, one of the largest sawmill operations in the region. It processed shortleaf pine and oak for flooring and railroad needs. On July 4, 1895, a disastrous flood destroyed most of Winona. Eleven people drowned, and most of the property on Front Street, along Pike Creek, was destroyed. The town rebuilt on higher ground. Today sawmill employment continues to be of some importance, but Winona is primarily an agricultural trade and service center. The Eleven Point Ranger Station is located in Winona, on the east side of MO 19. Open during the workweek, the station offers information on recreational activities in the district.

Head south on MO 19 across rolling hills that are mostly forested with white oak, post oak, black oak, and shortleaf pine. After 4.3 miles, the character of the road changes. There are stretches of highway from here to the Eleven Point River, where the road leaves the ridges and travels across slopes of hills, following the contour of the land. You may find this road is like a roller coaster as you go up and down the drainages. If you can tolerate the effect, the view along the way will set this road apart from many that use cut-and-fill to level out the road. The forest and its wildflowers, flowering shrubs, and towering trees hug the road. It is a special natural corridor that almost makes you forget about the ribbon of black asphalt over which you are traveling.

After just over 9 miles from the start of the drive, take FR 3170 on the left, then after 0.1 mile, turn left again onto FR 3164. Proceed 2.3 miles to **Falling Spring Recreation Area.** Use caution just before the recreation area for the road narrows to a single lane and has two sharp turns. Go slow because it is hard to see oncoming traffic. Falling Spring is unusual because the water shoots out of an opening in the cliff some 15 feet above ground. The water once provided power for two mills. The present mill was built in the late 1920s. The waterpower was used to produce electricity, grind corn, and make shingles. This site was settled before the Civil War and the old log cabin, which was the first home built on the site, is more than a hundred years old. A 650-foot trail leads along the edge of the lower pond, which offers fishing. There are no facilities here except for one picnic table and a fire ring.

Return to MO 19. After 3 miles, turn right onto FR 3155 toward **McCormack Lake Recreation Area,** which offers camping, fishing, hiking, and picnicking. At the recreation area, you can hike the McCormack Greer Trail, a 3.7-mile foot trail that links McCormack Lake with the Eleven Point River at Greer Access. A highland segment from Greer to Duncan Hollow offers an additional 2.1-mile loop. An interpretive brochure with trail map is available at the Winona Ranger District Office in Winona.

Back on MO 19 and heading south, the road continues on its roller coaster ride. A potential side trip begins in 2 miles: Turn left onto FR 3152 and then FR 3190, and go 8 miles to **Turner Mill Recreation Area,** the site of an old gristmill. The mill building and wooden flume are gone today, but the wheel and cement flume by the spring outlet still stand. Turner Mill Spring has an average flow of 1.5 million gallons per day. The area has two picnic tables, pit toilets, and access to the Eleven Point River.

Falling Spring issues out of a cliff beside an abandoned mill.

GREER AREA SITES

After another 1.3 miles on MO 19, the road enters the Eleven Point National Scenic River. On the left, the **Greer Crossing River Access** provides camping, picnicking, and access to the Ozark Trail and the Eleven Point River. This is a popular put-in and take-out area on the river. It is said that the Eleven Point was named by a French fur trader for the eleven points, or bends, in a particular stretch of the river. The Eleven Point River was included in the National Wild and Scenic Rivers Act in its initial passage by Congress in 1968. The river is protected from Thomasville to MO 142, a distance of 45 miles. The river is classified as permanent flow for 50 miles of its length. The upper reaches are fed by a number of springs, the largest being Greer Spring, which doubles the volume of the river as it joins the Eleven Point. The Missouri Department of Conservation stocks trout in the Eleven Point below the spring. Floating this river provides a wild, scenic experience with opportunities to see deer, turkey, beaver, belted kingfishers, and other wildlife inhabiting the corridor.

Continuing the drive, MO 19 crosses the Eleven Point Bridge and climbs out of the river hills. In just over a mile, you will see an access to **Greer Spring.** A 1.8-mile round-trip hiking trail leads to the spring. With a flow of 220 million gallons per day, Greer Spring is the second largest in Missouri and the third largest in the Ozarks, when Arkansas's Mammoth Spring is included. Greer Spring has much wild beauty, having escaped dams, mills, and other structures since 1921. Greer Spring flows from two openings, an upper cave outlet and a lower opening in the bed of the spring branch several hundred feet downstream. The Forest Service has developed a brochure explaining the history of Greer Spring. If the brochure is not available at the parking area, stop by the Winona Ranger District Office or write for a copy.

MO 19 continues south passing through the community of **Greer.** About 2 miles beyond Greer, a gravel road on the right goes about 3 miles to **Cane Bluff Access and Picnic Area.** This access to the Eleven Point River has the towering 250-foot Cane Bluff directly across the river. Upstream 100 feet, a rock slide occurred in 1991, knocking down trees and scarring the bluff to the river's edge.

Continuing on MO 19, MO AA leads 11 miles to **Turner Mill South Recreation Area,** a canoe access to the Eleven Point River. Continue on MO 19 another 2 miles to **Alton,** established in 1859 as a central location for the new Oregon County seat. The original courthouse was burned in 1863 during the Civil War. The present courthouse is made of Missouri red granite from Graniteville, which is featured on Drive 4. Many old buildings still crowd around the square.

THAYER AREA SITES

Proceed another 15 miles across a broad, level plateau to Thayer. Stay on MO 19, crossing over US 63. This area was once thriving orchard land and the home ground of "Ma" Barker and her boys, notorious criminals of the 1920s and 1930s.

After a mile, turn right onto MO W and follow it for 6 miles to **Grand Gulf State Park,** which is considered one of the most spectacular geologic features in the Ozarks. The major feature of the 159-acre park is the collapsed remains of a major cave system, with a sinkhole, cave, natural bridge, and a gulf that is often called Missouri's "Little Grand Canyon." The park does not have facilities for camping but does provide picnic tables and interpretive exhibits on how this impressive gulf was formed. Although the dolomite bedrock here was deposited in seas that covered much of the Ozarks 480 million years ago, the Grand Gulf cave system may be only one or two million years old. The deep valleys are actually the result of a cavern system, the roof of which collapsed several thousand years ago.

Today the gulf is a three-quarter-mile-long canyon. A portion of the cave roof that did not collapse remains as a natural bridge. Bussell Branch, which previously flowed above the intact cave system, now flows through the canyon

The collapsed roof of a huge cavern reveals part of a water-filled cave system at Grand Gulf State Park.

and into a part of the cave that did not collapse; its waters eventually reappear at Mammoth Spring in Arkansas, 7 miles away. The cave used to be accessible up to a length of 500 feet, but in 1921 a tornado filled the gulf with debris, blocking the cave passage. Heavy rains often back up in the gulf, forming a deep lake that slowly drains through the cave into an underground water system. There are four overlooks, one of which is accessible to the disabled. There is also a quarter-mile loop trail around the chasm with a primitive trail that crosses the natural bridge.

Return on MO W until you reach MO 19, then enter **Thayer.** The town was founded in 1882 by George Nettleton as a division point for the Kansas City, Springfield, and Memphis Railroad. The line from Memphis to Thayer had easy curves and a flat grade, while the Thayer to Springfield line had many sharp curves and a steep grade. Heavy trains from Memphis had to be divided to pass through the mountains to Springfield, and Thayer was a halfway point between the two cities. The town was actually called "Division" until George Nettleton proposed Augusta, the name of his second wife. Upon incorporation in 1885, the residents discovered there was already an Augusta, overlooking the Missouri River. In 1886 the name "Thayer" was chosen in honor of Nathaniel Thayer, a director of the railroad. Today the town is a thriving community with plenty of recreational activities within a short drive.

MAMMOTH SPRING

MO 19 ends at US 63 in Thayer. Follow US 63 south to the Arkansas State Line and **Mammoth Spring.** The spring is located in **Mammoth Spring State Park,** which is on the east side of the road. The state park has an information center that is a good place to find out about activities in the area. It also features exhibits, brochures, rest rooms, and souvenirs. On the grounds there are trails (including one to an 1886 depot), playgrounds, historical objects (such as a Frisco caboose), remnants of the mill, and a hydroelectic plant near Spring Lake.

Mammoth Spring is the second-largest spring in the Ozarks, with an average flow of 234 million gallons per day. The main source of the spring's water comes from rainfall over the high plains of southern Missouri. The water seeps into the water table and flows along a vast system of interconnected pathways. Water from Grand Gulf, 7 miles away, has been found to emerge at Mammoth Spring.

The spring was shown on early nineteenth century maps as "Great Spring." It was also called "Big Spring" in the 1820s by area settlers who established a village there known as "Head of the River." An early gristmill powered by the spring's water contributed to the town's growth. In 1886 the Frisco Railroad built lines into the area and constructed one of its first train depots in the town, which is now called Mammoth Spring. The town flourished with the railroad and a dam built by the Mammoth Spring Milling Company (a wheat mill) in the 1880s. The Arkansas-Missouri Power Company bought rights to the dam in 1925 and constructed a hydroelectric plant that provided electricity to the area until 1972. In 1957 legislation established Mammoth Spring State Park.

The **Mammoth Spring National Fish Hatchery,** established in 1904, is located in the back of the state park. Operated by the U.S. Fish and Wildlife Service, the hatchery draws from the 58-degree-Fahrenheit water of Mammoth Spring to raise more than three million fish a year. In its fifteen ponds and raceways, the hatchery has the unique ability to produce warm-, cool-, and cold-water fish. The hatchery raises trout, smallmouth bass, channel catfish, and striped bass for release in nearby streams. A display aquarium shows native fishes, amphibians, and reptiles. The hatchery is open during the workweek.

Speaking of fish, one of the best catfish and hush puppy dinners in the Ozarks is found at Fred's Fish House in Mammoth Springs. Expect more than the normal amount of food at a reasonable price.

Mammoth Spring flows into the **Spring River,** which begins as the Warm Fork Spring River north of Thayer. At the point of contact, Mammoth Spring

Although the depot at Mammoth Spring is now a museum, the railroad line remains active.

adds tremendously to the volume of the river. The water is ideal for trout and is stocked by the Arkansas Game & Fish Commission from below Mammoth Spring to Many Islands Camp. You can canoe on the Spring River from **Dam 3 Access** to the Black River, a distance of 61 miles. The Spring River has distinctive characteristics not found on other Ozark rivers. Long pools are broken by waterfalls that range from 1 to 5 feet in height.

Old Mill Run

GAINESVILLE TO U.S. HIGHWAY 160, MISSOURI

GENERAL DESCRIPTION: A 58-mile drive beginning in Gainesville and proceeding through scenic hills and valleys visiting glades, historic old water mills, springs, and clear-flowing streams along the way.

SPECIAL ATTRACTIONS: Caney Mountain Conservation Area, Rockbridge Mill, Zanoni Mill, Hodgson Mill, Dawt Mill, Bryant Creek, North Fork River; scenic views, showy glade wildflowers, fall colors, hiking, swimming, canoeing, hunting, and fishing, including trout.

LOCATION: Central Ozarks. The drive begins at Gainesville at the intersection of Missouri Highway 5 and U.S. Highway 160, travels mostly along Missouri Highway 181 and some secondary roads, and eventually ends back at U.S. Highway 160.

DRIVE ROUTE NUMBERS: U.S. Highway 160, Missouri Highways 5, 181, N, H, and PP.

CAMPING: There are no national forest recreation areas along the drive. At Caney Mountain Conservation Area, primitive camping is permitted only in designated areas. Public camping is also available at the U.S. Army Corps of Engineers' Theodosia Park, which has 36 sites, 12 of which can be reserved. The sites have water, electricity, fireplaces, tables, parking spaces, and rest rooms, but no showers are available. Rockbridge Trout and Game Ranch has modern sleeping rooms with 2 double beds and full bath. Zanoni Mill Inn provides bed-and-breakfast accommodations. Dawt Mill has camping, RV hookups, and lodging.

SERVICES: All services provided at Gainesville and Theodosia.

NEARBY ATTRACTIONS: Hercules Glades Wilderness Area, Devils Backbone Wilderness Area, Mark Twain National Forest, Norfork Lake, Bull Shoals Lake, and Glade Top Trail Scenic Drive.

THE DRIVE

Traveling through this part of the Ozarks takes you back to an earlier life when "goin' to mill" was a common event for backwoods families. For more than a century, these old mills not only ground their corn and wheat but also provided other services. The power used to turn the grinding stones, and with a system of belts and pulleys, drove rock crushers, cotton gins, wool-carding machines, lumber mills, woodworking equipment, and, later, electricity. The

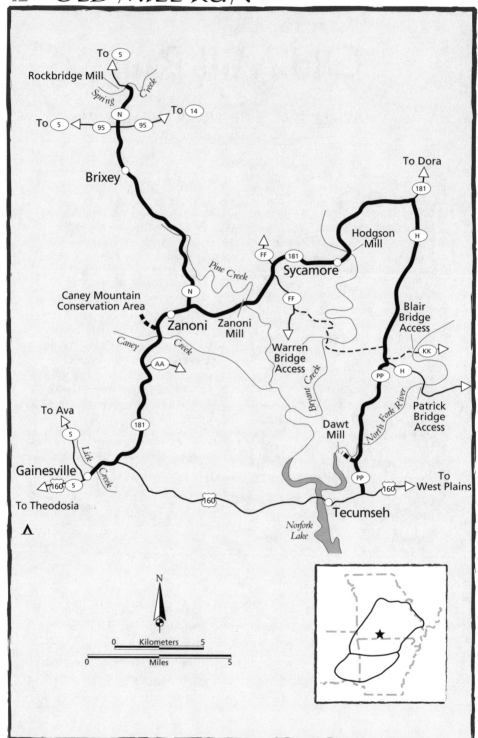

mill was also a gathering place where folks could visit, exchange stories, and catch up on the latest news. Beside the mill was usually a general store that supplied tea, coffee, yard goods, and simple clothes. A blacksmith shop and a post office were nearly always a part of the scene.

In the early part of the twentieth century, many of the mills' customers began to turn to store-bought flour. By the middle of the century, with easy access by automobile to city markets, the mills no longer could compete. Today the few remaining Ozark mills offer us a chance to step back in time and visit a way of life that is now mostly revealed to us only in old photographs and books.

GAINESVILLE AND CANEY MOUNTAIN

The drive begins at the intersection of US 160 and MO 5. **Gainesville** was established in 1857 when Ozark County was reduced in size, replacing Rockbridge as the county seat. Gainesville, which was more centrally located in the county, was primarily settled by Georgians and named for General Edmund P. Gaines. General Gaines, who arrested Aaron Burr on suspicion of treason, also commanded Fort Erie during the War of 1812. Gainesville's early history is somewhat vague due to the destruction of its county records by four courthouse fires in the town's early history.

Turn east on US 160 at the intersection of US 160 and MO 5. In about half a mile, after crossing over Lick Creek, you begin climbing a hill. Notice the massive road cuts. This bedrock is dolomite, a sedimentary rock that was deposited at the bottom of an ocean more than 350 million years ago. In another half a mile, turn left onto MO 181 and proceed 5.5 miles to **Caney Mountain Conservation Area.** Follow the gravel road into the conservation area about half a mile to the headquarters on the right. A bulletin board displays current information and an area brochure is available from a map box. Caney Mountain Conservation Area was acquired in 1940 as a wild turkey refuge. The turkey population had declined to fewer than forty birds across the whole state, and this area was seen as a stronghold from which to rebuild the population.

Caney Mountain Conservation Area is 7,899 acres and contains several interesting features including unusual geologic formations, a state-champion tree, caves, a nature trail through a large glade, and scenic views. Gravel roads provide access to these features. Although these roads are well maintained, travel by low-clearance vehicles, vehicles pulling trailers, and motor homes is not recommended. At the headquarters, pit toilets are provided, and primitive camping is available in designated areas.

Proceed past the area manager's house across from the headquarters and turn right onto the Main Trail. On this drive you will be encountering a series of low-water crossings. This is a common Ozark feature that should not be attempted when creeks are rain-swollen. Go another 0.2 mile and notice the sign and entrance on the left to the **Leopold Cabin.** It is easiest to back up a little and park along the side of the road or drive over the creek and park in the forest opening. After crossing the creek, go about 30 feet and on the left, notice some scattered stems of giant cane, a type of bamboo that inspired the name for the conservation area. Giant cane was once more common along creeks, but disturbances such as grazing has led to its decline throughout the Ozarks. A picturesque north-facing cliff provides shelter for wild hyacinth, Christmas fern, and mosses, with spice bush and pawpaw below it. Just to the left of the cliff, notice the spring box that was built to provide water for the cabin users. Follow the stone steps leading up the hill to the cabin.

The cabin was built in 1940 using pine logs harvested off the area. The first biologist to live in the cabin was A. Starker Leopold, son of Aldo Leopold, the pioneer of modern wildlife conservation. Starker Leopold was hired to implement the first wild turkey restoration plan. The success of his early efforts and of others that followed can be seen throughout the Ozarks; sitings of wild turkeys are now considered a common occurrence.

Another half mile down the gravel road past Food Plot #34, the High Rock Trail, about half a mile one way, leads to a viewing area with large boulders. It is not well marked and is strenuous at the end. Just beyond the High Rock Trail is the Spout Spring Trail, which leads to a small spring and beyond for a total of 1.5 to 2 miles. This trail is also not well maintained.

Continue down the gravel road and in about 1 mile notice the state-champion black gum on the right side of the road. Black gum is the first tree in the Ozarks to turn color in the fall. Often, as early as August, the dark green glossy leaves change to a brilliant scarlet color that can be easily seen in scattered blotches across wooded hills. The dark, blocky, "alligator skin" appearance of the bark is distinctive. Difficult to split because its wood fibers are cross-woven and not straight, black gum has been used as handles for heavy-duty tools and also for furniture, crates, lumber, and gun stocks.

Just down the road, a Red Wolf Camp sign marks the unmaintained trail to a shelter bluff about a quarter of a mile away that was once used by residents in the 1930s to search for signs of red wolves that were last sighted in the area. On the left side of the road, the Bear Cave Trail leads to a small cave a quarter of a mile away.

Farther down the road after crossing a creek, in a short distance there is a parking area on the left. Across the road, a quarter-mile trail leads to **Onyx Cave.** This is a recreational cave open to the public, but at least two flashlights and a hard hat are recommended. The cave has a crawlway entrance but opens to a room 6 feet high and 15 feet long. The passageway continues for 250 feet before it becomes too small to maneuver.

In about half a mile, the road splits; bear right. The road leads through some large boulders to Preston Flat Ridge. On the left, **Southwest Vista** offers a scenic view. The hills on the skyline are part of the Glade Top Trail Scenic Drive. All of the hills within view are part of what is known as the Monadnocks. Tightly clustered, knobby hills like these can be encountered at other locations in the Ozarks. They are remnants of a broad plateau that has weathered around the edges, leaving only a center high spot with fragmented hills that will eventually level off.

Continuing on the gravel road, in half a mile, the **East Vista** offers another view of the Monadnocks. Just to the left of the scenic view, **Preston Flats Trail,** about a three-quarter-mile loop trail, follows the ridge around Preston Flats. The trail is not maintained, and some of the white rectangular markers on the trees may be absent, so you may not want to go out on this one unless you feel venturesome. Beyond the entrance to the trail, a demonstration area

A view from East Vista of the Monadnocks.

explains how wild turkeys and white-tailed deer were once trapped for relocation to establish new populations in other parts of Missouri.

After another mile, turn left on a small road. It is a little difficult to locate, so if you encounter the sign FOOD PLOT 22 and a clearing on the right, you have just missed the turn. Go slowly down this short hill, which leads to a valley and a parking lot in about half a mile. A mowed, half-mile trail winds through part of the 1,330-acre **Caney Mountain Natural Area.** This area features a savanna (open grown trees with a grassy understory) and a large dolomite glade with interesting animals and showy wildflowers blooming throughout the season. For a description of glades and their interesting inhabitants, refer to the introduction to the Glade Top Trail Scenic Drive (Drive 13). The trail ends at the gravel road. Turn right and proceed to the parking area.

After leaving the parking lot, continue on the gravel road for about 1 mile. At an intersection, the South Road, to the right, provides another route back to the headquarters, but the features along the way are not very interesting. The road to the left leads back the way you came. If you return this way, in less than half a mile, bear right at the next intersection and continue to the headquarters.

ZANONI TO ROCKBRIDGE MILL

Leaving Caney Mountain Conservation Area, turn left onto MO 181. Drive cautiously along this scenic but windy road. In just over 1 mile, you enter the small community of **Zanoni.** Flooding at the old Zanoni mill site, seen later on in the drive, forced residents to relocate to this higher ground. Continue on MO 181 and turn left on MO N, passing through Brixey and crossing MO 95 in 7.5 miles. Staying on MO N, in about 2 miles, turn left at the entrance to the Rainbow Trout and Game Ranch, which leads to **Rockbridge Mill.**

Rockbridge, reportedly named for a rock bridge crossing, was once the county seat of Ozark County. After the county was shrunken in size, Gainesville became the county seat in 1857. Rockbridge's first post office was established in 1842. The entire town was burned down during a Civil War battle, so a new Rockbridge was established near Morris Spring, which flows into Spring Creek. The first structure was a water mill built in 1868. A millpond was originally established on Spring Creek with a log and stone dam that washed away in 1887. In 1895 the present stone dam was built. The water comes from damming the flow of four springs that produce a maximum flow of fifteen million gallons per day. The mill owner, B. V. Morris, originally began with a two-story building and added a third story in 1900. The water mill produced up to fifty barrels of flour per day. The mill also operated a sawmill, a planing mill, and a cotton gin. Rockbridge also had a general store, a bank, and a church.

An angler hooks a trout below Rockbridge Mill.

In 1954 Lile, Edith, and Ray Amyx purchased the property a few years after the mill's closing and established a private trout hatchery and fishing resort, called the Rainbow Trout and Game Ranch. They originally operated out of the 1890s general store, but it was destroyed by fire in 1986. Today a new general store houses a gift shop and restaurant. Dining by the windows offer views of the mill, its rock dam, and dozens of ruby-throated hummingbirds that come to the window feeders. Be sure to try the fresh rainbow trout boneless filets for lunch or dinner. It is a treat you won't forget! See Appendix A for its address. Lodging is also available.

Return to MO N, turn right, and head back to MO 181. Turn left on MO 181, go 2 miles, and turn left at the bottom of a steep hill. A U-shaped drive follows the edge of a large pond back to a large residence. The **Zanoni Mill** is to the left of the residence. The property is now owned by Dave and Mary Morrison. Dave is the grandson of A. P. "Doc" Morrison, who built the mill in 1905. The Morrisons operate a bed-and-breakfast (see the appendix for their address) in their new home, which is patterned after the house at South Fork Ranch near Dallas, Texas, that was made famous by the television show *Dallas*. They don't mind visitors who just want to stop and see the mill. Unfortunately, the old mill was recently removed because it was beyond reconditioning. You can still see the large waterwheel and the flume that carried the water over the wheel. A new building stands on the original mill site, and it is available for weddings and conferences. Be sure to look in back of the building and notice the spring flowing out of the rock face 20 feet above the base. The spring sends forth a maximum 400,000 gallons daily. Zanoni Mill, with its big waterwheel, was the only true water mill. The others, Rockbridge, Hodgson, and Dawt, were all roller mills and were powered by turbines.

The first mill was built of logs in the early 1860s. In 1900 the property was sold and the new owners replaced the mill and added a sawmill. Around 1905 the mill burned and "Doc" Morrison built the two-story building you see today. He first used the mill to grind corn and wheat but added a cotton gin a year later. In 1920 Morrison developed a waterpowered generator that supplied lights and electricity to run ten industrial sewing machines on the second floor used to make overalls carrying the label "Blue Jay."

Besides the mill, the small community of Zanoni also had a post office, general store, and several residences. Today the old country store and post office is still used as a local polling place. Morrison's original house is still intact and can be seen just behind his grandson's new home.

BRYANT CREEK

Return to MO 181 and turn left. In 1.5 miles, MO FF leads 4 miles to Warren Bridge Access. This seven-acre public area provides access to Bryant Creek. There is no boat ramp. In 2.5 miles on MO 181 you pass through the little community of Sycamore, which was once located at Hodgson Mill but moved to higher ground after flooding. Continue on and in half a mile, you cross a bridge over **Bryant Creek.** Just before the crossing, a road on the right leads to Sycamore Access. This sixteen–acre access to Bryant Creek provides fishing and wading opportunities. There is no boat ramp. Bryant Creek is considered an excellent fishing stream. It is also a relatively wild stream that begins north of MO 76 in Douglas County and flows approximately 40 miles to Norfork Lake. The creek begins as a perennial stream at Bryant Spring near Ava. The spring averages about 600,000 gallons daily. Bryant Creek is generally floatable beginning at the Bell School low-water bridge on MO 95. The slow-moving stream offers time to view wildlife and enjoy the exceptional scenery.

Just beyond the MO 181 bridge over Bryant Creek, you will find **Hodgson Mill** on the right. The mill is currently available for close viewing Monday through Saturday 10:00 A.M. to 5:00 P.M. and Sunday 1:00 to 5:00 P.M. There is a gift shop inside the mill with antiques, Ozark crafts, books, and more. It took a considerable amount of work to repair the mill and surrounding area after the record flood of early December 1982, when water from Bryant Creek

A view of historic Hodgson Mill.

reached the second floor of the mill. By the way, the turning waterwheel on the first level is for decoration; the mill was powered by turbines. The Missouri Department of Tourism has identified this mill as the most photographed mill in the state. It is also said that this premier example of a turbine-driven water mill is probably the best-known mill in America. The present mill, built in 1894, remained in operation until 1977. The building and the fact that it was still in operation made it the subject of pictures and stories between 1971 and 1975. The mill also appeared in several national magazines such as *American Farmer, Gourmet Magazine,* and *Ford Times.* The late Euell Gibbons once came to the mill for a cereal commercial. Unable to meet the demand for the mill's products, the Harringtons, who owned the mill at the time, moved the business to Gainesville. The Hodgson Mill label on packages of flour and meal can be seen in stores today.

The first mill was built in 1861 to capture the massive flow of the spring that flowed into Bryant Creek. At around twenty-four million gallons per day, this spring ranks fifteenth in size among the springs of Missouri. The mill was forced to close during the Civil War. Alva Hodgson constructed the present mill around 1894. Much of the building is built of hand-hewn pine and utilizes mortise joints. The huge wooden support beams were locked in place with wooden pins. The mill ground white flour, unbleached flour, and corn meal. It took thirteen years for Hodgson to complete the mill, build a general merchandise store, and finish a cotton gin and sawmill. In the general store, which still stands today, he established a post office named "Sycamore" for the trees in the area. Hodgson sold an interest to his brother, George, and moved to property he acquired along the North Fork River and developed Dawt Mill in 1900. Hodgson Mill was later sold and changed hands several times. In 1934 the last buyer was Charles T. Aid of West Plains. The mill continues in the ownership of the Aid family. It has often been referred to as the Aid-Hodgson Mill since the purchase.

Continue on MO 181 for about 3.5 miles and turn right on MO H. Travel about 5.5 miles to MO PP. Along the way you pass a gravel road to the Warren Bridge Access mentioned earlier in the drive. Another entrance, just down MO H and on the left, leads to the Blair Bridge Access. This public access is seven acres with a boat ramp on the North Fork River. Just beyond this entrance, MO PP begins on the right. If you continue on MO H, in a little over a mile, you come to Patrick Bridge Access, which contains 161 acres of mostly forested public land along the North Fork River. There is a canoe launching site, campground, picnic area, and short trail to Althea Spring. This spring, which was once an old mill site, discharges around fifteen million gallons daily. This stretch of the river is also a trophy trout management area.

DAWT MILL

Continuing on MO PP, in a little over 3 miles, a road to the right leads to **Dawt Mill** located on the North Fork River. The Dawt Road entrance is located next to Clear Springs Church and Cemetery. It is said that the first mill was built as early as 1866, but the first documented mill was built in 1892. In the early 1900s the present mill was built by Alva Hodgson after fire destroyed the original building. By 1906 Hodgson had in operation a three-story mill, cotton gin, sawmill, general store, blacksmith shop, and family residence. A year later, he established a post office in the store. Dawt Mill is powered by a long angling dam across the North Fork River. The angle eases pressure on the dam caused by the fast-flowing stream and directs some of the water into the forebay. A turbine in the forebay powers the mill, which still grinds meal and flour for sale at the general store.

The origin of the word "Dawt" is uncertain, but it has been suggested that it is a combined word using the first two letters of dam and the first and third letters of water. Whatever the case, Dawt Mill now provides a variety of services and recreational opportunities. You can camp in one of fifty campsites, stay in Hodgson's original house that has been divided into six units, rent a cabin, or check into the recently built lodge. Canoeing, tubing, and fishing on the North Fork River are also available. See Appendix A for Dawt Mill's address.

The **North Fork River,** or North Fork of the White River as it is sometimes called, begins in the Mark Twain National Forest. From there it flows 78 miles before it empties into Norfork Lake, which begins just beyond the bridge crossing at Dawt Mill. The North Fork River is considered to have some of the best white-water action for paddlers in the Missouri Ozarks. There are plenty of towering bluffs, fast waters, rocky ledges, long riffles, and gravel bars. The protected watershed in the national forest provides clear water together with several large springs that empty into the river along its journey at a rate of 4 miles per hour. The springs keep the water temperature around 55 degrees Fahrenheit, which makes the river suitable for trout. The North Fork River is ranked by Trout Unlimited as one of the top one hundred trout-fishing streams in the nation. It has the largest wild rainbow trout population in Missouri and is supplemented by annual stockings of brown trout. There are no native trout populations in the Ozarks, but they are often stocked in spring-fed waters cold enough to support them.

Returning to MO PP, another mile brings you to US 160 and the end of the drive.

Glade Top Trail

AVA TO LONGRUN, MISSOURI

GENERAL DESCRIPTION: A 38-mile drive beginning in Ava and proceeding south to a scenic ridge-top gravel road that is designated as a Forest Service Scenic Byway.

SPECIAL ATTRACTIONS: Glade Top Trail and Fall Festival, and Mark Twain National Forest; scenic views, colorful glade flowers throughout the season, wildlife, fall colors, hiking, hunting, and horseback riding.

LOCATION: Central Ozarks. The drive begins at Ava on Missouri Highway 5 and ends at Longrun on Missouri Highway 95.

DRIVE ROUTE NUMBERS: Missouri Highways 5, 14, and A and Forest Roads 147 and 149.

CAMPING: There are no national forest recreation areas along the drive. Primitive camping is available at the Corbit Potter Campground and along the Glade Top Trail except at the picnic areas. Public camping is available at the U.S. Army Corps of Engineers' Theodosia Park, which has 36 sites, 12 of which can be reserved. The sites have water, electricity, fireplaces, tables, parking spaces, and rest rooms, but no showers are available.

SERVICES: All services provided at Ava and Theodosia. Gas and store in Thornfield.

NEARBY ATTRACTIONS: Hercules Glades Wilderness Area, Caney Mountain Conservation Area, Bull Shoals Lake, Old Mill Run Scenic Drive, Assumption Abbey, and Laura Ingalls Wilder home in Mansfield.

THE DRIVE

The most interesting and unique parts of the White River Hills are their glades. Glades evoke thoughts of the desert Southwest with their harsh, dry conditions in the summer and wet, seepy soils and lush vegetation in the spring. These Ozark deserts have cactus plants, scorpions, tarantulas, black widow spiders, pygmy rattlesnakes, lizards (including eastern collared lizards), and roadrunners—similar to the arid lands of the Southwest. Although some of these animals are potentially dangerous, knowledge of their presence should not prevent you from exploring glades. One rarely encounters these animals, and their "horror movie" depictions are greatly exaggerated. Many glade animals escape the fierce summer heat in the cool, moist environment beneath rock slabs. That

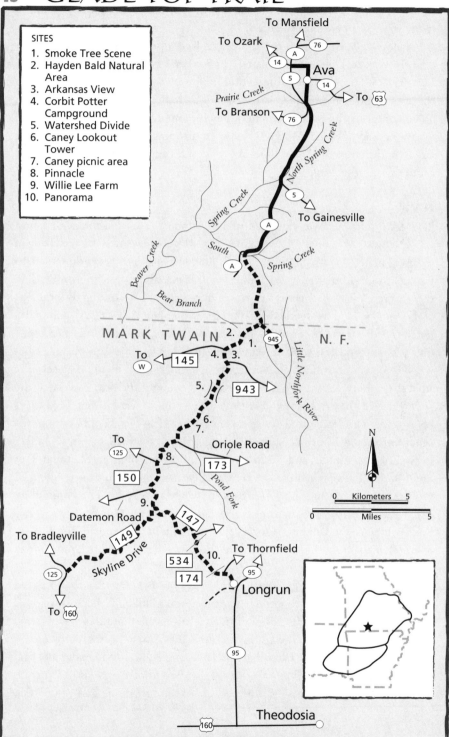

SITES
1. Smoke Tree Scene
2. Hayden Bald Natural Area
3. Arkansas View
4. Corbit Potter Campground
5. Watershed Divide
6. Caney Lookout Tower
7. Caney picnic area
8. Pinnacle
9. Willie Lee Farm
10. Panorama

To Mansfield
To Ozark
76
A
14
5
Ava
14
To 63
Prairie Creek
To Branson
76
North Spring Creek
5
To Gainesville
Spring Creek
A
South
Spring Creek
Beaver Creek
Bear Branch
MARK TWAIN N. F.
2.
945
1.
To W
145
4. 3.
Little Northfork River
5.
943
6.
7.
To 125
Oriole Road
8.
173
150
Pond Fork
9.
147
Datemon Road
To Bradleyville
149
Skyline Drive
534 10.
To Thornfield
174
95
125
Longrun
To 160
95
N
0 Kilometers 5
0 Miles 5
Theodosia
160

is why it is important to avoid "rock-flipping"; it destroys the microhabitat of many of these interesting creatures.

Glades are open areas in the forest that have thin soils with bedrock at or near the surface. They are dominated by plants and animals that can survive the hot, dry conditions of the summer and the moist, sometimes saturated soils of the spring and winter. The Ozarks have an incredible diversity of glade types. There are glades on sandstone, chert, igneous, novaculite, shale, dolomite, and limestone bedrocks. The White River Hills section of the Ozarks contains the largest and best examples of dolomite glades, a sample of which you will see on the Glade Top Trail.

AVA

The drive starts at **Ava.** Founded in 1849 upon the establishment of a post office, it was first named "Cow Skin" after a local creek. It was later changed to "Ava" in 1870, for a city in the Old Testament of the Bible. Early settlers to the area came from Kentucky, Tennessee, Indiana, and points south. By 1857 there were enough pioneers to organize into a county. According to local legend, Douglas County (named for statesman Stephen A. Douglas) endured a fierce rivalry for the claim of county seat. Both Ava and Vera Cruz, a community 8 miles southeast of Ava, wanted the honor. Ava was successful in its bid when three commissioners, appointed to lay out the town in 1871, successfully stole the county records from Vera Cruz and brought them to Ava. Then the rivalry literally heated up, with each would-be county seat burning the other's courthouse. The feud lasted well into the 1900s. However, Vera Cruz suffered other setbacks in its brief history. On June 1, 1876, Bryant Creek rose 25 feet in twenty-five minutes and washed away all of the buildings in the town. This flood started the slow demise of Vera Cruz; perhaps the town was destined for problems, for in Spanish, Vera Cruz means "edge of sorrow." The community lasted until the late 1950s, when new road improvements allowed cars to travel longer distances and the need for smaller communities dwindled. Today there is little left to show the traveler where the town actually existed, just a small cemetery and portions of the Old Vera Cruz Road.

Ava is the world headquarters of the Missouri Fox Trotting Horse Breed Association and its breed registry. The fox trotter is a "hillbilly" horse developed in the Ozarks. Because the hills demanded a sturdy, surefooted, even-tempered horse, the early settlers bred high-spirited, five-gaited horses with slower, calmer Tennessee walkers. Later they used mustang mares to add endurance and decrease size. The fox trotters were bred as a workhorse and also to furnish transportation. They are easy to ride because of their rhythmic gait—they walk with their front feet and trot with their hind feet. The name comes from the fox, which, like the horse, leaves only two tracks: its hind foot steps in the track left by the front one. Two annual fox trotting shows are held in Ava, one the second weekend of June and the other during Labor Day week.

At the intersection of MO 5 and 14, turn east on MO Business Route 5/MO 14 and take a tour through town. The road soon heads south into the center of town and the public square. The **Douglas County Museum,** open Saturday from 10:00 A.M. to 2:00 P.M., provides opportunities to view local history and culture. The museum is located on the south side of the road, 1 block east on MO 14 from the intersection of MO 14 and MO Business Route 5.

As you continue south on MO Business Route 5, look for the Forest Service's Ava Ranger District Office located on the east side of the road. Open during weekday business hours, the rangers there can provide information and maps on recreational opportunities in the forest. Be sure to pick up the Glade Top Trail Map.

The road continues and intersects with MO 5; head south. In a mile, the view on the horizon straight ahead is of a formation called a "monadnock." These mountains are erosional remnants of a broad plateau that has weathered around the edges, leaving only the center high spot to eventually level off. The Glade Top Trail travels along the crest of such a monadnock.

GLADE TOP TRAIL

Proceed south 8 miles and turn west onto MO A. After 3.5 miles, turn south on a gravel road and follow the signs for 3 miles to the **Glade Top Trail.** The first stop is a picnic area with an information sign orienting you to the area. Continue on the well-maintained gravel road, which was built by the Civilian Conservation Corps back in the 1930s. After crossing a cattle guard, the next stop is **Smoke Tree Scene.** To viewers looking out over the glades in the spring, this small tree wears what looks like puffs of bluish-grey smoke. The "smoky" parts have been described as feathery blooms but are actually hundreds of fruits and their bracts all arranged in a loose cluster. The small, inconspicuous flowers bloom earlier in the spring. The leaves turn a bright red-orange in October, adding to the rusty red color of the glade grasses. Smoke tree is also called "yellowwood" for its inner color, the sap of which was once used to make a yellow dye.

Fire is an important tool used to maintain the openness of the glades. Prior to settlement, natural fires, spread by lightning and assisted by Native Americans, easily maintained these open areas. Today prescribed fire, not wildfire, can be safely handled during low winds and moderate humidity with fire lines.

Without occasional fires, woody plants will eventually outcompete and over-shadow glade plants, eliminating habitat for glade species.

Eastern red cedar is the most aggressive of the woody invaders; as you look across the glades you can see that the glades are slowly losing their integrity as the cedars intrude. Because the government has deprioritized this matter and cut funding, the Forest Service has not been able to direct as much attention to this area as it deserves, but hopefully this will change. Some of the cedars are so tall that fire would only burn their lower branches. Now, after more than fifty years of fire suppression, the best method of removal is to cut the trees down and burn the debris. Once a fire maintenance schedule of burning every three to five years is initiated, the younger cedars and other small trees can effectively be controlled. (For a glade management success story, visit the natural area at Caney Mountain Conservation Area north of Gainesville. See Scenic Drive 12.)

Across from the Smoke Tree Scene, the forty-acre **Hayden Bald Natural Area** is visible. You can reach it by walking west a quarter of a mile from the road. Unfortunately, there is no designated trail. With dolomite glades on west, north, and east slopes, it is a good representative of the White River Hills section of the Ozarks.

Missouri coneflowers blanket the grass-covered glades along the Glade Top Trail in July.

SCENIC DRIVING THE OZARKS

In another 2 miles, the **Arkansas View** provides a scene of the Ozark Mountains near Mountain Home, Arkansas, some 40 miles away. The area around this stop is heavily forested with white oak, post oak, black oak, chinquapin oak, white ash, and various hickories.

After 0.4 mile, the **Corbit Potter Campground** is available for primitive camping. Proceed another 2 miles to the **Watershed Divide,** where the ridge divides two watersheds; water flows east into the Little Northfork River and west into Beaver Creek.

The **Caney Lookout Tower,** although closed to the public, provides a popular resting spot of the local turkey vulture population. The picnic area just beyond the tower is the site for the popular annual Glade Top Trail Festival (also called the Flaming Fall Review), which is usually held during the second weekend in October. On Sunday the town of Ava puts on a barbecued chicken dinner with free entertainment and a craft show. There is music and square dancing on Friday and Saturday, as well as a sausage and pancake breakfast Saturday. During the last half of April, another celebration called the Spring Flowering Tour is sponsored by Theodosia. It celebrates the dogwood, serviceberry, redbud, and wild plum flowering season. North of the parking lot at the **Caney picnic area,** a trail leads to a small but interesting cave.

The relatively gentle slope at the picnic area offers a good opportunity to walk through the glade and observe the plants and animals. The grasses here also grow on prairies further west. Big bluestem, little bluestem, Indian grass, switch grass, and sideoats grama are commonly seen. From late March through October, a variety of wildflowers cast a rainbow of colors over the glade. In the spring you will find Indian paintbrush, downy phlox, blue indigo, and yellow star grass. These give way to pale purple coneflower, Missouri primrose, Missouri coneflower, and butterfly weed in early summer. Yellow is the dominant color through summer, as prairie dock, compass plant, and various sunflowers brighten the scene. Fall brings varied hues of asters, goldenrods, and the striking rust-red color of the grasses set against the bright leaves of smoke tree, sumac, and flowering dogwood.

Several lizards are found in the glades; they venture forth in early morning or midevening, thus avoiding the relentless midday sun. Since they are cold-blooded, outside temperatures regulate their body temperatures. Lizards cool off by seeking shade under rocks on the glade. The eastern collared lizard, or "mountain boomer," is the largest lizard in the Ozarks. When startled, they can stand up on their hind legs and swiftly run to avoid predators. Their preferred food is other lizards. Look for a gray to green body and head, green legs, a

A collared lizard basks in the early morning sun.

length of up to 14 inches, and a dark band around the neck. Other lizards found on glades include the northern fence lizard, five-lined skink, ground skink, and six-lined race runner. Snakes include the red milk snake, speckled kingsnake, great plains rat snake, eastern yellowbelly racer, and the secretive pygmy rattlesnake.

A host of birds use the glades for nesting, feeding, and resting. One bird of particular note is Bachman's sparrow, which is endangered. As habitat diminishes, their numbers are declining dramatically. Past sightings of Bachman's sparrow have been made on Hayden Bald. Other birds include wild turkey, quail, several species of warblers, nighthawk, whippoorwill, yellow-breasted chat, blue-gray gnatcatcher, and northern cardinal, to name a few.

In the forest close to the edge of the glades, look for gray and fox squirrels, chipmunks, white-tailed deer, and gray and red fox. Recently a black bear was seen crossing the road and ambling across the glades.

In another mile the **Pinnacle,** which is a small hill to the left of the road, is the site of an abandoned gold mine. According to legend, a Mrs. Murray from Kansas City had a vision that told her to dig on the Pinnacle, where she would find gold. Mrs. Murray hired help and dug for years, but found no gold. The scars from her activities can still be seen. The Pinnacle, which was once a "bald," or hilltop lacking vegetation, used to serve as a gathering place for local mountain people each first Sunday in May. The religious services often drew a crowd of around 500 people for the daylong event. There is a trail at the base of the Pinnacle, but it soon loses definition and you are left to explore the hill on your own.

For the rest of the drive, the Forest Service road crosses stretches of both public and private land. Please access private land only with permission.

Following FR 147, in a couple of miles the road passes the **Willie Lee Farm.** The homestead, which was abandoned during the depression, served as a schoolhouse for more than forty children during the 1930s. Just beyond this site, at the intersection of Forest Service Roads 149 and 147, there is a picnic area, playground, and privy.

The road branches, with FR 149 heading southwest across additional Forest Service land. Called the **Skyline Drive,** the road ends in about 5 miles at MO 125 near Hercules Lookout Tower and Wilderness Area, which you can reach by traveling another 3 miles north on MO 125.

Continuing on FR 147, the next and last stop is **Panorama,** a lookout point that offers a broad eastward view across glades, forest, pasture, and farm-steads.

In another couple of miles, the drive ends at the small community of **Longrun.** At the three-way intersection in Longrun, turn east and proceed 0.1 mile to access MO 95.

14

Branson Area

SPRINGFIELD TO BRANSON, MISSOURI

GENERAL DESCRIPTION: A 56-mile drive beginning at Springfield and heading south through the scenic and rugged White River Hills to Branson.

SPECIAL ATTRACTIONS: Fantastic Caverns, Dickerson Park Zoo, Bass Pro Shop's Outdoor World, American National Fish and Wildlife Museum, Springfield Conservation Nature Center, Busiek State Forest and Wildlife Area, Branson, Ruth and Paul Henning Conservation Area, Shepherd of the Hills Outdoor Theater, Silver Dollar City, Shepherd of the Hills Fish Hatchery, Table Rock Lake and State Park, Dewey Short Visitor Center, Lake Taneycomo, and College of the Ozarks; scenic views, hiking, camping, fishing (including trout), boating, swimming, spring and fall colors, and country music and entertainment.

LOCATION: Western Ozarks. The drive begins at Springfield off of U.S. Interstate 44.

DRIVE ROUTE NUMBERS: U.S. Interstate 44, U.S. Highway 65, and Missouri Highways 13, 248, 76, 165, 265, and V.

CAMPING: Table Rock State Park has more than 165 campsites, including basic, improved, and full-hookup sites. Facilities include modern rest rooms, hot showers, a coin-operated laundry, and trailer dumping facilities. The U.S. Army Corps of Engineers has 21 recreation areas around Table Rock Lake with public campgrounds. Most parks have modern and complete facilities. Primitive camping is allowed at Busiek Conservation Area in designated areas. There are plenty of commercial campgrounds in the Branson area. Check the Branson Chamber of Commerce office for locations.

SERVICES: All services at Springfield, Ozark, Branson, and Hollister.

NEARBY ATTRACTIONS: Wilson's Creek National Battlefield, Boston Ferry and Drury-Mincy conservation areas, Hercules Glades and Piney Creek wilderness areas, Bull Shoals Lake, Kissee Mills Watchable Wildlife Site, and Ashe Juniper Natural Area.

THE DRIVE

This drive begins in a part of the Ozarks known as the Springfield Plateau. When land was uplifted over a period of time to form the Ozarks, this region of primarily limestone bedrock took the shape of a broad dome. Creeks and streams flow out in all directions from the high point of the plateau, which

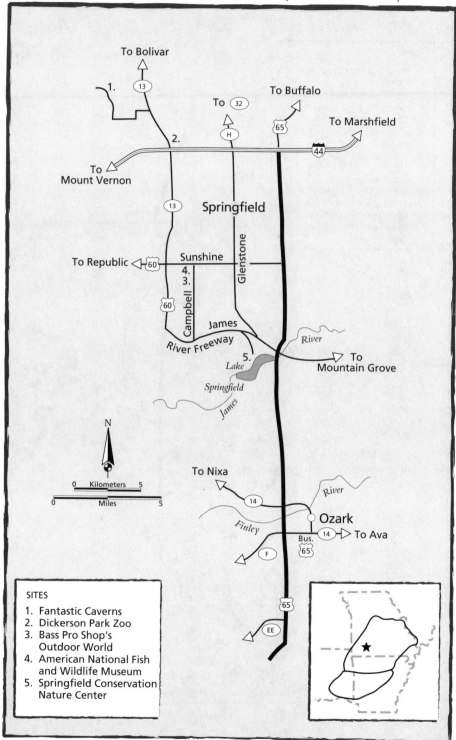

To Bolivar

1. ⑬

To ㉜

To Buffalo

To Marshfield

⑥⑤

H

2.

㊹

To
Mount Vernon

⑬ Springfield

Glenstone

To Republic ◁ ⑥⓪ Sunshine

4.
3.

Campbell

⑥⓪

James

River Freeway

River

5.

To
Mountain Grove

Lake

Springfield

James

N

| 0 | Kilometers | 5 |
| 0 | Miles | 5 |

To Nixa

River

⑭

Ozark

Finley

Bus.

⑭ ▷ To Ava

F

⑥⑤

⑥⑤

EE

SITES
1. Fantastic Caverns
2. Dickerson Park Zoo
3. Bass Pro Shop's
   Outdoor World
4. American National Fish
   and Wildlife Museum
5. Springfield Conservation
   Nature Center

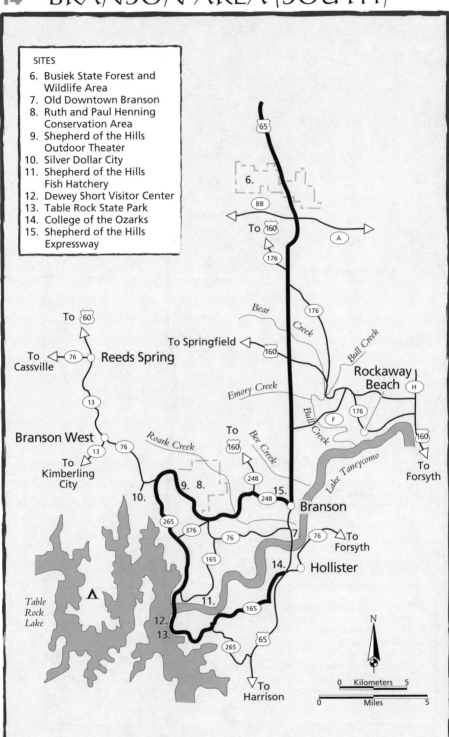

SITES

6. Busiek State Forest and Wildlife Area
7. Old Downtown Branson
8. Ruth and Paul Henning Conservation Area
9. Shepherd of the Hills Outdoor Theater
10. Silver Dollar City
11. Shepherd of the Hills Fish Hatchery
12. Dewey Short Visitor Center
13. Table Rock State Park
14. College of the Ozarks
15. Shepherd of the Hills Expressway

65

6.

BB

To 160

A

176

Bear Creek

176

To 60

To Springfield

160

Bull Creek

To Cassville

76

Reeds Spring

Rockaway Beach

H

Emory Creek

13

176

F

Branson West

Roark Creek

Bull Creek

160

76

To

To Kimberling City

13

160

Bee Creek

Lake Taneycomo

To Forsyth

248

9. 8.

15.

10.

248

Branson

265

376

7

76

To Forsyth

76

165

14.

Hollister

Table Rock Lake

11.

165

12.

13.

265

65

To Harrison

N

0   Kilometers   5

0   Miles   5

today is about 1,400 feet above sea level. Looking out from the city of Spring-field, which sits atop the Springfield Plateau, you will notice the land is rela-tively broad and level, lacking high hills and deep valleys. This was once prairie country. South of here, the White River and its tributaries have cut into the Springfield Plateau and exposed older bedrock of Ordovician age. Composed of dolomite, the hills are steep-sided with narrow, deep valleys. The slopes are forested, and grassy areas called glades are common on the more exposed south and west aspects of hills. Although much of the Springfield Plateau has been converted to pasture and row crops, the White River section still offers exten-sive wild areas and tremendous views.

SPRINGFIELD

Springfield, with its self-proclaimed cognomen of "Queen City of the Ozarks," has been the trading hub for a vast area, even since pioneer days. It was founded in 1829 by a homesteader from Tennessee named John Polk Campbell. He donated fifty acres for a public square and gave cabins to prospective settlers. In 1833 the settlement became "Springfield," as one story tells it, by way of a bribe of whiskey that was offered to each man to vote for the name. The town grew steadily; in 1858 the Butterfield-Overland stage offered passage to California from a depot on the northeast corner of the square. The Civil War divided the city, with major battles occurring over a two-year period. Just after the war, the town square was the site of the nation's first recorded shoot-out. A dispute over a gambling debt owed by "Wild Bill" Hickok to Dave Tutt ended in a gunfight, with Tutt on the losing end. Because of Hickok's fame as a Pony Express rider, the event made nationwide news. In 1870 the town's success and prosperity were guaranteed when the "Frisco," the St. Louis–San Francisco Railroad, arrived at its new station at Commercial and Benton Streets. Springfield is also recognized as the birthplace of Route 66, for it was here, in 1926, that officials first proposed the name of the new Chicago-to-Los Angeles highway. It was the first com-pletely paved transcontinental highway in America. It was finished in 1938.

There are many activities to enjoy in Springfield, the third-largest city in Missouri. There are some, however, that stand out above the rest. The first is **Fantastic Caverns.** To reach Fantastic Caverns, which is open year-round, travel on I–44 to MO 13 north and follow the signs to the caverns. The cave was discovered in 1862 by a farmer's dog, which had crawled through an entrance. However, five years passed before the first exploration took place. Twelve women from Springfield answered a newspaper ad seeking explorers, and they were the first to venture into the cave. Their names remain on a cave wall today. Now, jeep-drawn trams carry visitors on the mile-long, fifty-minute tour. No walking is necessary in this cave, and the trams easily accommodate wheelchairs. This may sound like an environmentally incorrect way to travel through a cave; however, these Jeeps are fueled by propane, which emits an exhaust of oxygen and water vapor. Only the front part of the extensive cave is used for tourism, and the water in the underground passages is monitored for pollution. The cave supports unique subterranean wildlife including the endangered Ozark cavefish, the rare cave crayfish, and the grotto salamander. Cave formations include stalactites, stalagmites, columns, soda straws, flowstones, cave pearls, and draperies.

If time permits, a tour of **Dickerson Park Zoo** offers an opportunity to see not only exotic animals but some native ones as well. The Missouri Habitats exhibit features black bear, deer, otter, and others. The zoo also has a bald eagle rehabilitation and breeding center, which worked with the Missouri Department of Conservation to release bald eagles back into the state. The zoo is located at the northeast intersection of I–44 and MO 13.

A good place to stop for outdoor recreational supplies is **Bass Pro Shop's Outdoor World.** Billed as the world's largest sporting goods store, the 150,000-square-foot building contains an incredible selection of merchandise for just about every outdoor activity. This is all showcased in a building studded with aquariums of up to 30,000 gallons, a 30-foot waterfall with stream, and numerous wildlife exhibits. To reach the store, take US 65 south to Sunshine Avenue, go east 4 miles to Campbell Street, turn left, and proceed 1 block to the parking area.

Right next to Bass Pro Shop's Outdoor World you will find the recently built **American National Fish and Wildlife Museum,** called "Wonders of Wildlife." The theme of the museum is to celebrate our interaction with nature and our responsibility to manage wildlife resources. The museum features 160 species of live animals, and cameras are allowed. "Wonders of Wildlife" is open daily from 9:00 A.M. to 6:00 P.M. except for Christmas Day. For more information call (877) 245–9543 or visit its Web site at www.wondersofwildlife.org.

Another recommended stop is the **Springfield Conservation Nature Center.** Sitting on eighty acres of woods, glades, and lakefront, nearly 3 miles of hiking trails weave their way through several exceptional habitats right within the city limits. The well-designed building features educational exhibits that give you a quick orientation to Ozark habitats and explains why they are special. It is well worth the time to take a hike, enjoy the outdoor setting, and learn about the Ozarks. The best way to find the nature center is to follow the signs beginning on US 65 south to US 60 west, which goes into Springfield. Turn onto the James River Freeway and exit on the frontage road, which heads south to the nature center. If you are already in the city, you can reach the center by finding Glenstone Avenue (MO Business Route 65) and heading south to the James River Freeway.

Continue south, taking US 65 to Branson. Just south of Springfield, the highway crosses the upper arm of Lake Springfield. This impoundment is part of the James River, a popular float stream that empties into Table Rock Lake. The best access to the river is off of MO 14 west of Nixa at the Delaware Town Access.

OZARK AREA SITES

The road continues another 5 miles to the town of **Ozark.** It can be reached by taking MO 14 east into town or, in another mile, US Business 65. The town was platted in 1843. It received national attention in 1889 when three members of the "Baldknobbers" were hung in the courthouse square. The Baldknobbers were a secretly organized band of vigilantes that formed after the Civil War to combat the lawlessness that swept the region. Because the group met on the treeless tops of nearby mountains, known as "bald knobs," they became known as Baldknobbers. Today bald knobs are called glades. The well-intentioned Baldknobbers eventually became a band of night-raiders conducting murders, whippings, and general disorder. They eventually disbanded after their leader, Nathaniel Kenney, was shot in 1888.

US 65 crosses over Finley River, a small but popular float and smallmouth bass fishing stream that is a tributary of the James River. In another 5 miles, the highway enters the White River section of the plateau. The relief now becomes more pronounced and the road begins to cut into the hills and valleys, exposing more bedrock. This Mississippian rock, called the Reeds Spring Formation, is layered with beds of white limestone and chert. Deep in the valleys an older, more solid rock appears called the Cotter Formation. It is a dolomite of Ordovician age and is characteristic of the White River section. The second deep valley the road enters is the most dramatic. Here the highway spans a 2-mile-wide valley in a nearly straight line, dropping 340 feet into the valley and up again. This feat of engineering makes this road the longest, straightest span of highway constructed across a valley in either the Ozarks or the Ouachita Mountains, and probably in the entire Midwest, for that matter.

At the bottom of the valley, the 2,505-acre **Busiek State Forest and Wildlife Area** offers primitive camping, hiking, self-guided nature trails, opportunities for nature study, and bird-watching as well as fishing, hunting, and horseback riding. The area, which is on both sides of US 65, contains typical Ozark features including streams, extensive forests, glades, and meadows.

As you travel south along US 65 notice that, although there are still plenty of forested hills, several of the hilltops are being cleared for pastures and homesites. This is increasingly evident the closer you get to Branson. There also seems to be no limit to the number of billboards; Busiek Valley is probably the only stretch that is billboard-free.

BRANSON AREA SITES

A new bypass around **Branson** is being developed; it's called the Ozark Mountain Highroad. It is designed to relieve traffic in Branson by offering an alternative route to the west side of town. When the road is completed, it will be an optional route on this drive, but it will be harder to reach the following highlights from it. However, the drive should be experienced, because if the Missouri Highway Department delivers what it has proposed, you should see a more environmentally sensitive highway with scenic pullouts and landscaping with native Ozark plants instead of traditional fescue, crown vetch, and lespedeza.

Branson began like most Ozarks towns, with a post office and country store, in 1882. About twenty-five years later the railroad came to town, bringing the first tourists to the area. In 1914 the first dam on the White River was completed, backing up water to form Lake Taneycomo. This triggered an influx of tourist and fishing camps, hotels, and boat docks along the new shoreline at Branson. The following decades were filled with gradual growth and change as the nearby towns of Hollister and Rockaway Beach became centers of tourism. The focus shifted back to Branson with the completion of Table Rock Lake in the 1950s. This new dam transformed the downstream Lake Taneycomo into a cold water impoundment. Taneycomo's waters now came from the bottom of Table Rock Lake, and the water's temperature of 48 degrees Fahrenheit was too chilly for swimmers and skiers. Such water recreation shifted to Table Rock Lake, and anglers found the new lake to be an outstanding source of bass, crappie, and other panfish. Meanwhile, Lake Taneycomo was stocked with trout by the Missouri Department of Conservation and soon became a popular lake for coldwater fishing.

Country music came to Branson in 1960 when the Baldknobbers began performing on the Taneycomo lakefront in town. They were joined in 1967 by the Presleys, who built a theater on West MO 76 in Branson, then the Foggy River Boys, the Plummer Family, and so on. Today there are more than sixty different shows, and Branson is known as "America's Live Entertainment Capital."

To see where it all began, take a side trip off US 65 and follow MO Business 65 into **Old Downtown Branson.** This is where the "locals" prefer to shop and eat; some of the historic brick buildings date back to the early part of the century. Since the 1960s, MO 76 west of town has been the center of activity for all modern development.

Of all the drives in and around Branson, the following is most recommended.

At the junction of US 65 and MO 248, start on MO 248 west; immediately to the left is the **Branson Chamber of Commerce Information Center.** It is a good place to stop for maps and brochures; knowledgeable staff can answer any questions you might have about activities in the area. The Chamber of Commerce plans to build a new visitor center at the intersection of US 65 and MO F after highway construction is completed. Continue on MO 248 west about 2 miles to Shepherd of the Hills Expressway. Follow the expressway another 3 miles, crossing over Roark Creek, to MO 76, also called "76 Country Blvd." Turn right onto MO 76. The large hill along the road is Dewey Bald, a common reference in Harold Bell Wright's classic book *The Shepherd of the Hills.*

Follow the highway around Dewey Bald and turn onto the drive to **Ruth and Paul Henning Conservation Area.** The land is named after the producer of the *Beverly Hillbillies,* a popular television program of the 1960s. Mr. Henning purchased this property, where he filmed some of the show's scenes featuring the characters' "Ozark home." Henning later sold the land, with a partial donation, to the Missouri Department of Conservation. The 1,534-acre area contains some of the best examples of glades remaining in the White River Hills today. There are several trails, with one leading up Dewey Bald to an observation deck. Another trail leads to the White River Hills Natural Area to view one of the "balds" that may once have been used by the Baldknobbers. Scenic views, interpretive displays, and a diversity of wildflowers showcase the

Watch for roadrunners seeking out lizards on the glades at Henning Conservation Area.

area's uniqueness. A naturalist is on duty during the busy season to answer questions, lead tours, and give programs.

Just down the road on MO 76, the **Shepherd of the Hills Outdoor Theater** reenacts the 1907 book written by Harold Bell Wright. The book was so successful that the Branson area became a popular attraction even before Lake Taneycomo was built in 1914. Tourists began to arrive as early as 1910 to see where the book was written and the places and people it was written about. The outdoor evening performance of Wright's story and daytime tours are both popular. A ride up the 230-foot Inspiration Tower provides a commanding view of the White River Hills and Table Rock Lake, even though the tower itself detracts from the beauty of the skyline.

Just beyond the intersection of MO 76 and MO 265, a side trip to **Silver Dollar City** will take you back in time to the 1880s. This theme park ranks as one of the nation's most popular entertainment facilities of its kind. Opened in 1960, Silver Dollar City features native craftspeople creating historic crafts that were once commonly found in the Ozarks. Silver Dollar City also has restaurants, specialty foods, free entertainment, and rides. Special festivals are scheduled throughout the year. To avoid traffic and crowds, come early in the day and avoid holiday weekends.

Return to MO 265 and travel 5.5 miles to the junction of MO 165. Turn left and follow the signs to **Shepherd of the Hills Fish Hatchery.** Operated by the Missouri Department of Conservation, the hatchery offers exhibits including aquariums, an introductory film, guided tours, picnicking, trails, and access to Lake Taneycomo for fishing. The hatchery produces between 350,000 and 400,000 pounds of rainbow and brown trout per year. You can also walk around the raceways and view the various sizes of trout before they are released into Lake Taneycomo.

Return to MO 165 and MO 265 and cross over Table Rock Dam. Immediately to the right, the **Dewey Short Visitor Center** offers four-seasons exhibits, a nature trail, a choice of six audiovisual programs in the auditorium, and tours of the Table Rock powerhouse. Just beyond the visitor center is **Table Rock State Park,** which provides access to the 43,000-acre lake. The 356-acre park is a great place for swimming, boating, fishing, hiking, picnicking, and camping. Bald eagles and loons are winter visitors to the area.

After 1.5 miles MO 165 and 265 divide. Turn left onto MO 165, and in 0.7 mile a scenic view overlooks Lake Taneycomo and, unfortunately, a resort development. This fairly new complex serves as a reminder of the rapid and seemingly unregulated housing and commercial development that has occurred in the Branson area over the past two decades. In addition to habitat

Viewing trout in rearing pools is a popular activity at Shepherd of the Hills Fish Hatchery.

loss, wastewater treatment cannot meet the needs of the increasing population. Water quality has noticeably declined, affecting the fisheries and other aquatic life in both lakes, especially Lake Taneycomo. As you stand at this overlook, you are on one of the table rocks that gave the larger lake its name.

In another 2.5 miles and just before US 65, turn left on Hollister Road, which is MO V. Proceed about a mile to the entrance of the **College of the Ozarks.** The school was established in 1907 by the Reverend James Forsyth to provide education in mechanical and commercial skills for young people from poor families. It grew in size from a boarding school for youngsters to a high school, then a junior college, and finally, in 1964, it became a fully accredited four-year college of liberal arts. The school continues its strong tradition of having a work-scholarship plan where students work for their tuition in the school dairy, print shop, water mill, museum, restaurant, or other college enterprises. Be sure to visit the working water mill, the Friendship House (which is a gift shop and restaurant), the Ralph Foster Museum, and other special attractions. The Ralph Foster Museum is dedicated to the history of the Ozarks region. The museum houses thousands of objects representing archaeology, natural history, fine arts, geology, and mineralogy. It even houses the car that was used in the *Beverly Hillbillies* television program. A tour map is available at most campus facilities.

An active water mill can be seen at College of the Ozarks.

Prairie Country

NIAWATHE TO PRAIRIE STATE PARK, MISSOURI

GENERAL DESCRIPTION: A 42-mile drive beginning 8 miles north of Lockwood on Missouri Highway 97, traveling west through prairie landscapes and the towns of Lamar and Liberal, and ending at Prairie State Park.

SPECIAL ATTRACTIONS: Niawathe Prairie Natural Area, Harry S Truman State Historic Site, and Prairie State Park; prairie wildflowers and wildlife, and hiking.

LOCATION: Western Ozarks. The drive begins at the junction of Missouri Highways 97 and E 8 miles north of Lockwood.

DRIVE ROUTE NUMBERS: Missouri Highways 97, 43, K, E, and P and U.S. Highway 160.

CAMPING: Stockton State Park has 45 basic campsites and 38 campsites with electrical hookups. The camping area, which is not far from the edge of Stockton Lake, has a dumping station, modern rest rooms, shower houses, and laundry facilities. Prairie State Park has 6 basic campsites and a pit toilet.

SERVICES: All services at Lamar. Gas and food at Liberal.

NEARBY ATTRACTIONS: Truman Lake, Schell-Osage Conservation Area, and several public prairies (consult *Public Prairies of Missouri*, available from the Missouri Department of Conservation).

THE DRIVE

The western part of the Ozarks in Missouri and Oklahoma was predominately prairie until the time of European settlement, which began in this region about 200 years ago. As the prairie was divided and farmed, what was not plowed was overgrazed by cattle or allowed to grow up in trees. Trees were not at home on the prairie. The gently rolling hills and hot, dry, westerly winds provided ideal conditions to carry wildfires. Prairie plants are adapted to fire, because their growing centers are below the soil. However, the growing points of trees are fully exposed, making them vulnerable to fire. Occasional fires are good for a prairie. The grasses and wildflowers (called forbs) have adapted to the cycle of fire over thousands of years and actually depend upon this natural event for their survival.

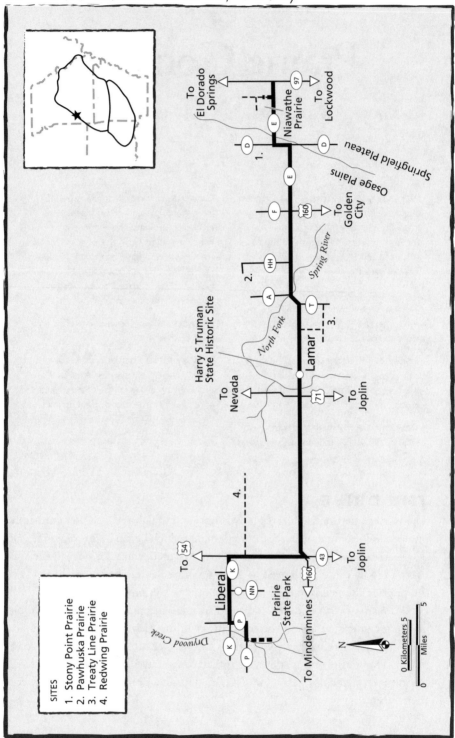

SITES

1. Stony Point Prairie
2. Pawhuska Prairie
3. Treaty Line Prairie
4. Redwing Prairie

Plains Indians were very keen observers of nature and knew how important fire was in maintaining a healthy prairie. Fire, either ignited by lightning strikes or set by Indians, kept the trees in check and removed the dead leaf litter that can cause a prairie to stagnate. Like thatch in a lawn, if dead plant leaves are allowed to accumulate, they can choke out new growth. With leaf litter removed, the soil is exposed and can better absorb the sun's warmth in the spring, allowing a flush of green growth. The Plains Indians saw that this attracted game, especially bison, which meant more successful hunts.

Today public prairies are managed mostly by haying and conducting prescribed burns on a rotational basis. A few prairies are occasionally grazed by cattle to mimic the effects that were once created by bison. Prescribed burns usually take place anytime from late summer to spring, and haying is usually done in July to allow the prairie vegetation to recover before the onset of winter. Some of the prairies that you visit may have various stages of such management occurring.

Missouri has been a leader in prairie protection. The notes of the original land survey indicate that Missouri once contained fifteen million acres of prairie, mostly in the northern and western part of the state. Now much of the prairie is gone from northern Missouri because its deeper soils were well suited to plowing. Western Missouri has characteristically shallow soils over bedrock, so grazing or cutting hay for cattle has been the common practice. Of the estimated 70,000 acres of native prairie remaining in the state, about 25,000 acres have been acquired, restored, and protected, in large part by the Missouri Department of Conservation but also by Missouri State Parks, The Nature Conservancy, and the Missouri Prairie Foundation. For descriptions and maps of the more than sixty prairies, write to the Missouri Department of Conservation and request *Public Prairies of Missouri* (see Appendix A for address).

This drive crosses prairie country on the western edge of the Ozarks' Springfield Plateau and enters a region called the Osage Plains. This allows for a visit to Prairie State Park, which was created to reclaim lost prairie heritage through interpretive exhibits and trails and is situated in the heart of a prairie. The Osage Plains region is distinguished from the Springfield Plateau by its bedrock of sandstone and shale of older, Pennsylvanian age, while the Springfield Plateau is composed of limestone and chert rocks of Mississippian age.

NIAWATHE PRAIRIE

Begin the drive at the junction of MO 97 and E, 8 miles north of Lockwood. Travel west on MO E for a mile and turn right onto a gravel road that continues for about half a mile to a parking lot on the left. This is **Niawathe**

Prairie, a 320-acre prairie named for the Osage Indian term for "life-giver." There are no trails, so wander freely across the prairie. As in any grassy area, chiggers may be present; using an insect repellent would be a good idea. During the growing season, you can see the showiest and best variety of wildflowers in the areas west and north of the parking lot. For the best view, walk toward the north end and look southwest. From there a beautiful prairie landscape unravels that is devoid of power lines, barns, silos, communication towers, and other reminders of civilization. Walking west to the high point provides more extended views of the landscape and its farmsteads.

Looking over the prairie, notice the mounds rising 2 to 3 feet above the ground and up to 10 feet across. These mounds are typical of many prairies in western Missouri and eastern Kansas and Oklahoma. Commonly called pimple mounds or Mima mounds (after a site south of Olympia, Washington), their origin is a mystery. There are several possible explanations for the mounds. They could be Indian burial sites, remnants left by wind or water erosion, seismic activity, or glacial outwash. Another popular theory involves pocket gophers—small mammals that dig their burrows by piling excavated soil into mounds. The plains pocket gopher exhibits this mound-building capability, but on a smaller scale than that required to create these mounds. It is possible that a larger pocket gopher once existed but is now extinct. Whatever caused these mounds is still a mystery because new mounds have been created, at least since the beginning of recorded history.

Prairies are remarkable for their diversity of plants and animals. Grasses such as big and little bluestem, Indian, switch, sideoats grama, and prairie dropseed dominate. A high-quality prairie is typically home to more than 150 forbs; species in the sunflower, legume, and rose families are the most numerous. You can also find representatives of the iris, orchid, spurge, mint, parsley, figwort, and many other families. Flowering begins on the prairies in April and ends in late October, guaranteeing a show of colors throughout the season. October is especially brilliant when the prairie grasses turn rusty red and gold. Although a variety of animals live on the prairies, birds are especially noticeable. Nesting birds include dickcissels, yellowthroats, American goldfinches, eastern meadowlarks, quail, and several types of sparrows. Less common but still sometimes seen are northern harrier, short-eared owl, prairie chicken, Henslow's sparrow, and upland sandpiper. Many species of insects inhabit the prairie, including beautiful butterflies such as the monarch and the rare regal fritillary.

Because prairies have drastically declined throughout their former thirteen-state range, many plants and animals that are exclusive to this habitat are also becoming rare. Even with 17,000 acres of protected prairie in Missouri, animals such as the prairie chicken are losing ground. Fewer than 500 of these birds are left in the state. Public involvement is essential for fostering support for measures that prevent the further decline of prairies.

PUBLIC PRAIRIES AND
HARRY S TRUMAN HOME

From Niawathe Prairie, return to MO E and proceed west for 3 miles to the junction of MO D. A mile north of here is the 640-acre **Stony Point Prairie.** MO E merges with US 160 in 4 miles. Follow US 160 west; in 3 miles a side trip on MO HH leads to the seventy-seven-acre **Pawhuska Prairie.** After another 4 miles on US 160, another side trip on a gravel road south leads to **Treaty Line Prairie,** a 168-acre area.

Return to US 160 and proceed into the town of **Lamar,** home of President Harry S Truman and Wyatt Earp. Lamar was settled in 1852 by George E. Ward, who built a sawmill and operated a small general store. Lamar was incorporated in 1867 and was named by Mrs. Ward in honor of President Mirabeau Lamar of the Republic of Texas. The focal point of the town is the large town square. The county courthouse, built in 1888, still functions as the center of county government. The square is the site of the annual Lamar Fair, which is billed as the "Largest Free Fair in the State of Missouri" and has been in continuous operation for one week each August for the past sixty years.

Upon entering Lamar, follow the signs to the **Harry S Truman State Historic Site.** This one-and-a-half-story house, built around 1881, is listed on the National Register of Historic Places. Truman's father, John Anderson, and mother, Martha Ellen, bought the house in 1882 for $685. Two years later, on May 8, Harry was born. Six years later, the family moved north to Independence, Missouri, where the future president began his schooling. The United Auto Workers of America bought the house from descendants of the famous Wyatt Earp (who was once the constable of Lamar) in 1957. The house was donated to the state in 1959. The historic site is open to visitors from 10:00 A.M. to 4:00 P.M. Monday through Saturday and from noon to 4:00 P.M. Sunday. An interpreter provides tours of the house, which is decorated with furnishings from the period of the Trumans' occupancy. A temporary visitor center and parking area are now available across from the Truman house. Recently the rest of the city block was purchased by the Missouri Department of Natural Resources, with future plans to include a new visitor center as well as a mule barn and other structures appropriate for the era.

The recent Hollywood movies *Wyatt Earp* and *Tombstone* have triggered renewed interest in Earp's days in Lamar. He followed his parents from Illinois

*A naturalist stands ready to guide visitors through the late president
Harry S Truman's first home in Lamar.*

in 1869 and became the town's first constable the following year, at the age of
twenty-two. For $15 a month, he served warrants, broke up fights, and hauled
drunks to jail. Earp left Lamar around 1872, apparently after a barroom brawl
with some of his in-laws; he stole a horse and never returned. Later, his legendary status grew in Wichita and Dodge City in Kansas and at the infamous
shootout at the O.K. Corral in Tombstone, Arizona, in 1881.

LIBERAL AND PRAIRIE STATE PARK

Continue west on US 160 for about 10 miles to the junction of MO 43. Turn
right and proceed north 3.5 miles. A 2.5-mile side trip east on a gravel road leads
to the 160-acre **Redwing Prairie.** Proceed another mile on MO 43, then turn
west onto MO K and continue to the town of **Liberal.** Founded in 1880 by
George H. Walser, Liberal was established as a "Free-thinker" town. It was
designed to be a place where Free-thinkers could live in a sort of colony and
enjoy their beliefs in a quiet, unmolested way. What is more remarkable is that
churches and saloons were not allowed within the town limits. At one point, to
keep Christians from settling in the town and eventually outnumbering the
Free-thinkers, the latter established a high-post, barbed-wire fence around the
entire town, including the public highway. When railroad authorities telegraphed
that they would remove the depot if the lunacy was not abandoned—it was

abandoned. Today the town of 689 residents exhibits little of its early beginnings. Follow MO K for 2 miles west of Liberal and turn south onto MO P and follow the signs to **Prairie State Park.** Covering just over 3,500 acres, the park began with a purchase of 1,500 acres of prairie in 1982. Today the park supports a visitor center, complete with interpretive exhibits and programs, 7 miles of trails, and naturalist-led walks. Of particular interest is the opportunity to see bison roaming the prairie much as they did more than 200 years ago. (For your safety, be sure to obey the signs indicating the current location of bison.) The bison, once numbering more than sixty million, almost became extinct before a few hundred animals were found and protected by law. Bison were eliminated from Missouri in the 1870s. Now, in addition to bison, the park supports elk, which were also an original component of the prairie.

Ask a park staff member for an animal checklist that lists 150 birds, 23 mammals, 10 fishes, 12 amphibians, 23 reptiles, and 88 butterflies and moths. Observers have also documented more than 350 species of grasses and forbs that live in the park. The once extensive prairies have been carved up, leaving only small isolated patches, causing plants and animals dependent on prairies to suffer. At least twenty-five plant and animal species listed as rare or endangered are finding refuge at Prairie State Park. Additional efforts to protect prairie across its former range must continue so that future generations can also experience the awe and excitement of this unique ecosystem.

American bison, once numbering in the millions, can still be seen at Prairie State Park.

Prairie Country

Roaring River State Park

CASSVILLE TO EAGLE ROCK, MISSOURI

GENERAL DESCRIPTION: A 15-mile drive beginning in Cassville and dropping into the White River Hills to Eagle Rock.

SPECIAL ATTRACTIONS: Roaring River State Park and Fish Hatchery, Roaring River Cove Hardwoods Natural Area, Sugar Camp Scenic Drive, and Mark Twain National Forest; hiking trails, trout fishing, glades, wildflowers, scenic views, fall colors, camping, canoeing, horseback riding, and hunting.

LOCATION: Western Ozarks. The drive begins on Missouri Highway 112 in Cassville on the east side of town.

DRIVE ROUTE NUMBERS: Missouri Highways 112, 248, and F; Forest Road 197; and Table Rock Road 86-97.

CAMPING: Roaring River State Park has the newly built Roaring River Inn and Conference Center that features lodging and dining. Cabins are also available that can accommodate up to 6 persons. The state park also provides 180 tent and trailer campsites, both basic and with hookups. Facilities in the camping area include two sanitary dumping stations, ice machines, hot showers, modern rest rooms, and laundry facilities. Motel and cabin reservations are required and may be made by calling the park concessionaire's office. The U.S. Army Corps of Engineers' Table Rock Lake has 21 recreation areas with modern campground facilities. Three local Corps of Engineers recreation areas are Eagle Rock, Viney Creek, and Beaver. Primitive camping is allowed in the Mark Twain National Forest.

SERVICES: All services at Cassville.

NEARBY ATTRACTIONS: Flag Spring Conservation Area, Piney Creek Wilderness Area, Eureka Springs, Table Rock Lake, Beaver Lake, and Pig Trail and Ozark Highlands scenic drives.

THE DRIVE

The first part of the drive crosses the southwestern part of the Springfield Plateau. The hills are only slightly dissected and rolling. This is a transition region, where prairies from the plains once graded into the forests of the rugged Ozarks. The bedrock is Mississippian limestone, known for its sinkholes, caves, and springs. About 4 miles south of Cassville, on the way to Roar-

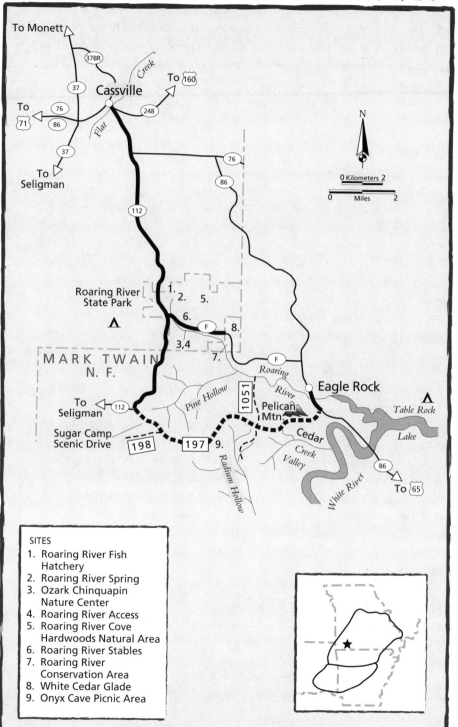

SITES
1. Roaring River Fish Hatchery
2. Roaring River Spring
3. Ozark Chinquapin Nature Center
4. Roaring River Access
5. Roaring River Cove Hardwoods Natural Area
6. Roaring River Stables
7. Roaring River Conservation Area
8. White Cedar Glade
9. Onyx Cave Picnic Area

ing River State Park, the road leaves the plateau and descends into the watershed of the White River section. For millions of years the White River has been cutting into the Springfield Plateau, creating deep, steep-walled valleys and exposing various layers of sedimentary rock, including limestone, shale, dolomite, and chert. Today the hilly White River section still contains extensive forests with some clearing for pastures on the broader ridges and wider valleys.

CASSVILLE

The drive begins in **Cassville.** Originally platted in 1845, the town was once a stop for the Butterfield Overland Mail and briefly served as the Confederate capital of Missouri. During the Civil War, the secessionist governor and Confederate members of the Missouri General Assembly fled Union troops and met here the first week of November 1861. They considered the ordinance of secession, which was approved at nearby Neosho by eleven senators and forty-four representatives. Both the ordinance and the act of affiliation to the Confederate States were signed here, and the Confederate flag was hoisted above the courthouse. During the war, Cassville was attacked several times by both sides. The courthouse, having suffered from its use as a fort and horse stable, was eventually torn down in 1910 and replaced with the existing building in 1913.

Recently named one of the top one hundred retirement areas in America, Cassville (ranked 49th) was one of only two Missouri towns to receive the honor—the other being Branson at 34th. Cassville received high ratings on quality of life, affordability, housing, safety, and law enforcement. The town is a service center for the surrounding farms and settlements, as well as a gateway to Roaring River State Park and the upper portion of Table Rock Lake.

Before leaving Cassville, a good place to stop for information on recreational opportunities in the Mark Twain National Forest is the Cassville Ranger Station. The office is located on the north side of MO 248 just three-quarters of a mile east of the five-highway intersection in midtown. It is open Monday through Friday.

ROARING RIVER SITES

On the east side of town, take MO 112 south to **Roaring River State Park.** After about 4 miles the road drops off the relatively flat Springfield Plateau and begins its descent into the White River watershed. Be careful as you enter the park: The last mile drops 400 feet into the Roaring River valley, offering some scenic views but no turnouts. A busy intersection awaits at the bottom of the hill; turn left to go to the spring and hatchery. Trout fishing is the most popular activity here, but the deep hollows, extensive forests, and open glades provide an exceptional diversity of plants and animals that can be seen on the six trails that total 9.7 miles. Although elk, bison, and wolves are gone, armadillos, bobcats, and black bears still roam here. Armadillos and other typically "southern" animals such as the painted bunting and roadrunner have been extending their range northward over the past twenty years due to the mild winters. This may be evidence of global warming.

The road up Roaring River Hollow parallels the spring run. At the end of the road, the Missouri Department of Conservation's **Roaring River Fish Hatchery** offers the chance to see trout grouped by various sizes in rearing pools. Guided tours are given, mostly on weekends. Check at the hatchery for information on tour times. A trail leads past the trout rearing pools to **Roaring River Spring.** An average of twenty-two million gallons of water per day emerges from the base of a grottolike gorge beneath a high dolomite cliff. Ranked as the tenth-largest spring in Missouri, divers have measured the vent, which directs the spring upward, to be 215 feet long. At the bottom there are several cave passageways from which the water collects. It has been said that before the dam was built in 1880 to pool the spring, the waters rushed from the grotto over rocks with a sound and splash that gave merit to the spring's name.

Rearing pools offer a chance to see and feed trout before they are released into Roaring River.

The first mill to use the Roaring River Spring was built in 1836. Another mill was built in 1845 where the lodge now stands; it was destroyed during the Civil War. Rebuilt in 1886, the mill carded wool, ground grain, and sawed logs. When the milling business declined, the building was converted to a hotel. By the early 1920s, it had become a popular vacation spot for residents of Kansas City and St. Louis. The inn was later destroyed by fire. A private resort and trout hatchery were soon established but met an early demise. Finally, in 1928, a wealthy businessman from St. Louis purchased the entire tract of 2,400 acres with elaborate plans to develop the area as a tourist resort. Within a year he changed his mind and donated the land to the State of Missouri. Today, with additional purchases, the park includes 3,354 acres.

Before leaving Roaring River Spring and the hatchery, the 0.2-mile **Deer Leap Trail** begins along the spring walkway and leads to a great overlook. From there you can view the hatchery and the spring grotto. The name of the trail comes from an incident in which someone observed a deer being chased by dogs; the dear leaped to its death from the towering cliff overlooking the spring. The first part of the hike is a strenuous climb up stone steps built by the 1930s Civilian Conservation Corps. The CCC also constructed the attractive stonework around the lodge. The trail takes you along the base of a huge rock cliff with interesting rock slabs that have broken away from the wall. After spending time at the overlook, continue on the trail, which descends and exits by a cabin near the spring pond.

Another trail, the 1.5-mile **Devil's Kitchen Trail,** begins at the small picnic area across from the lodge or can be accessed from the hatchery road near the junction of MO 112. It was named for a huge cavity in a rock outcrop; legend has it that this feature was once used by Civil War bushwhackers. Before them, Native Americans probably used the alcove as a campsite, for they were observed as late as 1830 hunting in this area along the spring-fed river. A self-guided interpretive brochure for this trail is available at the nature center.

Back on the hatchery road, follow the signs to the **Ozark Chinquapin Nature Center,** which is located just off MO F. The nature center contains exhibits interpreting the natural history of the area. It has field guides for sale, and be sure to ask for a map showing the hiking trails. In front of the building, the staff maintains an excellent display of native wildflowers that can be found growing in the park. The plants have labels for easy identification.

For the more adventuresome, ask about access to the **Roaring River Cove Hardwoods Natural Area.** A 120-acre portion in the northern part of the park was designated in 1978 as a state natural area. The area features old-growth, dry upland forest of black oak, white oak, red oak, post oak, and

Roaring River Spring issues twenty-two million gallons of water per day from the base of a towering dolomite cliff.

shagbark hickory on rocky chert slopes, with an understory of flowering dogwood and serviceberry. The richer, more protected coves contain basswood, walnut, and sugar maple.

Spring floaters can reach the **Roaring River** off MO F through campground "C," past the restricted fly-fishing area. The river, which is actually a spring-fed creek, has a permanent flow of 6.5 miles and passes the MO 85 bridge at Eagle Rock before emptying into Table Rock Lake.

Continuing down MO F, the road passes **Roaring River Stables.** Located in the park, its guided one-hour rides leave every half-hour throughout the day. Past the stables and on the right, the 439-acre **Roaring River Conservation Area** contains forest, pasture, and half a mile of the Roaring River. There is no developed access to the river here. The parking lot does offer a convenient place to stop and walk across the highway to see the **White Cedar Glade** restoration project. Trees are being removed, and prescribed fire has been used to help restore this overgrown glade and savanna. No trails have been developed yet, so visitors should be prepared for cross-country hiking across the state park and Forest Service land. Walking south along the slope, which parallels MO F, the glade begins to show its true character in about 200 yards. A quicker access to the best part of the glade can be reached by driving 0.1 mile beyond the Roaring River Conservation Area parking lot on MO F and parking along the road in a pullout that accommodates two or three vehicles. Be careful crossing the highway; most vehicles tend to drive much faster than the posted speed limit along this stretch. Particularly attractive in the spring and early summer, the glade features an abundance of wildflowers and unusual animals such as collared lizards, or "mountain boomers," tarantulas, scorpions, painted buntings, and roadrunners. The rare white cedar tree also grows here, not to be confused with the more common eastern red cedar, which is one of the main threats to the glade.

SUGAR CAMP SCENIC DRIVE

Return to the main part of the park and turn onto MO 112 south. You immediately begin climbing a steep hill and just to the right encounter the **Roaring River Inn and Conference Center**—a new facility that features lodging, dining, conference rooms, and a gift shop. For advance reservations call (800) 334-6946. Continuing on MO 112 for about 2 miles, a scenic overlook is located on the east side of the road. In another mile and on the left, Forest Road 197 starts the **Sugar Camp Scenic Drive.** The 8-mile drive derives its name from a popular activity of the early twentieth century—tapping sugar maples and camping. The well-maintained gravel road is now a popular route,

A commanding view along Sugar Camp Scenic Drive.

having been featured on a national cable television show and in a recreation magazine. The first vista overlooks Pine Hollow and, in the distance, Roaring River Hollow.

Continuing on FR 197, the road follows a narrow ridge that supports short-leaf pine, white oak, black oak, red oak, hickories, and sassafras. In springtime the steep, cherty slopes light up with the colors of redbud and flowering dogwood. The next vista overlooks **Radium Hollow** to the south. The valley derives its name from Radium Spring. Water from the spring was bottled and sent to Germany during the 1930s for medicinal purposes. The site is also said to have been a tomato cannery. Foundations from the old structures can still be found on the site.

After about half a mile, **Onyx Cave Picnic Area** overlooks Cedar Creek Valley. A short trail opposite the picnic area leads to Onyx Cave, a crawling-only cave that has about 100 feet of passageway. In 2 miles, passing another vista along the way, the road crosses FR 1051. The flat open areas along the road are actually small limestone glades. The thin soil, with lots of exposed limestone bedrock, supports special plants that are adapted to the harsh conditions. Plants like the prickly pear cactus, glade onion, widow's-cross sedum, Trelease's larkspur, and the fragrant calamint grow here. In another mile a vista shows a section of the White River as it courses its way to Table Rock Lake. In 1.5 miles the gravel road comes to FR 2275; turn left and in 0.1 mile the drive ends at MO 86 and the small community of Eagle Rock.

The Christmas City

ANDERSON TO NOEL, MISSOURI

GENERAL DESCRIPTION: An 11-mile drive along the scenic overhanging bluffs of the Elk River to Noel, the Christmas City.

SPECIAL ATTRACTIONS: Elk River, Indian Creek Roadside Park, Mt. Shira Stream Access, and Noel; overhanging bluffs, canoeing, swimming, and fall colors.

LOCATION: Western Ozarks. The drive begins at the intersection of U.S. Highway 71 and Missouri Highway 59.

DRIVE ROUTE NUMBERS: Missouri Highway 59.

TRAVEL SEASON: Year-round.

CAMPING: Private campgrounds are located along the Elk River. Primitive camping is available at Huckleberry Ridge Conservation Area, but no services are provided.

SERVICES: All services at Noel. Food and gas at Anderson.

NEARBY ATTRACTIONS: Buffalo Hills Natural Area.

THE DRIVE

This part of the Ozarks is known as the Elk River section. The region is a combination of rolling plains and rugged hills that drain into the Elk River. Historically there were extensive upland hardwood and pine forests with a few prairie openings, which mostly occurred on the broad, rolling plains. Today there are still large forested areas, but with fire suppression, pine trees and prairie openings are fewer in number. These are two natural communities that depend on fire to keep them healthy and viable; otherwise they lose ground to hardwood forests. Although the Elk River had lost its namesake by the 1830s, there are reports of thirty or more elk roaming the hills near here, having escaped from an elk ranch. Much like the Rocky Mountain elk that were released along the Buffalo River in Arkansas, these elk also seem to be adjusting to the Ozarks.

The drive takes place in McDonald County, a county that gained fame in 1961 by declaring itself the McDonald Territory after the county name was left off the official Missouri highway map that year. Although the county officials

144

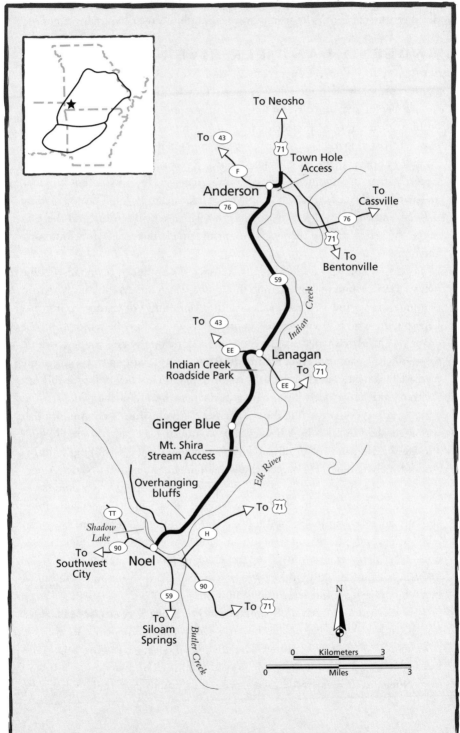

have since forgotten their anger, and the added publicity they generated has declined, the exceptionally scenic overhanging bluffs over the highway endure.

ANDERSON AND ELK RIVER

Starting at the intersection of US 71 and MO 59, proceed on MO 59 to **Anderson.** Nestled in the valley of Indian Creek, this small town is a retail and service center for the surrounding farms. Supplies for tourists and outdoor enthusiasts are also an important part of the retail trade. Indian Creek is an excellent fast-flowing run in the spring. The gradient is 8.6 feet per mile with 26 miles of permanent flow. Unlike the Elk River into which it drains, Indian Creek has few developments along the way. Access to Indian Creek is provided at **Town Hole Access,** which is on Main Street in Anderson. Located toward the east end of Main Street at the end of a large parking lot behind the post office, the access offers a nice view of Spring Creek, interesting rock outcrops, and a picnic area.

Leaving town, MO 59 follows the Kansas City Southern Railroad, the line that was so instrumental in opening the remote Ouachita Mountains. The road continues down Indian Creek valley to the community of **Lanagan.** Just past Lanagan, the road is forced to take an upland route because the railroad and the creek are already crowded against the bluff, occupying the best route. Once on top of the hill, **Indian Creek Roadside Park** is an interesting stop. Notice the picnic tables made out of huge slabs of limestone rock. They will probably last for thousands of years, making them a permanent fixture of the park.

Proceeding down the hill, the road passes **Ginger Blue,** a community that was established in 1915 by a Kansas City Southern Railroad tycoon. He built a lodge on the banks of the Elk River to provide a place for fishing enthusiasts and their families. He named the lodge Ginger Blue after a Native American chief who lived near the site in the 1700s. The lodge was expanded over the years to include a restaurant that was once known for its excellent cuisine and offered a beautiful view of the Elk River from the dining room. After several owners and a declining structure, the lodge was used as a barracks in the mid-1990s for workers from a nearby chicken processing plant. In the late 1900s it was purchased by new owners who had plans to renovate the building; unfortunately, it burned to the ground in July 2003.

In less than a mile, turn at the entrance to **Mt. Shira Stream Access.** Since it is the only public access along the drive, this is the best opportunity to get a close-up view of the **Elk River.** The Elk River, along with Big Sugar and Indian Creeks, drains much of McDonald County. The Elk flows northwest from Noel and then turns southwest, making its way to Lake of the Cherokees in Oklahoma. With its 22 miles of permanent flow, it is sought out by canoeists and anglers year-round. The best floating is below the mouth of Indian Creek; the scenery is exceptional, with rugged hills, craggy overhanging ledges, and unusually clear water. During the summer season the river receives intensive recreational use. This can be hard on wildlife, because increasing contact with humans causes the animals stress. The fish community in the Elk River section is the most distinctive of the Missouri Ozarks. Unusual fish such as the cardinal shiner, Neosho madtom, Neosho orangethroat darter, and redspot chub are found in this area.

Continue on MO 59 and after 1.5 miles you will be driving under impressive **overhanging bluffs.** Such features are unique to this drive; this craggy limestone bluff line overshadows the highway in dramatic fashion. In the spring and after heavy rains, there is even a small waterfall cascading off the bluff that splatters the windshields of southbound motorists. The overhangs were formed as the Elk River cut into the bluff in the not-too-distant geologic past. The softer, 6-foot layer at the base is Chattanooga shale, which is highly erodible. This shale, which is derived from mud, and the massive overlying limestone, which originated from shell fragments, were deposited more than 340 million years ago in a vast sea. Over millions of years the accumulations of mud and shell fragments were compressed by the weight of additional layers to form rock. Land animals had not yet appeared, but trees, ferns, and other plants were flourishing. In the oceans, primitive fish, sharks, and amphibians were abundant. It is difficult to find a pulloff along here from which to observe the overhangs in more detail, but midway down there is a shoulder wide enough to pull over. Also, just south of the bluff line, there is an area sufficient to park three or four cars.

It is easy to imagine the attraction these shelters held for the early inhabitants of this region. These overhangs and nearby caves were used by Ozark Bluff Dwellers during a period from 500 to 2,500 years ago. A 1922 expedition of archaeologists from the Museum of the American Indian in New York found, in excellent condition, numerous objects crafted from bone, clay, stone, plants, and feathers. In the 1930s scientists from the University of Arkansas explored the bluff shelters and found baskets and mats woven of reeds and also small quantities of acorns and corn that were used for food. To learn more about the life of these early people, visit the commercially operated **Bluff Dweller's Cave and Browning Museum,** located 2 miles south of Noel on MO 59. It offers cave tours and displays of Indian artifacts. It's open March to November from 8:00 A.M. to 6:00 P.M.; winter schedules may vary. For more information call (417) 475–3666 or visit www.4noel.com/bluffd.

Impressive overhanging bluffs lead to Noel.

NOEL

In another mile the road leads to **Noel,** one of the oldest resort centers in the Midwest. The Elk River in Noel forms Shadow Lake, due to a low-lying dam about half a mile downstream from here. After crossing the Elk River, turn left and you will be approaching a rather spectacular bluff overhang. This setting, especially from the opposite direction, has been the location for many travel brochure photos.

Noel is known as "The Christmas City." Each year the town receives widespread publicity when the post office is deluged with more than a half million Christmas cards to be postmarked with the town's yuletide name. As an added decoration to the "Noel" cancellation, volunteers stamp a tiny green Christmas tree on every piece of mail. To receive this special postmark, package up your Christmas cards and mail them to Postmaster, Noel, MO 64854. Children who send their Christmas letter to "Santa Claus," Noel, MO 64854, along with a self-addressed, stamped envelope, will receive a personal message from Old Santa himself.

Two Mountains

MOUNTAIN HOME TO MOUNTAIN VIEW, ARKANSAS

GENERAL DESCRIPTION: A 59-mile drive starting at Mountain Home, traveling south to the scenic river hills of the White River, and ending at Mountain View.

SPECIAL ATTRACTIONS: Blanchard Springs Caverns, Ozark Folk Center State Park, Norfork National Fish Hatchery, Norfork Lake, North Fork and White Rivers, and Ozark National Forest; scenic views, hiking, canoeing, swimming, fishing (including trout), hunting, cave tour, camping, and horseback riding.

LOCATION: Southeastern Ozarks. The drive begins on Arkansas Highway 5 in Mountain Home and heads south.

DRIVE ROUTE NUMBERS: Arkansas Highways 5, 9, 14, and 177.

CAMPING: Norfork Lake and Bull Shoals Lake have several modern camping sites. The Sylamore Ranger District of the Ozark National Forest has campsites at the Blanchard Springs (32 sites), Gunner Pool (27 sites), and Barkshed (5 sites) recreation areas.

SERVICES: All services found in Mountain Home, Mountain View, and Calico Rock. Food and gas at Norfork.

NEARBY ATTRACTIONS: Bull Shoals Lake, Buffalo National River, and Leatherwood and Lower Buffalo wilderness areas.

THE DRIVE

This area of the eastern Arkansas Ozarks has a lower elevation than its western counterpart. The White River and its tributaries have been carving into this region of the Ozark uplift for more than one hundred million years, exposing prominent dolomite cliffs, sandstone outcrops, rugged wooded hills, and canyonlike valleys.

MOUNTAIN HOME TO NORFOLK

The drive begins at **Mountain Home,** one of the fastest-growing communities in northern Arkansas. Most of this growth has been stimulated by tourism and recreation developments associated with Norfolk and Bull Shoals Lakes. The town was first called Rapp's Barren for 1839 settler "Rapp" Talburt, who settled in an area barren of trees. Then Colonel Orrin L. Dodd, another early

settler, came into the area in the early 1850s and developed a plantation along the White River. Accompanied by his slaves, Dodd traveled back and forth from his Augusta, Arkansas, home in the Mississippi River bottoms to his place at Rapp's Barren. Along the journey, Dodd's slaves talked about returning to their "mountain home." When the post office was established in 1857, its name was officially listed as Mountain Home. The town was incorporated as the county seat in 1888.

Leaving Mountain Home, head south on AR 5 for 11 miles and turn east onto AR 177 at the small town of Salesville. Proceed 2 miles to the **Norfork National Fish Hatchery,** which is below Norfork Dam. The federal hatchery, one of the largest of its kind east of the Rockies, was established in 1957 to produce trout for restocking the cold tailwaters below Norfork, Bull Shoals, and other dams. The water in these reservoirs is more than 100 feet deep at the dam, and the lower depths average between 44 and 56 degrees Fahrenheit. This temperature is ideal for raising trout. The hatchery supplies more than 1.5 million trout of catchable size annually. Dry Run Creek, which runs just outside the fenced-in area of the hatchery grounds, is the site of a catch-and-release program for properly licensed disabled individuals and those under sixteen years of age. A wheelchair-accessible ramp, paved walk, and picnic tables are located in this area. Hatchery hours are from 7:00 A.M. to 3:30 P.M. daily, and tours are available to large groups.

Follow the road signs to **Norfork Lake;** the road offers overlooks of the lake and the dam that was completed in 1944 to hold back the North Fork River. Built for flood control and the generation of hydroelectric power, the project provided jobs and boosted the economy of a region that was still reeling from the depression. Recreational opportunities on the 22,000-acre lake include fishing, boating, skiing, swimming, and wildlife viewing. Below the dam, the North Fork River courses through wooded hills for 4 miles before joining the White River at the town of Norfork. Along this stretch, rainbow trout in the fifteen-pound class can be caught.

Return to AR 5 and continue south for 2 miles to **Norfork.** One of the oldest settlements in Arkansas, the town was founded at the junction of the North Fork and White Rivers during the riverboat days. Because of the shoals and rapids where the two rivers joined, only flat-bottomed boats could navigate beyond that point. Although steamboats could later ascend the White River to Forsyth, Missouri, Norfolk remained the normal unloading point. From here, loads of salt and other goods were freighted over the "Old Salt Road," which led northwest along the White River to Branson, and then north to Springfield. In Norfork, the Wolf House, which was built in 1809, is closed and is being restored. Just before the Wolf House, a road leads down the hill to the Norfork Access to the White River. This provides you with an opportunity to see the river firsthand.

CALICO ROCK

Leaving Norfork, the road climbs steeply and offers dramatic views of the surrounding hills and river valley, which is often shrouded with morning fog. Continue on AR 5 about 12 miles to the town of **Calico Rock.** Many of the buildings here are built into the hill above the White River, making for a picturesque setting. Like many other points along the river, Calico Rock was named by boatmen prior to any settlement. They often referred to the "calico rock" landmark well before the town was established on the bluff. At one time, multihued mineral stains on the bluff's sandstone face looked similar to calico, the multicolored fabric used to make dresses and shirts. Unfortunately, the original face of the bluff was blasted away to make room for a railroad bed. Centuries from now, with the continual leaching of minerals onto the face of the bluff, the calico effect will probably once again be evident.

Calico Rock affords good views of the **White River.** This stretch of the White River below Bull Shoals Lake is almost always floatable due to daily power generation and has become one of the most famous trout streams in the world. This is one of the positive aspects of the many impoundments upstream from this point. The most powerful and destructive miles of the White are now impeded by a chain of dams forming lakes Beaver, Table Rock, Taneycomo, and Bull Shoals. Flood control and recreation benefited, whereas Ozark plants and animals and their habitats along the river were eliminated.

Although the river's straight-line distance from its source near Boston (in northwest Arkansas) to where it empties into the Mississippi River is 225 miles, its natural meandering causes the water to travel more than 800 miles to complete the same journey. The White River was named by the early French explorers in the 1730s, who called the river *La Rivière au Blanc,* referring to the foaming white-water shoals that, prior to impoundment, were common along the river.

OZARK NATIONAL FOREST TO MOUNTAIN VIEW

After crossing the White River, AR 5 enters the Sylamore Ranger District of the **Ozark National Forest.** The next 26.5 miles to Blanchard Springs Caverns is designated as a National Forest Scenic Byway. For this national program, the Forest Service has selected exceptional stretches of highways across the nation that offer scenic drives and recreational opportunities on Forest Service land. The Sylamore Scenic Byway, from Calico Rock to Blanchard Springs Caverns, has such a designation. The 175,000 acres in the Sylamore Ranger District offer several recreational opportunities, including an 89-mile trail for horseback riding, hiking, and mountain biking. Most of the trail is located on maintained forest roads. Maps and descriptions of the hiking, biking, and horse trails are available at the Blanchard Springs Caverns Visitors Center and at the Sylamore District Office in Mountain View.

After 16 miles, the road crosses over Sylamore Creek just before the creek enters the White River. Turn right onto AR 14 in Allison and begin a steep, 6-mile climb to the **Blanchard Springs Caverns** entrance. Note that the dolomite and sandstone outcroppings seen from Mountain Home to Calico Rock have changed to chert and limestone rock. The latter bedrock is more recent in geologic history and thus higher in elevation. Also, notice more pine trees along this drive; they favor the acidic, cherty soils. Below the chert, the permeable limestone bedrock harbors caves, springs, and openings to sinkholes, and hence the formation of Blanchard Springs Caverns.

For a general orientation to the area, be sure to stop at the visitor center. Follow the road signs off AR 14 leading down a steep hill to the visitor center on the right. A guided tour of the caverns and two trails are available. The Dripstone Trail is wheelchair accessible and no more than 0.7 mile long. However, inclines are steep, and strong assistants are needed to control wheelchairs. The trail passes through two huge rooms filled with an incredible abundance of crystalline cave formations including sparkling flowstone, towering columns, and delicate stalactites. The Discovery Trail follows the path of the first explorers through water-carved passages, under the natural entrance, and along the cave stream. The longer, more strenuous tour is 1.2 miles long, with nearly 700 stairsteps. Do not take this trail if you have walking, heart, or breathing difficulties. The Discovery Trail is open from Memorial Day weekend through Labor Day.

The visitor center also has a bookstore, interesting exhibits, and information on other activities in the recreation area. For hiking, be sure to ask about the North Sylamore Creek Trail. The trail is 15 miles long and can be accessed at Barkshead, Gunner Pool, and Blanchard Springs campgrounds, and at the main trailhead, off AR 14 near Allison. This is one of the most scenic backpacking or day-hiking trails in Arkansas. It follows North Sylamore Creek, a crystal-clear, spring-fed stretch of water winding past impressive limestone bluffs and large trees. Canoeing is possible on this proposed Wild and Scenic River, but only when most other streams are in flood.

Anglers try their luck fishing for trout in Blanchard Springs Caverns' Mirror Lake.

Before leaving the recreation area, follow the road to **Blanchard Springs,** passing by Mirror Lake, a trout-fishing area built by the Civilian Conservation Corps. Proceed to a parking area and walk the short, level trail to a deck overlooking Blanchard Springs. The spring tumbles out of an opening in the limestone wall. Here, in 1971, scuba divers entered to explore the watercourse all the way to the natural cave entrance, which is a large sinkhole half a mile up and on the other side of the mountain, some 4,000 feet away from the spring outlet.

Return to AR 5, head south 6 miles, and turn right on AR 382, which leads 1 mile to **Ozark Folk Center State Park.** The center is a unique facility that works to preserve the heritage and way of life of the Ozark mountain people. More than twenty pioneer skills and crafts are demonstrated to a background of live mountain music. A gift shop, restaurant, and lodging are also available. The season extends from May through October.

Nearby, the town of **Mountain View** is appropriately named for the precipitous bluffs hovering over it 2 miles to the south. The "view" is of the Boston Mountains, the highest and most dramatic part of the Ozarks, which extend westward into Oklahoma. Mountain View offers a variety of activities, primarily around the courthouse square. Weekend afternoons and evenings offer jam sessions by folks who bring both instruments and lawn chairs to hear

A craftsman at the Ozark Folk Center carves a wooden chair leg.

or make music, dance, and visit. The nearby shops sell antiques, crafts, musical instruments, iron-forged products, and flour from a working mill. A scenic hiking trail, far removed from the busy highway, leads from the city park (north of the square) to the Ozark Folk Center.

The **Sylamore Ranger District Office** is also located in Mountain View on the north side of town along AR 5. It has maps and brochures, and books for sale.

Scenic 7 Byway North

HARRISON TO RUSSELLVILLE, ARKANSAS

GENERAL DESCRIPTION: An 84-mile drive from Harrison south to Russellville through the picturesque Boston Mountains.

SPECIAL ATTRACTIONS: Buffalo National River, Pruitt River Access, Koen Interpretive Trail, Mystic Caverns, Hilary Jones Wildlife Museum, Roundtop Mountain Scenic Hiking Trail, Scenic 7 Byway, Alum Cove Natural Bridge, Pedestal Rocks and Long Pool recreation areas, Buffalo River Trail, Ozark Highlands Trail, and Arkansas Grand Canyon; scenic views, fall colors, hiking, horseback riding, canoeing, camping, fishing, hunting, and swimming.

LOCATION: Southern Ozarks. The drive begins on Arkansas Highway 7 at Harrison.

DRIVE ROUTE NUMBERS: Arkansas Highways 7 and 16 and Forest Roads 1206, 1801, 1804, and 1838.

CAMPING: Ozark, Erbie, and Hasty offer camping on the Buffalo National River. Long Pool, Haw Creek Falls, Richland Creek, and Fairview recreation areas provide camping in the Ozark National Forest.

SERVICES: All services at Harrison, Jasper, and Russellville.

NEARBY ATTRACTIONS: Hurricane Creek and Richland Creek wilderness areas; Haw Creek Falls, Sam's Throne, Twin Falls, and Dismal Hollow recreation areas (in the Ozark National Forest); and Lost Valley, Steel Creek, Kyles Landing, and Tyler Bend Visitor Center (on the Buffalo National River).

THE DRIVE

On April 5, 1994, Arkansas's first National Scenic Byway was dedicated at a ceremony in Russellville. Called the Scenic 7 Byway, AR 7 has long enjoyed a reputation as one of the nation's most scenic drives. Meandering from its origin at Bull Shoals Lake near Diamond City, through the Ozark Mountains to the spa city of Hot Springs and the pine forests of the Ouachitas, the attractions along the highway are as varied as the scenic views. Because of this, the 153 miles of the byway are divided into two separate drives: The first begins at Harrison, which is considered the best place to start. For information on **Harrison,** see Drive 20.

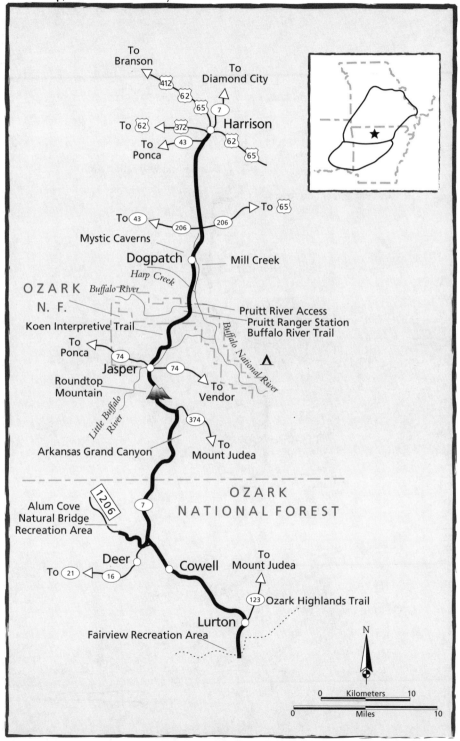

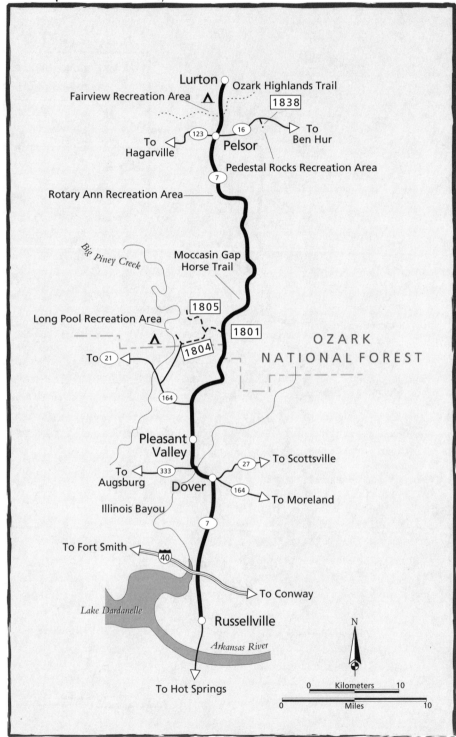

Begin the drive on AR 7 on the south side of Harrison. The road travels across the Springfield Plateau from Harrison to Jasper. The broad valleys and low hills were once covered by prairie and grassy woodlands that have been converted to pastures, row crops, and forest. Thanks to the efforts of the Arkansas Natural Heritage Commission, a prairie remnant on the west side of Harrison is now protected. Future generations will be able to see and learn about what the region was once like. See Drive 20 for directions to Baker Prairie.

MYSTIC CAVERNS TO KOEN INTERPRETIVE TRAIL

Located about 8 miles south of Harrison, **Mystic Caverns** offers a commercial tour of two caves at one location. First discovered in 1968, the caves were opened for public viewing in 1982. The caves have been gradually carved out of limestone, which is the principal bedrock of the Springfield Plateau. Interesting features include calcium deposits of soda straws, flowstone, rimstone, an eight-story crystal dome, and large underground chambers. The tour is available beginning at 9:00 A.M. daily March through November.

Continuing on AR 7 you will notice the deteriorated theme park called Dogpatch, U.S.A. Conceived in 1967 by Harrison businessmen, the 825-acre tract was built around Al Capp's comic strip "Li'l Abner." Although Dogpatch was a popular attraction at one time, the meteoric rise of Branson as a major tourist stop undoubtedly took its toll on the theme park, together with unsuccessful business investments. On the west side of the highway, just past the entrance to Dogpatch, a historical marker commemorates the Arkansas marble that was taken from this site in 1836; it was used to help build the Washington Monument in Washington, D.C.

After another 5 miles, you cross the **Buffalo National River.** Just beyond the bridge, turn right and park at the **Pruitt Ranger Station.** Information is available on naturalist programs, places to hike and camp, and river floating opportunities. Walk the path that leads to the Buffalo River for a good view of the river with its pools, riffles, and gravel bars against a backdrop of a cedar-covered dolomite cliff. Notice the cedar trees with the old-man's-beard lichen hanging from the branches. From a distance, this lichen closely resembles Spanish moss, which is commonly found in the more warm and humid southern states.

The Pruitt Ranger Station picnic area is the trailhead for the **Buffalo River Trail.** The 25.5-mile one-way trail to Ponca Access traverses the scenic Buffalo National River hills and valleys. Several access points along the way allow for shorter hikes. Information on trail conditions and hiking opportunities, including shorter hikes, is available at the ranger station.

A shorter trail can be reached by heading north on AR 7, crossing over the Buffalo River, and turning right at the entrance to the **Pruitt River Access.** Follow the road to the parking lot where the 2.2-mile **Mill Creek Trail** begins. A relatively easy walk along Mill Creek valley leads past old homesites, a cemetery with headstones dating back to the 1860s, and opportunities to see wildlife along a bottomland hardwood forest. An interpretive map can be obtained either at the Pruitt Ranger Station or the superintendent's office in Harrison.

About a mile past the Pruitt Ranger Station on AR 7, a road to the right leads to the Ozark Access. A 1-mile drive takes you to a primitive camping area with water, pit toilets, a telephone, and access to the river. Drive another 2.5 miles on AR 7 to the Erbie Access road, on the right. Follow the gravel road 0.3 mile and turn right, following the signs to the **Koen Interpretive Trail.** This trail is part of the Ozark National Forest's Henry R. Koen Experimental Forest. The experimental forest was established in 1950 to develop scientific principles for forest management and to define and evaluate land management concerns in the Forest Service's Southern Region. Henry R. Koen is known as the "Father of Forestry" in the Arkansas Ozarks. Once the forest supervisor of the Ozark National Forest, his active conservation career spanned four decades in the first half of the twentieth century. The Koen Interpretive Trail provides an opportunity to see and identify more than forty native and non-native trees and shrubs planted along the half-mile, wheelchair-accessible trail.

JASPER AND THE ARKANSAS GRAND CANYON

Return to AR 7 and proceed south to **Jasper.** Just before Jasper and on the right, the Visitor Information Center of the Buffalo Ranger Station, Ozark National Forest, can supply you with maps, books, and specific information on activities in the forest. Just south of the Visitor Information Center, the recently constructed Arkansas Fish and Game's **Hilary Jones Wildlife Museum** contains four large aquariums exhibiting native fish of the Ozarks and brochures and publications relating to Arkansas wildlife, including elk. Jasper lies in a cove at the base of the Boston Mountains escarpment to the south. Jasper is the county seat of Newton County, the only county in Arkansas that has never had a single mile of railroad track. Because of its rugged topography, Newton County supports a tremendous diversity of plants and animals. With more than half of its total area devoted to public lands, this mountainous area is renowned for being the home to more than 1,500 species of plants, 65 species of mammals, 79 species of amphibians and reptiles, 90 species of fish, and 190 species of birds.

The Jasper/Newton County Chamber of Commerce is very active in promoting and supporting festivals and events; write for its directory to help plan your trip. Also, the Newton County Resource Council sponsors the development of ecotourism as a means of improving the local economy. Guided tours include such activities as photography, birding, nature hikes, genealogy, and visits to historic sites. For more information on how to contact these organizations, see Appendix A.

Leave Jasper and begin a long, steady climb up **Roundtop Mountain,** which is the beginning of the Boston Mountains. About three-quarters of the way up the mountain, a road to the right leads to the **Roundtop Mountain Scenic Hiking Trail.** Two hiking trails are available: One is a 1.6-mile loop trail to the top; the other is an outer loop trail of 2.78 miles. The trail is strenuous at first but gets easier and offers great views of the countryside. A rest room is available at the parking lot. Returning to AR 7, in a couple of miles, a side trip on AR 374 offers great scenic views as the road descends Judea Mountain. This drive is especially rewarding in October, when the leaves turn their fall colors. Returning to AR 7, the next stop is Cliff House Inn and a view of the **Arkansas Grand Canyon.** A remarkably steep drop of more than 600 feet and an expansive view of several miles across Big Creek valley give this site its reputation. The quaint restaurant there is especially known for its desserts and biscuits. In addition to the restaurant, lodging is available with five units. For more information you can access www.mcrush.com/cliffhouse or call (870) 446–2292.

Within a couple of miles, two scenic overlooks offer more views of Big Creek valley. The first pullout provides picnic tables; in addition to a nice view, the second pullout shows interesting layering of sandstone and shale in the roadcut. This rock dates back to a time before the Ozark Mountains were uplifted, to the Pennsylvanian Period more than 300 million years ago. This was when great coal-forming swamps flourished and reptiles began to appear. Dinosaurs would not evolve for another seventy million years.

Continue south and after about 5 miles, notice the Ozark National Forest **Scenic 7 Byway** sign. The next 36.3 miles have been designated by the Forest Service as part of the National Forest Scenic Byways.

ALUM COVE TO RUSSELLVILLE

The next stop is the **Alum Cove Natural Bridge Recreation Area.** Turn right onto AR 16, which is 14 miles south of Jasper. Proceed west for about a

Hikers admire the huge 130-foot span of Alum Cove Natural Bridge.

mile and turn right onto FR 1206 for 3 miles to the entrance road to the recreation area. Picnic tables and a rest room are provided, but no overnight camping is allowed. The 1.1-mile round-trip trail leads to the natural bridge and other points of interest along the bluff line, including a wet-weather waterfall. The natural bridge is 130 feet long and 20 feet wide. The formation is actually a natural arch that was carved from the rock bluff when a fracture was gradually widened by the forces of wind, rain, and ice. Natural bridges are formed from the erosive force of water cutting through cracks in the rock's interior and usually have streams flowing through the opening.

The forest is rich with spring wildflowers growing under stately American beech trees spread out over the canopy. The rare umbrella magnolia can be observed along the trail, especially at the natural bridge. Look for whorls of large leaves up to 18 inches long and 8 inches wide clustered at the ends of branches. Wild azaleas bloom in mid-to-late April at about midslope on the trail.

Return to AR 7 and proceed 12 miles to the **Fairview Recreation Area.** Along with providing eleven campsites, the campground is the crossing for the **Ozark Highlands Trail,** rated one of the top-ten trails in the United States. The 160-mile national recreation trail follows a scenic east-west route. A portion of the trail can be hiked for 5 miles west of here to the Hurricane Creek Wilderness Area, or for about 17 miles east through Richland Creek Wilderness Area to the Richland Creek Campground.

Continue on AR 7 to Pelsor and the intersection with AR 16 east. A side trip down AR 16 east for a little over 5 miles leads to FR 1838 and **Pedestal Rocks Recreation Area.** The trails offer two loops to some unique sandstone bluff formations. Because there are bluffs, take care with small children. The Pedestal Rocks Loop Trail, to the left, is 2.2 miles and passes scenic overlooks and large sandstone pedestals that stand apart from the bluff line. The Kings Bluff Loop Trail, to the right, is 1.7 miles and comes out on top of Kings Bluff. It offers a good view of a wet-weather waterfall nearly 100 feet high. Roughly 4 miles of trail are available if you hike both loops.

Back on AR 7, the road crosses Piney Creek Wildlife Management Area, home to deer, turkeys, black bears, and ruffed grouse. The next pullout is the **Rotary Ann Recreation Area,** which offers a great view of Indian Creek valley and the surrounding mountains. Picnic tables and a rest room are provided.

Continuing on AR 7, the road passes **Moccasin Gap Horse Trail,** a series of loops totaling 28 miles through Forest Service land. A horse camp with seventeen graveled parking spurs, pit toilets, and well water for horses is also provided. A map and more information are available from the Bayou Ranger District.

Proceed 2 miles for a side trip to the **Long Pool Recreation Area.** Follow FR 1801 and 1804 to the recreation area on Big Piney Creek. For low-

Arkansas Highway 7 is rated as one of the top-ten scenic byways in the nation.

Fascinating sandstone rock formations await hikers visiting Pedestal Rocks Recreation Area.

clearance vehicles, campers, and motor homes, continue on AR 7 to AR 164. After about 3 miles on AR 164, watch for a sign and road on the right to Long Pool Recreation Area. Long Pool offers picnicking, a swimming beach, canoe access, rest rooms, and nineteen campsites. Daily user fees are charged for parking and camping. **Big Piney Creek** received congressional designation in 1992 as a National Scenic River. Considered one of the most popular bait-fishing and swimming streams in Arkansas, the 67-mile Big Piney Creek National Scenic River is also a popular float stream. One of the more challenging streams in Arkansas, the paddler can experience rapids up to Class III in difficulty. An interpretive sign at the river explains what to expect based on the current water level. (The recreation area can also be reached by following signs for 8 miles starting on AR 164.)

Return to AR 7 and begin the long descent out of the Boston Mountains of the Ozarks to the Arkansas River valley, which is considered a subsection of the Ouachita Mountains. After 10 miles, the road crosses the Illinois Bayou. "Bayou" is a deceptive name, since it is a white-water stream for most of its length as it courses through the Boston Mountains. The stream becomes slow and silt-laden as it flattens out in the Arkansas Valley, eventually emptying into the backwaters of Lake Dardenelle.

Continue to **Russellville.** For information on Russellville and the Arkansas River valley of the Ouachita Mountains, see Drive 24.

20

Buffalo Hills

HARRISON TO JASPER, ARKANSAS

GENERAL DESCRIPTION: A 39-mile drive starting at Harrison, heading southwest into the rugged Buffalo River hills, and ending at Jasper.

SPECIAL ATTRACTIONS: Baker Prairie, Gaither Mountain, Ponca Elk Education Center, Boxley Valley, Buffalo National River, Lost Valley, Buffalo River Trail, Ponca Access, Steel Creek, Kyles Landing, and Ponca Wilderness Area; scenic views, hiking, canoeing, camping, fishing, and hunting.

LOCATION: Southern Ozarks. The drive begins on Arkansas Highway 43 on the south side of Harrison and heads southwest.

DRIVE ROUTE NUMBERS: Arkansas Highways 43 and 74.

CAMPING: Lost Valley, Steel Creek, and Kyles Landing offer camping on the Buffalo National River.

SERVICES: All services at Harrison and Jasper. Food at Ponca.

NEARBY ATTRACTIONS: Alum Cove Natural Bridge, Arkansas Grand Canyon, Boxley Historic District, Hawksbill Crag, Ozark National Forest, Tyler Bend Visitor Center, Upper Buffalo Wilderness Area, Scenic 7 Byway North, and Ozark Highlands Scenic Drive.

THE DRIVE

The rugged hills of the Buffalo River offer scenic views and places to hike along the northern edge of the Ozarks' Boston Mountains. Of the four scenic drives in the Boston Mountains (Drives 19, 20, 21, 22), this drive offers the most dramatic transition from one major landform to another. The drive starts on the southern edge of the Springfield Plateau, with elevations varying from 500 to 1,500 feet. The bedrock is primarily limestone. The road then climbs onto the northern edge of the Boston Mountains, with a pronounced elevation ranging from 1,500 to 2,300 feet. Composed of sandstone and shale, much of the area is very rugged, with several sections reaching more than 1,000 feet in local relief. Relatively level land is confined to the valleys and to the mountaintops, which are remnants of the old plateau surface.

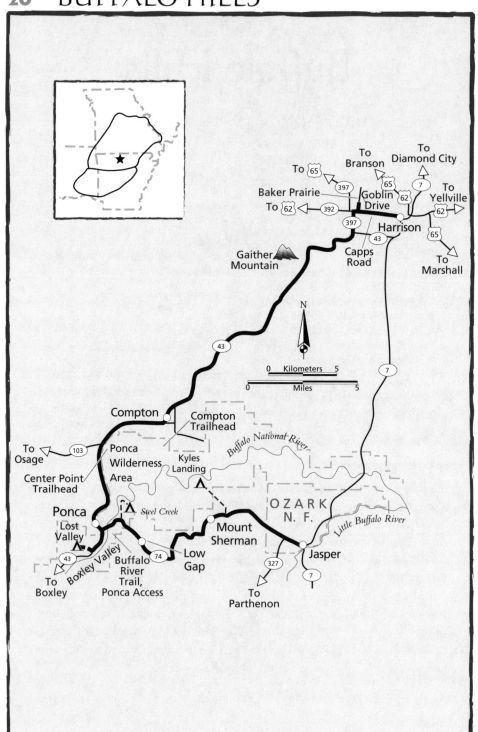

To 65
To Branson
To Diamond City
Baker Prairie
397
65
7
Goblin Drive
62
To Yellville
To 62
392
62
397
Harrison
43
65
Gaither Mountain
Capps Road
To Marshall
N
43
Kilometers 5
Miles 5
7
Compton
Compton Trailhead
Buffalo National River
To Osage
103
Ponca Wilderness Area
Kyles Landing
Center Point Trailhead
Ponca
Steel Creek
OZARK N. F.
Lost Valley
Little Buffalo River
Ponca
Mount Sherman
43
Boxley Valley
Low Gap
74
Jasper
To Boxley
Buffalo River Trail, Ponca Access
327
7
To Parthenon

HARRISON AREA SITES

The drive starts in **Harrison,** a town that was named for surveyor M. L. Harrison. He laid out the town in 1870 and, in lieu of payment, the town was named for him. A map and a self-guided walking tour of downtown Harrison leads to twelve historic buildings, some more than a hundred years old. The tour begins at the Boone County Courthouse, which is located on Main Street and Stephenson Avenue. The tour map is available at the courthouse or from the Boone County Heritage Museum at the corner of Central and Cherry Streets. Five miles north of Harrison on US 65, the Harrison Tourist Information Center is operated by the Arkansas Department of Parks and Tourism. This is a nice rest stop with picnic facilities. Numerous brochures of attractions throughout the state are available, and the friendly staff will provide routing assistance. The facility is open year-round.

Traveling on AR 7, on the south side of Harrison, take AR 392 (Capps Road) west for 1.4 miles to the first traffic light. Turn right (north) on Goblin Drive and, after half a mile, look for the newly constructed Junior High School on the right (east) side of the road. Park in the parking lot and walk downslope and onto **Baker Prairie,** which is located on both sides of the road. Designated in 1992, Baker Prairie is a state natural area owned by the Arkansas Natural Heritage Commission. This seventy-one-acre tallgrass prairie is a remnant of a much larger prairie that once covered much of Boone County. A variety of prairie grasses and wildflowers (called forbs) are on display throughout the growing season, with different flowers coming into bloom about every two weeks. Take time to explore the prairie and examine the diverse array of plants and animals. Because of its location within Harrison, this prairie offers an excellent opportunity for environmental education. Return on Goblin Drive to AR 392, turn right (west) on AR 392, and in less than 1 mile, turn left (south) on AR 397. Continue for 1 mile and turn right (west) onto AR 43.

As you head west, look at the prominent outcrop known as **Gaither Mountain.** After 3 miles, the road steeply ascends the eastern flank of the mountain. Notice the bands of shale and sandstone, characteristic of the Boston Mountains. A pulloff on the left offers a great view of Harrison Valley, which was once covered with prairie and grazing bison. The town of Harrison is to the left, just out of sight.

COMPTON AREA SITES

Continue another 9 miles, driving through the small community of **Compton.** This region has been getting considerable attention since July 1992, when a United States Department of Agriculture employee found a male gypsy moth in a trap just west of Compton. This was the first recorded outbreak of gypsy moths in Arkansas. The gypsy moth is one of the most notorious pests of hardwood trees in the eastern United States. Since 1980 the gypsy moth has defoliated close to a million or more forested acres each year. Trees that are defoliated two to three years in a row weaken and often die. The gypsy moth is not a native insect. It was introduced into the United States in 1869 by a French scientist living in Massachusetts, who was interested in developing a disease-resistant silkworm. Since then the moth has spread throughout the Northeast and, more recently, into Utah, Oregon, Washington, and California.

After the initial discovery of a male gypsy moth, a visual survey of the Compton area revealed an active breeding population producing an estimated 10,000 gypsy moth egg masses per acre. This twenty-five-acre core area was well established and probably dated back to an introduction in the mid-1980s. In 1993 additional trapping revealed male moths over a 200-square-mile area. Treatment with an insect growth regulator and a biological insecticide is being used to control the spread of this major threat to the Ozark forest.

A gravel road on the left, just before Compton, leads to the Compton Trailhead of the **Ponca Wilderness Area,** a part of the Buffalo National Scenic Riverway. One of the features along this trail is the Hemmed-in Hollow Falls, a 209-foot falls said to be the highest free-falling waterfall between the Appalachians and the Rocky Mountains. The trail to the falls is very steep and about 2.5 miles from the parking lot.

The 11,300-acre Ponca Wilderness Area is one of three wilderness areas on the Buffalo National Scenic Riverway. All have developed trails for hiking or horseback riding. No motorized vehicles are allowed. Maps and trail information are available at the Buffalo National Scenic Riverway superintendent's office in Harrison or at the Pruitt River Station, 8 miles north of Jasper on AR 7.

Continuing on AR 43, 0.8 mile past AR 103, look for the Ponca Wilderness's Center Point Trailhead. This trail also goes to Hemmed-in Hollow, as well as Big Bluff, which overlooks the Buffalo River. At a distance of 5.4 miles, it is longer than the Compton Trail but much easier to walk.

PONCA AREA SITES

Follow AR 43's steep descent into the Buffalo River valley to the community of **Ponca.** Sharing the narrow valley with the river, the village of Ponca is now a collection of canoe outfitters and lodges serving visitors to the Buffalo National River. The recently constructed **Ponca Elk Education Center,** operated by the Arkansas Game and Fish Commission, houses impressive exhibits on elk ecology and wildlife. Area information is also available. The center is open daily 10:00 A.M. to 5:30 P.M. March to Thanksgiving and Wednesday through Sunday the remainder of the year. For more information access www.agfc.com/education/ponca.htm or call (870) 861–2432.

South of Ponca is the "Big Buffalo Valley," also sometimes referred to as **Boxley Valley.** The valley is a distinctive cultural landscape, and as such, it was included in the National Register of Historic Places in 1987. More than two hundred structures of historical significance—houses, barns, a gristmill, and a community building—are "fine examples of regional vernacular architecture." Many date from the nineteenth century. Just past the intersection of AR 43 and AR 74 and on the right, the pre–Civil War log house of Beaver Jim Villines stands. Interpretive signs provide the history of this renowned trapper.

Just beyond Villines's cabin, follow the signs to **Lost Valley,** a National Park Service campground. In the campground, a 3.5-mile round-trip trail passes waterfalls, Clark Creek, cliffs, a large sandstone bluff shelter, and a natural bridge. The trail dead-ends at a cave that can be accessed (with a flashlight) for 200 feet. The cave ends in a large room with a 35-foot waterfall. Plan on spending two or three hours hiking the trail. The first mile is level and easy hiking, then the trail climbs steeply to the cave. It is a special trail that offers a variety of features and is well worth the visit.

Return to AR 43 and a short side trip to the right (south) down AR 43 leads you to a viewing area on the left that overlooks a valley where elk are known to graze. Continuing down AR 43 offers more opportunities to view elk, especially in October and November during the mating season. Then head north to Ponca. Just before the junction of AR 43 and AR 74, a road on the right leads to **Ponca Access.** Watch for elk in a field to the right of the gravel road. This access is a popular starting point for those canoeing the **Buffalo River.** It also offers a good view of the upper reaches of the river. The Buffalo River, which is about 150 miles long, flows entirely in Arkansas from its origins near Fallsville in the Boston Mountains to its confluence with the White River near Buffalo City. Here, at its upper reaches, the river courses through steep drops, hairpin turns, and swift chutes. Averaging a drop of 10 feet per mile, this stretch of the Buffalo River is primarily a springtime float. Below Pruitt, the lower stretch of the river drops 3 feet per mile and can be floated year-round. The Buffalo River, named for the buffalo (or bison) that roamed this area prior to 1820, is one of the few unchannelized and dam-free streams in the Ozarks. After several years of threats to contain its flow, in 1972 the river won enough public support to convince the government to authorize the creation of the Buffalo National River. Because of its protected status and its nat-

A short trail at Lost Valley leads to Eden Falls, which is made up of a series of four falls ending at this 40-foot drop into a plunge pool.

ural beauty, it is considered one of the most popular rivers in the United States.

Just across the low-water bridge and on the other side of the Buffalo River, the **Buffalo River Trail** begins. This 25.5-mile one-way trail now goes to Pruitt but will eventually run most of the length of the Buffalo National River. Plans call for the trail to someday connect with the Ozark Trail and go across Missouri all the way to St. Louis. When all the trails in the two states are completed, there will be more than 1,000 miles in one connected trail system. Information on the Ponca-to-Pruitt trail can be obtained from the Buffalo National River office or from Tim Ernst's hiking books, listed at the back of this book. When hiking this trail, it is not recommended that you leave vehicles at the trailhead overnight—rising floodwaters have been known to sweep them away. It is safer to park in Ponca.

Return to AR 43 and turn right onto AR 74. Drive with caution: This 14-mile stretch to Jasper is narrow and winding. After 1.3 miles a road to the left leads to **Steel Creek,** a campground and access to the Buffalo River and the Buffalo River Trail. The steep and winding gravel road to the river valley is worth the effort to see the grand, towering cliffs carved by the river. (Because of the narrow and sometimes steep descent, motor homes and travel trailers

Dolomite cliffs tower above the tree-shrouded Buffalo River at Steel Creek Campground.

Buffalo Hills   **173**

should not try this road.) Elk can sometimes be seen in the open valley that parallels the river. The eastern elk, a subspecies that lived along the Buffalo River, was overhunted and by 1840 became extinct in Arkansas. Between 1981 and 1985, a total of 112 Rocky Mountain elk were stocked at five release sites in Newton County by the Arkansas Game and Fish Commission. There are 300 to 350 elk presently living in or adjacent to the Buffalo National River corridor.

The campgrounds at Steel Creek and Kyles Landing can be extremely crowded during spring weekends because of those floating the river at this optimal time of the year. Both campgrounds provide pit toilets, fire pits, and water. **Kyles Landing** can be reached by returning to AR 74 and driving 7.4 miles to the gravel road entrance on the left. The 3-mile drive is slow-going, becoming very steep as it descends into the river valley. (Motor homes and travel trailers should not try this road.) About a mile down the gravel road, bear left at a fork in the road. (The road to the right leads to a Boy Scout camp.) Although not as dramatic as the road to Steel Creek, this road does offer another view of the Buffalo River valley.

Returning to AR 74, continue another 4.5 miles to **Jasper** and the end of the drive. For information on Jasper see Drive 19, Harrison to Russellville.

21

Ozark Highlands

EUREKA SPRINGS TO CLARKSVILLE, ARKANSAS

GENERAL DESCRIPTION: A 95-mile drive beginning at historic Eureka Springs, crossing the Boston Mountains, and ending at Clarksville.

SPECIAL ATTRACTIONS: Kings River, Eureka Springs, Boxley Valley, Hawksbill Crag, Upper Buffalo Wilderness, Buffalo National River, Ozark Highlands Scenic Byway, Ozark Highlands Trail, and Ozark National Forest; fall colors, scenic views, hiking, canoeing, fishing, hunting, and camping.

LOCATION: Southern Ozarks. The drive begins in Eureka Springs on U.S. Highway 62 to Berryville and south on Arkansas Highway 21.

DRIVE ROUTE NUMBERS: U.S. Highway 62 and Arkansas Highway 21.

CAMPING: Lost Valley, Buffalo National River; Ozone Recreation Area, Ozark National Forest; Spadra Park, Lake Dardanelle.

SERVICES: All services at Eureka Springs, Berryville, and Clarksville. Gas and food at Boxley, Fallsville, and Ozone.

NEARBY ATTRACTIONS: Beaver Lake; Lost Valley; Alum Cove and Haw Creek Falls recreation areas; Lake Dardanelle; and Mount Magazine, Buffalo Hills, and Pig Trail scenic drives.

THE DRIVE

The northern part of the drive is in a region underlaid by limestones and dolomites. For over hundreds of thousands of years, water seeping into cracks in the bedrock dissolved minerals in the rock, creating caves, sinkholes, and springs. This type of region is named "karst," after a similar area in the former Yugoslavia near the Adriatic Sea. The Ozarks are one of the best-known of karst regions worldwide, with more than 7,000 caves. Leaving the karst region, AR 21 just beyond Kingston climbs into the Boston Mountains, the highest part of the Ozarks. Composed of sandstone and shale, this rugged landscape offers great variations in elevation (from 1,500 to 2,300 feet) creating panoramic views and deep, moist valleys rich in wildflowers and crystal-clear streams.

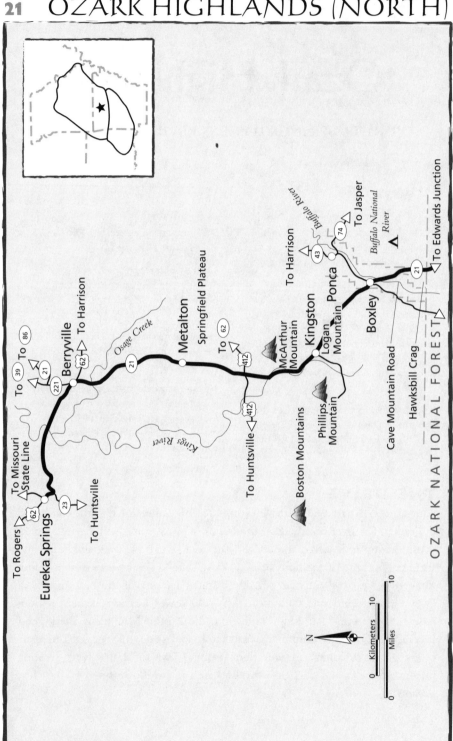

21 OZARK HIGHLANDS (SOUTH)

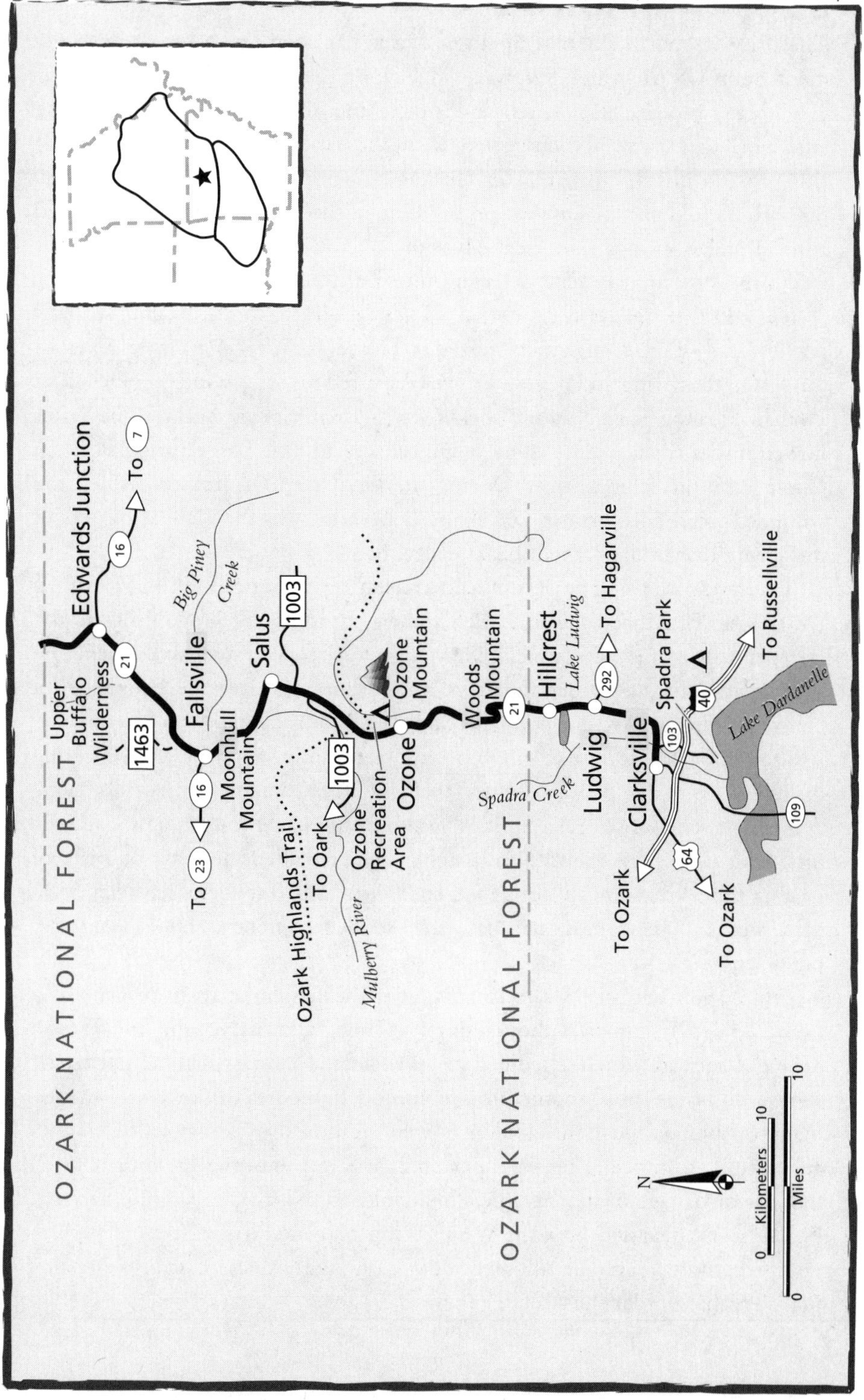

EUREKA SPRINGS

The drive begins in **Eureka Springs.** There has been much recent development along US 62, which follows a ridge along the south side of town. Modern hotels, motels, restaurants, and stores line the highway; however, the
attractions that spawned their growth lie in the narrow valleys that drop off the
ridge to the north. From US 62, take AR 23 north along the historic loop
through the old part of Eureka Springs. One of the first buildings encountered
is the Eureka Springs Historical Museum, on the west side of the road. It is
worth the stop for a general orientation to Eureka Springs.

It is said that the Native Americans knew about the "great healing spring,"
but few early European settlers visited it. However, in 1856 a Dr. Alvah Jackson found the spring and believed its waters cured his long-standing illness. The
"Indian Healing Spring" was also known as Basin Spring because the water
flowed into a small natural stone basin. Be sure to visit Basin Spring in Basin
Circle Park on Spring Street. During the Civil War, Dr. Jackson treated the
wounded from both armies, and many believed it was the curative waters of
the spring that brought them back to health.

The spring's healing powers remained relatively unnoticed until 1879, when
Dr. Jackson convinced the ill L. B. Saunders, a prominent judge from nearby
Berryville, to sample the waters. The judge was so delighted by the relief he
obtained that he proclaimed the news of his healing far and wide. People began
coming in droves—by horseback, in carriages, and by simple farm wagons, and
in a few months more than 4,000 people were camped nearby. At a meeting
on July 4, 1879, the people decided that the judge's young son Burton Saunders's suggestion of "Eureka Springs" was a fitting name for the new community. After only eight months, daily newspapers heralded the news of a city of
healing waters that already contained 10,000 to 12,000 residents. By May 1880
there were 2,000 dwellings plus daily mail service, churches, schools, and thirty
physicians.

From 1885 until 1910 the town was at the height of its popularity as a
health resort. It attracted thousands of visitors who arrived on the Eureka
Springs Railroad, which scheduled six trains a day. Health spas, motels, theaters,
shops, and homes mushroomed to accommodate the health-seekers. However,
many of these wood-frame buildings were destroyed by a series of four fires
and rebuilt again over a ten-year period. It was not until the last fire, in 1893,
that the next stage of the city's development ensured it against more than fire.
Native stone quarried near the White River was used to build more permanent structures, which are still seen today, along with miles of attractive retain-
ing walls that border the streets.

Unique and attractive stone and brick buildings await exploring along the narrow streets of historic Eureka Springs.

By 1904 the permanent population was 5,000, with fourteen doctors and six dentists. The health spas, however, began to decline because people began putting more trust in surgery and medicine than in the healing powers of the spring water. Gradually the visitors shifted from health-seekers to those seeking rest and relaxation. From 1907 through World War II, Eureka Springs barely kept alive. But tourism increased and funds became available for restoration of the many fine old Victorian homes, businesses, and public buildings. In fact, the entire town is listed on the Register of Historic Places.

The narrow city streets were laid out to accommodate pedestrians, horseback riders, and wagons—they are not multilanes for automobile traffic. To fully appreciate the Historic District, it is best to park and walk the streets, which are lined with shops, galleries, artists' studios, craft workshops, restaurants, and hotels. Open-air trolleys are available to take you through the Historic District. Information on their routes and a detailed brochure of things to do in Eureka Springs and the surrounding area are available at the Eureka Springs Chamber of Commerce (see Appendix A). The Visitor Information Center is located in a red caboose on the north side of the road at 2059d Highway 62 East.

Proceed east on US 62 towards Berryville. In 6.6 miles you cross over **Kings River,** a floatable stream from April to June, which empties into Table Rock Lake to the north. The river originates near the town of Boston, as do the Mulberry and White Rivers. Kings River's water quality is considered above average, and there is a greater feeling of wilderness on the Kings River than on the more heavily used rivers nearby.

BERRYVILLE TO FALLSVILLE

Continue to **Berryville,** which was founded in 1850 by Blackburn Henderson Berry of Alabama. During the Civil War, the town, except for a few houses, was burned by both sides. Two attractions of particular interest are the Saunders Memorial Museum and the Heritage Center Museum. The former, which is located just 1 block off the northeast side of the town square on Madison Street, was established with funds provided by C. Burton Saunders, who is credited with naming Eureka Springs. A world-champion sharpshooter by 1910, Saunders toured the country with Buffalo Bill's Wild West Show. He also traveled the world collecting antiques and firearms and bequeathed his collection, along with money to build a museum in his hometown of Berryville. Weapons on display include those used by Jesse James, Billy the Kid, Belle Starr, Buffalo Bill, Wild Bill Hickok, and Annie Oakley, to name a few. Besides its famous gun collection, the Saunders Museum has a great variety of other artifacts, including Native American relics.

Located on the town square, the Heritage Center Museum houses hundreds of historical items including a moonshiner's still, a pioneer schoolroom, a barbershop, and an undertaker's office. The museum is located in the 1881 courthouse, which is on the National Register of Historic Places.

Leaving Berryville, you may want to stop at the Tourist Information and Rest Area at the intersection of AR 21 and AR 62. Then head south on AR 21 for about 20 miles and enter the Kings River valley. The valley is flanked on both sides by the Boston Mountains as you proceed 4 miles to **Kingston.** Continuing past Kingston, the road leaves the Springfield Plateau and climbs Logan Mountain. After a couple of miles, following the crest of the mountain, the road descends steeply for 3 miles into the community of Boxley at the intersection of AR 21 and 43.

Boxley was first settled in 1838, when it was named "Whiteley." After the Civil War, a merchant, D. Boxley, moved to the site. In 1883 he established another post office, and the community later took his name. Just north of Boxley a gristmill was established in 1870 to replace an 1840 mill. The mill was closed in 1960 after serving the community for almost a century. It is now a part of the Buffalo National River system, and there are plans to restore it someday. A side trip north on AR 43 leads to Lost Valley, Villines Cabin, the Buffalo River Trail, and Ponca. For more details see Drive 20.

About 1 mile past Boxley on AR 21 and just before the bridge over the Buffalo River, there is a county road to the right called Cave Mountain Road. This road leads to Whitaker Point or what is more commonly referred to as **Hawksbill Crag,** one of the most photographed natural features in all of Arkansas. Cave Mountain Road is narrow, steep, and not recommended for low-clearance vehicles. If you do decide to visit Hawksbill Crag, proceed 5.4 miles along Cave Mountain Road passing Cave Mountain Church on the right and, in another half a mile, pull off into the Wilderness Access parking lot on the right. A trail begins across the road from the parking area, leads to the rock outcrop, and returns the same route for a total of 3 miles. The trail is moderately strenuous in places and leads to a precipice, so take special care with children. A spectacular view of the Whitaker Creek Watershed and the Buffalo River Valley rewards the adventuresome traveler.

Continuing on AR 21, the road crosses the **Buffalo River.** The river is seasonally dry at this location because it is close to its headwaters. The 150-mile river is floatable in the spring from Ponca to Pruitt and year-round from Pruitt to the White River. The Buffalo River, because of its protected status and natural beauty, is considered one of the most popular floatable rivers in the United States.

*The rock outcrop called Hawksbill Crag is one of the
most photographed icons in Arkansas.*

In 4.5 miles, AR 21 enters the boundaries of the Ozark National Forest and the **Ozark Highlands Scenic Byway.** For the next 35 miles, this scenic byway traverses some of the highest elevations of the Ozarks and offers several panoramic views. A National Forest Scenic Byway, its special status helps provide funding for hiking trails, scenic overlooks, camping and picnic areas, brochures, and interpretive displays.

Just west of here the boundaries of the 11,094-acre **Upper Buffalo Wilderness** begin. Protecting the headwaters of the Buffalo River, the wilderness contains extensive hardwood forests with scenic sandstone outcrops, mountainous terrain, and nineteen waterfalls. Access is best off Forest Road 1463, a mile north of Fallsville on AR 21.

The scenic byway continues south through **Edwards Junction,** where AR 16 joins AR 21 for 8.5 miles. There is a roadside scenic view along the east side of the highway half a mile north of Fallsville. The road runs along high ridges through **Fallsville,** paralleling Moonhull Mountain and the headwaters of the Mulberry River, which has premier canoeing farther downstream, beginning in Oark.

OZARK AREA SITES

Eleven miles south of Fallsville and just before Ozone Recreation Area, AR 21 crosses the **Ozark Highlands Trail.** Parking is on the west side of the road. The trail begins at Lake Fort Smith State Park on the western edge of the national forest and travels eastward 165 miles to the Buffalo National River. At the Ozone Campground Trailhead, the westward trail goes 29 miles to Lick Branch Trailhead. This is the longest section of the Ozark Highlands Trail. The trail crosses the Mulberry and Little Mulberry Rivers and passes a number of waterfalls, valleys, and steep hills. The trail east goes 20 miles to Big Piney Trailhead. A mile-long walk from the trailhead leads to Little Piney Creek and in another mile crosses the creek. Moss-covered boulders and bluffs add interest along the way.

Ozone Recreational Area provides eight campsites. It was a Civilian Conservation Corps camp during the 1930s, and foundations from the original buildings remain.

Continuing on AR 21 the road passes through Ozone, over Woods Mountain, and leaves the boundaries of the Ozark Highlands Scenic Byway. Leaving the Boston Mountains of the Ozarks, the road eventually levels out in the

*A roadside pulloff just north of Edwards Junction offers a
far-reaching view of the Boston Mountains.*

Arkansas River valley, which is part of the Ouachitas. The **Ozark Forest Visitor Information Center** is located just south of Ludwig. Maps, brochures, books, and information on recreational opportunities on the national forest are provided. AR 21 and, thus, the scenic drive ends at Clarksville.

CLARKSVILLE

Clarksville was incorporated in 1848. Once the third-largest coal producer in Arkansas, it also has natural gas reserves. The Johnson County Courthouse contains one of the most impressive and best-preserved courtrooms in Arkansas. Built during the Great Depression, the second-story courtroom accurately reflects the look and atmosphere of the 1930s. The Walton Fine Arts Center has exhibits and shows at the University of the Ozarks, which was founded in 1834. Among special events, the Johnson County Peach Festival, held in July, has the distinction of being the oldest continuing outdoor festival in Arkansas, dating back to July 1936. Just south of Clarksville on AR 103, the U.S. Army Corps of Engineers' Spadra Park offers camping, picnicking, rest rooms, showers, electrical hookups, and access to Lake Dardanelle.

Pig Trail

OZARK TO EUREKA SPRINGS, ARKANSAS

GENERAL DESCRIPTION: A 78-mile drive from Ozark north across the rugged Boston Mountains to Eureka Springs.

SPECIAL ATTRACTIONS: Pig Trail Scenic Byway, Ozark Highlands Trail, Ozark National Forest, White Rock Mountain Recreation Area, Mulberry River, White River, and Reed Mountain Park; fall colors, scenic views, hiking, canoeing, fishing, hunting, and camping.

LOCATION: Southwestern Ozarks. The drive follows Arkansas Highway 23 north from Ozark.

DRIVE ROUTE NUMBERS: Arkansas Highways 23 and 215 and Forest Roads 1003, 1501, 1505, and 1504.

CAMPING: Ozark National Forest campgrounds at Redding, Shores Lake, and White Rock Mountain recreation areas; Withrow Springs State Park has 25 campsites, 17 of which have water and electrical hookups. Aux Arc Park at Ozark Lake Dam Site 13 has campgrounds, water, and comfort stations.

SERVICES: All services at Ozark and Eureka Springs. Food and gas at Huntsville. A small store, gas, and canoe rental at Turner Bend.

NEARBY ATTRACTIONS: Mount Magazine, Ozark Highlands, and Roaring River State Park scenic drives; Haw Creek Falls Recreation Area; Upper Buffalo Wilderness; Buffalo National River; Arkansas River; and War Eagle Mill.

THE DRIVE

Climbing out of the Arkansas River valley, AR 23 scales the rugged **Boston Mountains,** offering breathtaking views of a densely forested, seemingly never-ending landscape. This region is the highest and most deeply dissected of the Ozarks, with local relief sometimes exceeding 1,500 feet. Sandstone bedrock forms bluffs and rocky slopes that favor shortleaf pine, the Ozark region's only native pine. In sheltered deep ravines, moist, cool conditions provide habitat for such uncommon trees as American beech and umbrella magnolia. In the lush understory, ferns, orchids, and spring wildflowers carpet the ground.

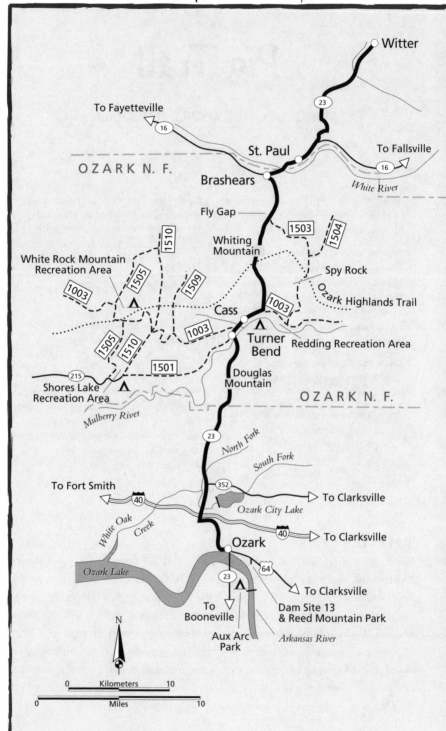

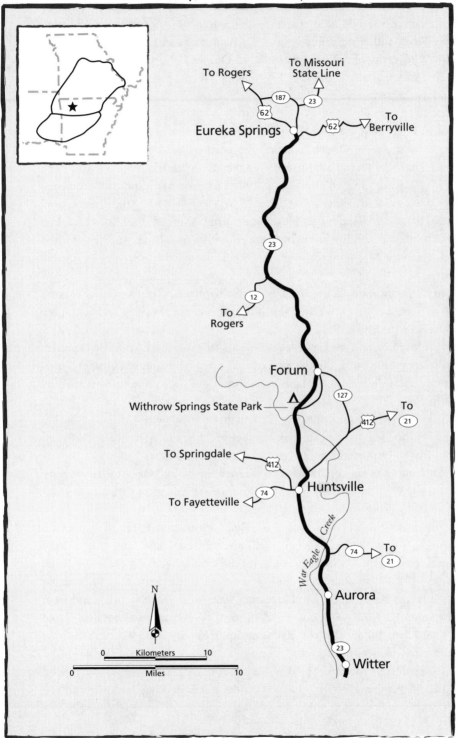

To Rogers

To Missouri
State Line

187

23

62

62
To
Berryville

Eureka Springs

23

12

To
Rogers

Forum

127

Withrow Springs State Park

412
To
21

To Springdale

412

Huntsville

74

To Fayetteville

74
To
21

War Eagle Creek

Aurora

23

Witter

N

0 Kilometers 10

0 Miles 10

This section of AR 23 is known as the Pig Trail. Those traveling this route in the autumn should be prepared to encounter football fans, especially from Little Rock and Hot Springs, who are driving to Fayetteville to attend games of the University of Arkansas Razorbacks. Do not be surprised to see carloads of fans wearing bright red hog hats yelling "Wooo-pig-sooee!" out of their windows as they drive by.

OZARK AREA SITES

The drive begins in **Ozark,** which is the northernmost point of the Arkansas River. There are several explanations for the name "Ozark," which is said to be derived from the French *Aux Arc*. In 1909 Professor Marinoni of the University of Arkansas theorized that "Ozark" was derived from the French *Aux Arkansas,* which he translated to mean "from amongst the Arkansas." The French called the Indian tribes in this area the *Arkansas* or the shortened name *Arcs*. Professor Marinoni felt that the French named this area after its inhabitants.

In his publication *Geography of the Ozark Highlands,* Carl O. Saure theorized that this word comes from the French phrase *pays aux Arcs,* or "land belonging to the Arcs [Indians]."

Aux Arc can also be translated to mean "the big bow." French explorers reported that the Indians in this area carried extra-large hunting bows. According to this interpretation, "Ozark" comes from the large hunting bows used by the Indians.

Another explanation of "Aux Arc" is that the translation means "the big bend" or "the big bow" of the Arkansas River. This is in reference to the sharp bend that the Arkansas River makes at the town of Ozark.

Although it is not certain what the French meant by "Aux Arc," the "Ozark Mountains" appeared on maps long before the settlement of Ozark was established in 1838 along the Arkansas River.

Two miles east of town on US 64, **Reed Mountain Park** offers a scenic overlook, picnic and playground facilities, and the mile-long River Bluff Nature Trail. From US 64, turn south on the Ozark Lock and Dam and Reed Mountain Park entrance road. Follow the signs to the park. Reed Mountain was named after Randall Reed, a former slave who purchased the land from Fort Smith Railroad Company in 1880. For those wanting a closer look at the lock and dam, follow the road down to the Arkansas River, where there is an observation platform.

Returning to town, proceed north on AR 23. The office of the Boston Mountain Ranger District is located on the north end of Ozark. Its staff can provide information and maps on recreational opportunities in the Ozark National Forest. In another 4.5 miles the road passes under I–40. While crossing White Oak Creek valley, you will have a good view of the Boston Mountains lying straight ahead.

In about 6 miles, the **Pig Trail Scenic Byway** sign marks the boundary of the Ozark National Forest. The next 19 miles of highway are designated as a National Forest Scenic Byway. This special designation helps provide funding for hiking trails, scenic overlooks, camping and picnic areas, brochures, and interpretive displays.

TURNER BEND AND CASS AREA SITES

After a steep climb over Douglas Mountain, the road drops into the Mulberry River valley. The **Mulberry River,** known by some as the state's "wildest" river during spring, pours over ledges, shoots through willow thickets, and whips around sharp turns. Much of its 70-mile run to the Arkansas River has been given a Class II/III (medium to difficult) rating by its floaters. Just before the Mulberry River bridge, **Turner Bend** store offers canoe rentals, shuttles, camping, and groceries.

Turner Bend offers access to the scenic Mulberry River.

Prominent sandstone cliffs rim White Rock Mountain Recreation Area.

Cross the bridge and after 0.3 mile, FR 1501, on the left, offers a side trip to **White Rock Mountain Recreation Area.** Because of the narrow roads, recreational vehicles are not recommended beyond the Shores Lake Recreation Area. The 18-mile distance is easily forgotten when you drive right up on top of one of the highest mountains in the Ozarks (2,260 feet). White Rock Mountain is named for the white lichen found growing on the sandstone rocks. Whether you take the 2.1-mile Rim Walk Trail or the shorter 1-mile loop, the views are some of the finest in the Ozarks. Four stone-and-timber shelters along the trail provide scenic picnic areas. There are three cabins and a lodge that can be reserved by calling the White Rock Mountain Concessionaires (see Appendix A). Camping spaces are also provided, and there is a trailhead for the Ozark Highlands Trail on White Rock Mountain.

To return to AR 23 from White Rock Mountain, FR 1003 offers an interesting, less-traveled route. However, the often single-lane gravel road is not recommended for low-clearance vehicles, campers, or motor homes.

Before reaching White Rock Mountain, FR 1501 goes to **Shores Lake Recreation Area.** This eighty-two-acre lake, built by the Civilian Conservation Corps in the 1930s, provides swimming, fishing, camping facilities, and picnic areas. A 14.4-mile loop trail runs from Shores Lake past several nice waterfalls, up to White Rock Mountain, and then returns to the lake through

The tranquil Shores Lake Recreation Area offers camping, fishing,
and a hiking trail that leads to White Rock Mountain.

the Salt Fork drainage. This would be a nice weekend hike, especially if you reserve a cabin at White Rock Mountain.

Continue 1 mile on AR 23 to the small community of **Cass.** Settled by Elias Turner and called "Turner's Bend" until the 1850s, from 1915 to 1920 Cass reportedly produced more wooden wagon wheels than any other place in the world. Today the Cass Job Corps Center and canoe outfitters produce income for the community. The Cass Job Corps Center trains more than 200 young people a year in various occupational skills such as carpentry, plumbing, masonry, painting, and heavy equipment operation. Visitors may tour the facilities.

The next Forest Service road to the east, FR 1003, goes 3 miles to **Redding Recreation Area,** another side trip. This is a popular access point for floaters on the Mulberry River. An 8.8-mile trail to **Spy Rock** is also available. For a shorter trip to Spy Rock take FR 1504, just past the turnoff to Redding Recreation Area. Follow FR 1504 approximately 2.5 miles to a trail on the left. It may be difficult locating the trailhead that leads up to Spy Rock. Contact the Boston Mountains Ranger District Office for directions and trail conditions. Legend has it that Spanish gold was buried in this area and that a lookout was stationed at Spy Rock while others buried the gold. Spy Rock offers a nice view of the Mulberry River valley.

Proceeding on AR 23, the road climbs up and over Whiting Mountain; just 4 miles before you reach FR 1003, the **Ozark Highlands Trail** crosses the road. Parking for the trail is on the east side of the road. The 165-mile trail begins at Lake Fort Smith State Park, on the western end of the national forest, and goes out the northeastern edge of the forest to the Buffalo National River. Rated as one of the top-ten trails in the United States, the trail offers great vistas, enchanting streamside walks, bluffs, boulders, rich forests, and hundreds of waterfalls. Eventually, the Ozark Highlands Trail will join the Buffalo River Trail, go across to the Sylamore Ranger District, then go along Lake Norfork, join the Ozark Trail through Missouri, and end up at St. Louis for a total of 1,000 miles of hiking experience. If you wish to walk a portion of it going east, a steep climb goes to Cherry Bend Hollow and broad vistas. West of the road, the trail is easier and goes around the mountain past an old rock house beneath a bluff a quarter of a mile from the road.

Just north of the Ozark Highlands Trail, the road crosses **Fly Gap,** which is the highest spot on the drive at an elevation of 1,953 feet. In 4 miles the scenic byway portion of AR 23 ends at the Ozark National Forest boundary at AR 16.

WHITE RIVER TO EUREKA SPRINGS

After 3.3 miles, AR 23 crosses the headwaters of the **White River.** Just east of here at the community of Boston, the White River begins. The river starts its 225-mile journey by flowing west toward Fayetteville and then north, where its flow is checked by Lakes Sequoyah and Beaver. It then continues north into Missouri, where it is impounded by the Table Rock and Taneycomo Lake dams. It then flows into Bull Shoals Lake, and after emerging below the dam in Arkansas near the community of Mountain Home, it cuts a winding path south to the Mississippi River. In spite of all the alterations it is considered one of the finest fishing and floating streams in the Ozarks.

After 20 miles, the road crosses **War Eagle Creek.** Rising just east of Boston, it flows northwest to Beaver Lake. For most of its length it is considered a Class II (moderate) floating stream. War Eagle Creek is named after an Osage Indian, Hurachis the War Eagle, who signed treaties with the federal government during the 1820s.

In 3 miles, the road passes through **Huntsville,** the CROSSROADS OF THE OZARKS, according to the sign. It was named by pioneers from Huntsville, Alabama. The town was platted and made the permanent county seat in 1839. Mostly destroyed during the Civil War, it was incorporated in 1877.

North of Huntsville the road leaves the Boston Mountains and enters the

Springfield Plateau. This region is not as dramatic; its elevations vary from only 500 to 1,500 feet. The bedrock is limestone, with caves, springs, and sinkholes contributing to the Ozark landscape.

In 4 miles, after you again cross War Eagle Creek, **Withrow Springs State Park** appears on the west side of AR 23. This 786-acre park was named after an early settler, Richard Withrow, who came west from Tennessee in 1832 and established the first gristmill in the area. The park has three trails; one, the War Eagle Trail, is a 2-mile round-trip hike. The trail runs along War Eagle Creek, offers a chance to enter a cave, and climbs 150 feet to the top of a bluff overlooking the river and countryside.

Continue to Eureka Springs, which is 20 miles away. For details on Eureka Springs, see Drive 21.

Eastern Ouachitas

LITTLE ROCK TO HOLLA BEND, ARKANSAS

GENERAL DESCRIPTION: A 75-mile drive from Little Rock along the eastern edge of the Ouachita Mountains to the Arkansas River valley and Holla Bend National Wildlife Refuge.

SPECIAL ATTRACTIONS: Pinnacle Mountain State Park, Arkansas Arboretum, Ouachita National Recreation Trail, Ouachita National Forest, Winona Auto Tour, Lake Sylvia Recreation Area, Petit Jean State Park, and Holla Bend National Wildlife Refuge; hiking, scenic views, fall colors, camping, swimming, hunting, fishing, crystal prospecting, and bird-watching.

LOCATION: Eastern Ouachitas. The drive begins on Arkansas Highway 10 on the west side of Little Rock and heads west.

DRIVE ROUTE NUMBERS: Arkansas Highways 10, 9, 154, and 155 and Forest Roads 132, 152, and 324.

CAMPING: The U.S. Army Corps of Engineers' Maumelle Park contains 111 campsites with water and electrical hookups, tables and grills, pavilions, hot showers, and a dump station. Petit Jean State Park has Mather Lodge with 24 guest rooms, a swimming pool, a gift shop, and a full-service restaurant; 19 fully equipped cabins; and 127 campsites with water and electrical hookups. Lake Sylvia Recreation Area has 19 camping units with electricity, 9 basic camping units, picnic areas, rest rooms, showers, and swimming.

SERVICES: All services at Little Rock and nearby Morrilton and Russellville. Food and gas at Perryville, Perry, and Oppelo.

NEARBY ATTRACTIONS: Mount Nebo State Park, Lake Dardanelle, Lake Maumelle, Flatside Wilderness Area, Arkansas River, Lake Winona, and Scenic 7 Byway.

THE DRIVE

The drive, which begins just west of Little Rock, is on the extreme eastern edge of the Ouachita Mountains. These mountains began to form more than 300 million years ago, when the continental plates of South America and Africa began pushing from the south, uplifting the Ouachitas and the Ozarks at the same time. This uplifting, folding, and faulting lasted millions of years, producing the dramatic shapes and sizes of mountains unique to the Midwest. Over the last half of the drive, the road follows the Arkansas River valley, which is considered part of the Ouachitas. Here backwater areas provide habitat for more "southern" plants and animals such as bald cypress trees and alligators.

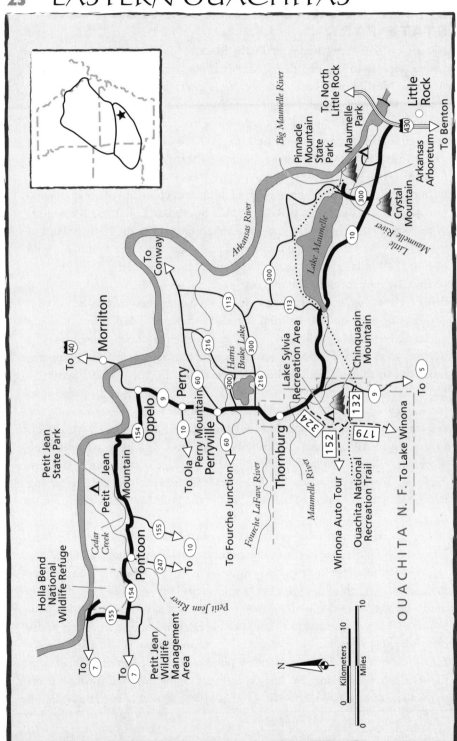

LITTLE ROCK TO PINNACLE MOUNTAIN STATE PARK

AR 10, on the western edge of **Little Rock,** begins the drive. Little Rock, with a population of more than 180,000, is the largest city and the capital of Arkansas. North Little Rock, located on the north side of the Arkansas River, is the third-largest city in the state, with more than 63,000 people. Historical accounts indicate that Little Rock's name originally referred to a moss-covered rock jutting out from the south bank of the Arkansas River. French explorers in the early 1800s noted that the location of this rock marked the transition from the broad lowland plains to the rugged mountainous region. In 1821 Little Rock was established on a bluff at the intersection of two major transportation routes: the Arkansas River and the Southwest Trail. Little Rock grew as successive waves of travelers passed through it. In 1836 there was a flood of migrants to the newly created state of Texas; then came the California gold rush of 1849 and the arrival of the Cairo and Fulton Railroad in 1870. Because of the city's accessibility, Little Rock grew to become the state's center of finance, education, transportation, industry, medicine, and government.

Traveling west on AR 10 from the intersection with I–430, you pass the entrance road to Maumelle Park after 2 miles. The park offers camping facilities and access to the Arkansas River. Continuing on AR 10, the prominent mountain lined with communication towers on the left of the highway is Crystal Mountain. At 1,085 feet above sea level, it is the highest mountain in the eastern Ouachitas. After 3 miles, turn right onto AR 300 and follow the signs to the entrance to **Pinnacle Mountain State Park.** Pinnacle Mountain, to the east of AR 300, is 1,011 feet above sea level. Although its cone shape suggests a volcanic origin, it is actually part of a ridge of the massive Jackfork sandstone formation, which has been gradually isolated by streams cutting through it. The main part of the ridge, called the Fulk Mountain chain, lies to the east.

For an orientation to the park, take Pinnacle Valley Road east 1.8 miles, turn left, and follow the road north to the visitor center. Upon entering the exhibit area, you will notice a huge stuffed alligator. These reptiles were once common in the southern half of Arkansas, but poaching for hides reduced their numbers until alligators were declared endangered in the state. Although they are now protected, habitat destruction continues to keep their population in low numbers. Alligators require quiet waters such as swamps, bayous, and lakes. Grassy Lake, west of Hope, Arkansas, is such a place, and it is one of the few areas in the state where alligators are known to breed. Individual animals have been sighted as far north as the Arkansas River, having migrated or been transplanted

American alligators occur as far north as the Arkansas River.

from the southern part of the state. Be sure to ask the naturalist if there is an opportunity to see one of these incredible living fossils in the quiet waters around the park.

Pinnacle Mountain State Park was established in 1977 and is Arkansas's first state park adjoining a major metropolitan area. Although not open to camping, the recreation area at the base of the mountain has shaded picnic tables, grills, water, a playground, rest rooms, and a large, open-air pavilion. Boat ramps allow access to the Big and Little Maumelle Rivers that border the park. The many trails lead you into bottomland hardwood forests, shaded boulder-strewn valleys, along cypress-lined rivers, and windswept mountaintops. The trail up and over Pinnacle Mountain, the steepest trail in Arkansas, offers a spectacular panoramic view of the Ouachitas, Lake Maumelle, and the Arkansas River. The other trails vary in difficulty from level, paved, and barrier-free to moderately difficult. Consult the trail map brochure and the knowledgeable staff at the visitor center. While at the center, be sure to walk to the scenic overlook just off the parking lot.

At the lower parking lot, the **Ouachita National Recreation Trail** begins its 225-mile route to Talimena State Park in Oklahoma. The Ouachita Trail is the longest trail in Arkansas, traversing mountains, valleys, lake and river overlooks, bottomlands, and pine/hardwood forests, with many plant and animal surprises along the way. The first segment of the trail, which is managed by Pinnacle Mountain State Park, extends 34 miles west to Lake Sylvia. A trail map is available at the visitor center.

About half a mile west of the entrance road to the visitor center on Pinnacle Valley Road, a sign marks the entrance to the **Arkansas Arboretum.** The arboretum is an ongoing project that is devoted to depicting characteristic plants found to occur in each of the six natural divisions of the state. A paved trail winds through different habitats that are identified by interpretive signs describing each natural division. Many of the trees, shrubs, vines, and herbaceous plants are also identified by plaques or labels. It is a good opportunity to see the diversity of plants that are especially adapted to the different regions of the state.

Return to AR 10 and proceed west, crossing **Lake Maumelle** after 7 miles. This 9,000-acre lake formed after the damming of the Big Maumelle River to provide an adequate water supply for Little Rock. The lake also provides boating and fishing and includes a wheelchair-accessible area just off the right side of the bridge.

LAKE SYLVIA AREA SITES

Continue on AR 10 for 11 miles to the junction with AR 9. A 3-mile side trip south on AR 9 will take you to FR 132 and the beginning of the **Winona Auto Tour,** which includes the **Lake Sylvia Recreation Area.** A self-guided interpretive brochure for the scenic drive is available at the Winona Ranger District Office at Perryville or by writing the Supervisor's Office, Ouachita National Forest, in Hot Springs. The 26-mile Winona Auto Tour features mountain vistas, quartz crystal hunting, displays of spring and fall color, lush forests, and wilderness experiences, and ends at AR 7. For a shorter drive that loops through Lake Sylvia Recreation Area, also take FR 132, 3 miles south of the intersection of AR 9 and 10. While traveling south on AR 9, you cross over the Maumelle River and the Ouachita National Recreation Trail. Turn west on FR 132, proceed about 4 miles, driving through the Chinquapin Mountain Walk-in Turkey Hunting Area, and turn right on FR 152. In about a mile, the road crosses the Ouachita Trail. After another mile, a parking lot to the right accesses a half-mile wheelchair-accessible interpretive trail. A side road just beyond the parking lot leads to the campground and to additional trails. Continuing on FR 152, another side road leads to a swimming area and bathhouse overlooking Lake Sylvia, a sixteen-acre Forest Service lake. FR 152 now becomes FR 324 and continues for 4 miles, ending at the junction of AR 9 and AR 10.

Continue to **Perryville,** passing the Harris Brake Lake and Wildlife Management Area and the Fourche LaFave River. Be sure to stop for information and maps at the **Winona Ranger District Office** in Perryville on the west side of town.

PERRY TO PETIT JEAN STATE PARK

Proceed 3 miles north on AR 9, over Perry Mountain, to **Perry.** On the north side of town, notice the roadcut on the right. Instead of horizontal rock strata, the layers are vertical, attesting to the tremendous pressures that squeezed the once-level landscape together like an accordion to form the Ouachita Mountains. This roadcut is one of the best in the Ouachitas that illustrates how the mountains were formed. After another 4 miles, turn west onto AR 154 at Oppelo. While driving across the Arkansas River valley, notice the prominent mountain straight ahead—this is the 1,100-foot Petit Jean Mountain. After 5 miles the road begins the climb to the mountain's plateau. After 2 miles, a road to the right leads to **Petit Jean's Gravesite.** Petit Jean, whose name has been given to numerous features in the region, was said to have lived during the period of French exploration of the New World. Legend has it that she disguised herself as a cabin boy so she could secretly accompany her fiance, a sailor, to the New World. Because of her diminutive size, the crew called her "Petit Jean" ("little John"). After exploring the region, she became fatally ill and requested to be buried on this mountain, which now bears her name.

After another 2 miles, you will reach the visitor information center of **Petit Jean State Park.** Be sure to stop, view the exhibits, and ask about recreational opportunities in the park. Set aside as parkland in 1923, before there was a park system, Petit Jean is considered one of the finest state parks in Arkansas. Interesting historic features add to the exceptional natural beauty of the mountain. A mountaintop motor-tour brochure, available at the visitor information center, guides you to interesting stone structures built by the CCC, scenic overlooks, exceptional geologic features, and cultural landmarks. The drive takes a minimum of two hours, depending on the length of stay at each stop.

There are seven trail systems at Petit Jean State Park. Be sure to visit the Cedar Falls Overlook if you do not have time to hike one of the trails. From the overlook, Cedar Creek can be seen as it plunges 100 feet into a box canyon. Depending on the time of year and the amount of rainfall, Cedar Falls can be spectacular. The Cedar Falls Trail, which begins at Mather Lodge, is a 2-mile round-trip hike into the canyon. This is the most popular trail in the park, even though the hiking difficulty is moderate to hard because of its steep descent into the deeply incised sandstone canyon. There is a great variety of

*An impressive roadcut just north of Perry gives testament to the massive forces
that uplifted and formed the Ouachita Mountains.*

vegetation in the canyon. The south-facing slopes are more exposed and provide habitat suitable for more drought-tolerant plants such post oak, blackjack
oak, shortleaf pine, and hickory. The more protected north-facing slopes have
red oak, white oak, sweet gum, and red maple. Two unusual plants, Ozark chinquapin and yellow ladyslipper orchid, inhabit the canyon.

The unspoiled beauty of Seven Hollows Trail inspired the establishment of
Petit Jean as Arkansas's first state park. In the early 1900s executives of the Fort
Smith Lumber Company, who owned the Seven Hollows area, recognized that
it should be preserved for everyone to enjoy. Unfortunately, in August of 2000
a forest fire swept through the Seven Hollows landscape, destroying the over-
story trees and changing the character of the area for some time to come. There
is now a lush growth of plants in the understory, with the hollows being mostly
recovered. The 4.5-mile Seven Hollows Trail is moderate to hard in difficulty.
Sites along the way include a natural bridge, grotto, turtle rocks, bluffs, and
desertlike sandstone glades. (Another place to see turtle rocks, which are
weathered sandstone shaped like the backs of turtles, is along the Rock House
Cave Trail.) Turtle rocks exhibit a variety of colors and weathering patterns
because of the varying iron deposits in the sandstone.

A shorter, easier, quarter-mile walk is the Bear Cave Trail, named for the last
bear killed on Petit Jean Mountain. Piles of huge sandstone boulders, rock shelters, and monoliths allow visitors to walk under, around, through, and over

these erosional features. A map showing the location of Bear Cave and the other trails in the park is available at the visitor center.

When leaving Petit Jean State Park, visit the Palisades Overlook opposite the intersection of AR 154 and 155. A commanding view of Cedar Creek Canyon, the towering Red Bluff above the canyon, and the vast Arkansas River valley lay before you. Continuing on AR 154 after 4 miles, the road passes Pontoon Park, which is maintained by the U.S. Army Corps of Engineers as an access to the Petit Jean River.

After another 3.5 miles, a gravel road on the south leads to **Petit Jean Wildlife Management Area.** Managed by the Arkansas Game & Fish Commission, the 15,000-acre area is best known for its duck hunting. There are additional opportunities to see wildlife, especially alligators, at Kingfisher Lake, located at the headquarters, and Pelican Pond, which is reached by a gravel road that eventually leads to AR 7.

HOLLA BEND

Continue on AR 154, turn north onto AR 155 for 3 miles, and take the entrance road into **Holla Bend National Wildlife Refuge.** A per-vehicle entrance fee is required for all visits. Be sure to stop at the office for informa-

Massive sandstone outcrops provide spectacular views of the Arkansas River valley near Petit Jean's grave site atop Petit Jean Mountain.

tion and a map of the area. The staff can suggest special wildlife viewing opportunities; these change depending on the season. The winter months offer viewing of up to fourteen species of ducks, four species of geese, and bald eagles. The numbers of these birds peak in December and January. Any time of year, especially during early morning and evening hours when wildlife are most active, may yield sightings of white-tailed deer, eastern cottontail and swamp rabbits, gray and fox squirrels, red fox, raccoon, beaver, coyote, bobcat, opossum, nine-banded armadillo, muskrat, and river otter. Refuge personnel have also identified 240 species of birds in the refuge. A checklist is available for your reference.

The refuge provides an 8-mile auto tour that is one of the best ways to see wildlife and learn about the refuge and its management practices. A self-guided tour brochure is available at the information station; there are also interpretive signs along the route.

Scenic 7 Byway South

RUSSELLVILLE TO HOT SPRINGS, ARKANSAS

GENERAL DESCRIPTION: A 69-mile drive south from Russellville across the Arkansas River valley, into the Ouachita Mountains, and ending at Hot Springs.

SPECIAL ATTRACTIONS: Lake Dardanelle State Park, Dardanelle Rock, Mount Nebo, Ouachita National Recreation Trail, Ouachita National Forest, Scenic 7 Byway, Hollis CCC Camp, Winona Auto Tour, Flatside Wilderness Area, Buffalo Gap Auto Tour, Iron Springs Recreation Area, and Hot Springs; scenic views, camping, hiking, mountain biking, horseback riding, swimming, crystal prospecting, fall colors, fishing, and hunting.

LOCATION: Eastern Ouachitas. The drive begins on Arkansas Highway 7 at Russellville and heads south.

DRIVE ROUTE NUMBERS: Arkansas Highways 7, 7S (a side road off Highway 7), and 22 and Forest Roads 132 and 11.

CAMPING: Lake Dardanelle, Mount Nebo, Petit Jean, Lake Catherine, Lake Ouachita, and DeGray Lake Resort state parks; Lake Dardanelle and Nimrod Lake of the U.S. Army Corps of Engineers; South Fourche and Iron Springs recreation areas in the Ouachita National Forest; and Gulpha Gorge in Hot Springs National Park.

SERVICES: All services are available at Russellville, Dardanelle, and Hot Springs. Gas and food at Centerville, Ola, Fourche Junction, Hollis, Jessieville, Blue Springs, and Hot Springs Village.

NEARBY ATTRACTIONS: Long Pool Recreation Area; Holla Bend National Wildlife Refuge; Petit Jean and Galla Creek wildlife management areas; Petit Jean State Park; and Eastern Ouachitas, Mount Magazine, Hot Springs National Park, and Crystal Trail scenic drives.

THE DRIVE

The drive begins in the Arkansas River valley, which is considered a subregion of the Ouachitas. The valley occupies a band running from 25 to 35 miles wide, separating the Ozarks to the north from the Ouachita Mountains to the south. Although it is composed primarily of the floodplains and terraces of the Arkansas, Fourche LaFave, Petit Jean, and Poteau Rivers and their tributaries, several ridges rise conspicuously above the valley floor. Examples include Mount Magazine, Mount Nebo, and Petit Jean Mountain; Mount Magazine, at 2,753 feet, is the highest point in Arkansas as well as in the Midwest.

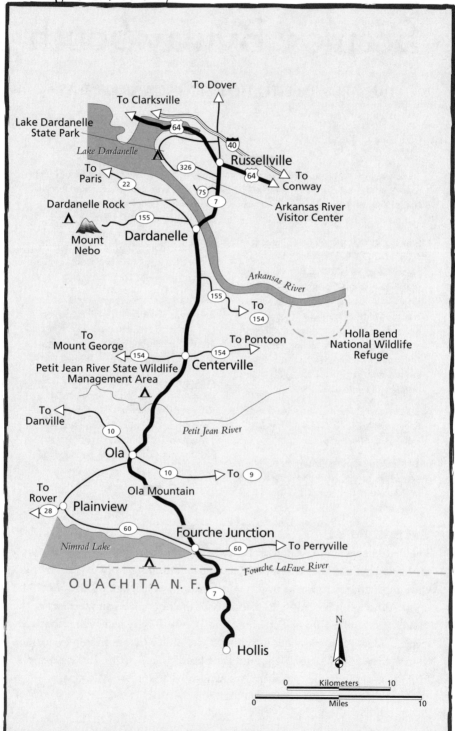

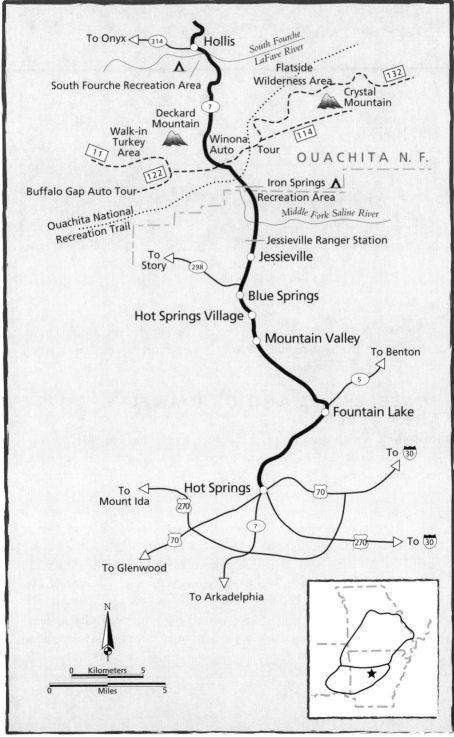

To Onyx ← 314 Hollis
South Fourche LaFave River

South Fourche Recreation Area

Flatside Wilderness Area

132

Crystal Mountain

7

Deckard Mountain

Walk-in Turkey Area

Winona Auto Tour

114

11

OUACHITA N. F.

122

Buffalo Gap Auto Tour

Iron Springs Recreation Area

Middle Fork Saline River

Ouachita National Recreation Trail

Jessieville Ranger Station

To Story ← 298 Jessieville

Blue Springs

Hot Springs Village

Mountain Valley

To Benton

5

Fountain Lake

To 30

To Mount Ida Hot Springs

270

70

7

70 270 To 30

To Glenwood

To Arkadelphia

N

0 Kilometers 5
0 Miles 5

*Scenic 7 Byway is also a nationally designated scenic route along
its 23 miles through the Ouachita National Forest.*

This part of AR 7, from Russellville to Hot Springs, is a continuation of the nationally designated **Scenic 7 Byway**—one of the nation's most scenic drives. The northern section of Scenic 7 Byway is described in Drive 19.

RUSSELLVILLE AND DARDANELLE AREA SITES

Russellville is the starting point for this drive. Incorporated in 1835, the town was named for Dr. T. J. Russell, a British-born and -educated physician who immigrated here in 1835. Russellville, the largest town between Little Rock and Fort Smith, is experiencing steady population growth due to its well-developed manufacturing sector. The headquarters for the Ozark National Forest is located here and is a convenient stop for those wanting advice and information on the national forest. The headquarters is easily located if you proceed on AR 7 to about the middle of town, turn right on Main Street, and go a few blocks, looking for a large building on the left at 605 West Main. This is also US 64, which leads to the west side of town and intersects with AR 326. By taking AR 326 south, you arrive at Lake Dardanelle State Park. The Ouachita National Forest headquarters are located in Hot Springs, the destination of this drive.

Lake Dardanelle State Park, located on the west side of Russellville, is worth a visit. There is a newly constructed visitor center that houses the largest indoor freshwater fish tank display in Arkansas. More than 7,000 gallons of water house a variety of fish, turtles, crawfish, and other species found in Arkansas waters. There is also a live beehive, history exhibits, and a variety of interpretive programs. You can reach the state park by starting at the intersection of I–40 and AR 7 and heading south to the first traffic light. Then turn right and follow AR 326 around the shore of Lake Dardanelle to the intersection of US 64. Turn left on US 64 and then right on AR 326 and follow the signs to the state park and visitor center. An alternative route is to take AR 7 into Russellville and turn right on Main Street, which is also US 64, follow the highway west to AR 326, turn left, and follow the signs to the state park.

You can continue on AR 326 or go back to US 64 to reach AR 7, turn right (south), proceed to AR 7S, turn right, and follow the road to the Old Post Road, which leads to the **U.S. Army Corps of Engineers' Arkansas River Visitor Center.** The visitor center has interpretive exhibits and information on recreational opportunities in the area, including several hiking trails maintained by the Corps. The area just below Dardanelle Lock and Dam is a favorite winter feeding location for large numbers of bald eagles. Eagles can be seen in the park most mornings between sunrise and 10:00 A.M. during December, January, and February.

Dardanelle Rock is visible from the visitor center looking south. A geologic natural area owned by the Arkansas Natural Heritage Commission, Dardanelle Rock has been a major landmark on the Arkansas River since the days of earliest exploration. Although the craggy sentinel offers some limited hiking, it is best viewed from the visitor center because the graffiti sprayed on its massive rock face is lost in the distance.

As you head back to AR 7, on the left side of the road you will find a building containing the Arkansas Game and Fish Commission's West Central Regional Office. Maps, brochures, and other information are available during normal business hours.

Return to AR 7, cross over the Arkansas River, and drive to the town of **Dardanelle.** The town's name stems from the resemblance of the landmark rock to the Strait of Dardanelles in Turkey. Originally established as a trading post, the settlement that grew up beside Dardanelle Rock in the early 1800s was one of the first in the Arkansas valley.

Proceed south on AR 7 to the intersection with AR 22. Turn right and then left on AR 155 and follow the signs to **Mount Nebo,** which rises 1,350 feet above the valley. A spectacular view of 34,000-acre Lake Dardanelle, the

Dardanelle Rock has been a major landmark along the Arkansas River since the days of earliest exploration.

Arkansas River, and the surrounding mountain ridges can be obtained from **Mount Nebo State Park.** Because of the steep climb up the mountain, no trailers or RVs more than 15 feet in length should be used. Seven trails and several overlooks draw the visitor to places such as Sunrise Point, Fern Lake, Nebo Springs, and Sunset Point.

Return to AR 7 and continue south across the Arkansas River valley. Patches of woods seen along the way are dominated by bottomland hardwoods such as sweet gum, willow oak, water oak, pin oak, and persimmon. Along the route, you will find access points to Holla Bend National Wildlife Refuge by way of AR 155 and 154. See Drive 23 for details.

OLA AND FOURCHE JUNCTION

Pass through Centerville; the next town is **Ola.** Situated in the Petit Jean River valley, the community is sustained by forest-related industries and by providing services to the nearby farmers and ranchers. South of Ola, AR 7 climbs out of the Arkansas River valley to the summit of Ola Mountain. A pull-off with picnic tables offers an expansive view across Nimrod Lake and the Fourche LaFave River valley.

Ola Mountain marks the northern boundary of the rugged Ouachita Mountains. These east-west trending mountains are unique in the United States as a result of folding when another continent from the south collided with the North American continent more than 300 million years ago. The mountain-building lasted millions of years, forming the Ouachita Mountains and the Ozarks. The Ouachita Mountains are composed of sandstone and shale and rise as many as 1,500 feet above the valley floor. Their more acid and well-drained soils are favored by shortleaf pine and upland hardwoods.

Continue on to **Fourche Junction,** which is on the eastern edge of **Nimrod Lake,** an 18,300-acre lake built in 1942 for flood control of the Fourche LaFave River that also provides recreational opportunities. The lake is a popular fishing site for largemouth bass, white bass, crappie, and large channel catfish. There is a public duck-hunting area and a 1,200-acre waterfowl refuge.

Proceeding on AR 7, the road enters the boundary of the Ozark National Forest. For the next 24.3 miles, this segment of Scenic 7 Byway is part of the system of National Forest Scenic Byways. This designation promotes special emphasis on varied recreational facilities such as hiking trails, camping and picnic areas, and lakes for boating and fishing; development of scenic overlooks and drives; and production of brochures, interpretive displays, and visitor centers on Forest Service land.

After 10 miles, the road crosses the South Fourche LaFave River; immediately to the left is the **South Fourche Recreation Area.** Camping and picnic areas are provided, with easy access to the river.

WINONA AND BUFFALO GAP AUTO TOURS

Proceeding another 2.4 miles, the **Hollis CCC Camp** exhibit is located on the right. Interpretive displays explain the Civilian Conservation Corps' role as an emergency employment program devoted to natural resource conservation work. A wheelchair-accessible paved trail weaves its way by exhibits under a canopy of tall shortleaf pine trees. Pit toilets are also available. About another 5 miles on the left, FR 132 marks the beginning of the 26-mile **Winona Auto Tour** between AR 7 and 9. This side trip offers an opportunity to get off the main road and see some of the backcountry. The route takes about one hour, one-way. The gravel road is two-lane, but caution is advised when you approach oncoming vehicles and curves in the road. Be sure to pick up an auto tour interpretive booklet, available from the Jessieville or Winona Ranger District offices, or from the Ouachita National Forest headquarters in Hot Springs. The route provides scenic mountain vistas and a chance to hunt for Arkansas "diamonds," which are veins of white quartz crystal considered to be the best-quality white quartz in the world. Surface collecting of a small amount of quartz is allowed on Crystal Mountain. Much of the road parallels the **Flatside Wilderness Area,** a 10,105-acre forested expanse featuring small creeks, panoramic views, rugged terrain, and a section of the Ouachita National Recreation Trail.

Back on AR 7 and across from the entrance to FR 132, another side trip, on FR 11, leads west to **Deckard Mountain Walk-in Turkey Area.** Two trails, the 9-mile Buffalo Gap Mountain Bike Ride and the 36-mile Bear Creek Horse Trail, have been developed. Maps are available at the Jessieville Ranger District office.

FR 11 also begins the 9-mile **Buffalo Gap Auto Tour.** A tour brochure is available at the Jessieville Ranger District office. The gravel road offers overlooks of Deckard Mountain, Blue Ouachita Mountain, and Buffalo Gap.

OUACHITA AND IRON SPRINGS TRAILS

Continuing south on AR 7, in 0.6 mile the **Ouachita National Recreation Trail** crosses the highway. Interpretive displays and a short, universally accessible trail offer visitors a chance to observe trees, shrubs, and wildflowers typical of the Ouachita Mountains. The Ouachita Trail spans 225 miles from Talimena State Park in Oklahoma east to Pinnacle Mountain State Park, west of Little Rock. A shorter, 4.3-mile trail called Hunts Loop can be accessed here, or from an easier trailhead 1.3 miles down the road at Iron Springs Recreation Area. This moderately difficult trail leads to panoramic views from Short Mountain Vista, interesting rock outcrops, and valleys lush with ferns and spring wildflowers. Plan on three to four hours with stops along the way.

Proceeding on AR 7, about 1 mile on the left side of the highway, the Jessieville Civilian Conservation Corps exhibit explains the recreation construction projects that 201 young men accomplished in the 1930s. In another half a mile, **Iron Springs Recreation Area** is on the right. The recreation area offers campsites, picnic areas, and places to wade and explore the clear-flowing Middle Fork Saline River. The National Forest Scenic Byway ends just south of Iron Springs Recreation Area.

After another 4 miles down AR 7, the **Jessieville Ranger Station** maintains a visitor information center with staff to answer your questions, plus an extensive supply of brochures on recreational opportunities in the area. Also, a 0.7-mile trail called the Friendship Barrier-Free Trail is marked with interpretive signs and a paved trail that winds through a mature pine and hardwood forest. This path offers everyone a good opportunity to relax in a natural setting before proceeding to Hot Springs.

Along the next 14 miles of AR 7, you may notice a gradual increase in the amount of tourist attractions and traffic as you approach **Hot Springs.** For details on Hot Springs and Hot Springs National Park, see Drive 26.

Mount Magazine

PARIS TO HAVANA, ARKANSAS

GENERAL DESCRIPTION: A 28-mile drive from Paris, to the top of Mount Magazine, and down to Havana.

SPECIAL ATTRACTIONS: Mount Magazine (highest point in Arkansas) and Cove Lake; Mount Magazine State Park; scenic overlooks, hiking, camping, fall colors, fishing, and hunting.

LOCATION: Northern Ouachitas. The drive begins on Arkansas Highway 309 at Paris.

DRIVE ROUTE NUMBERS: Arkansas Highway 309 and Forest Road 1606.

CAMPING: Cameron Bluff and Cove Lake recreation areas, both in the Ozark National Forest, have picnic tables, drinking water, fire grates, and pit toilets.

SERVICES: All services at Paris. Food and gas at Havana.

NEARBY ATTRACTIONS: Blue Mountain Lake, Lake Dardanelle, Mount Nebo State Park, and Scenic 7 Byway.

THE DRIVE

Mount Magazine, at 2,753 feet above sea level, is the highest point in the Midwest. Only the Appalachians to the east, the Rockies to the west, and mountains in western Texas attain higher elevations. Standing approximately 2,300 feet above the surrounding valley floor, it is truly an impressive site. From the top of the mountain there are scenic views of the surrounding Arkansas River valley, the Boston Mountains to the north, and the Ouachita Mountains to the south. Because of its exceptional scenery, AR 309, the highway that takes travelers up and over Mount Magazine, was designated as an Arkansas Scenic Byway in 1994. WARNING: Low-flying clouds and fog can sometimes cause poor visibility. Ice can form on the roads in winter.

PARIS

Begin the drive in **Paris**, a community that was settled about 1820 on the Old Military Road that connected Little Rock and Fort Smith. This road later became the Butterfield Overland Mail route. The village was incorporated in 1879 and was named for Paris, France. A side trip east on AR 22 takes you to

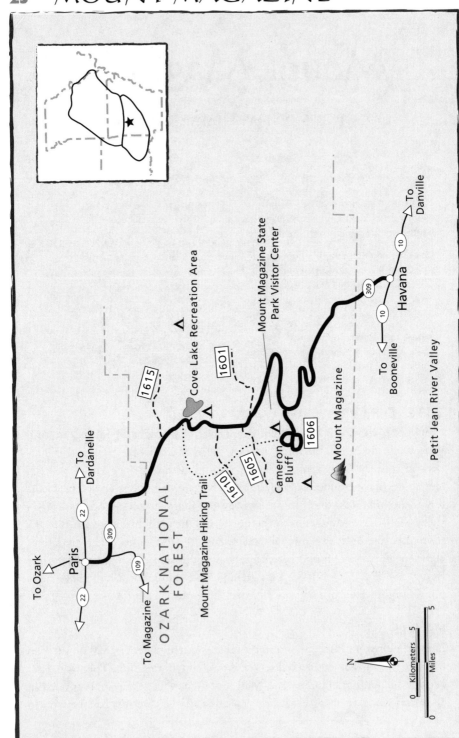

the Magazine Ranger District, located on the south side of the highway. Information and brochures on recreational opportunities in the national forest are available at the district office.

MOUNT MAGAZINE SCENIC BYWAY SITES
A few miles south of Paris on AR 309, you enter the Mount Magazine District of the Ozark National Forest. The next 24.9 miles are designated as the **Mount Magazine Scenic Byway,** which is part of the national system of National Forest Scenic Byways. This designation recognizes special scenic drives through national forest land and emphasizes the development of special recreational opportunities such as trails, picnic and camping areas, and scenic overlooks.

The road begins to climb, and in about 3 miles, **Cove Lake Recreation Area** comes into view. There are 28 campsites, rest rooms, and showers available in the summer. Cove Lake also has picnicking, swimming, fishing, a 3-mile loop hiking trail, and a boat-launch ramp. Interpretive programs are offered by naturalists in the summer.

Across the highway from the entrance to Cove Lake Recreation Area is the head of the Mount Magazine Trail. This moderately difficult, 14.2-mile trail climbs to the top of Mount Magazine and offers spectacular scenic views, dense stands of hardwoods and pine trees, glade openings, beautiful wildflowers, and strolls along picturesque streams. For shorter hikes, there are two other

Travelers from Texas have come to view the fall colors from the top of Mount Magazine.

trailheads (Corley Access and Green Bench Access) along the way that can be reached by Forest Service roads. The Magazine Ranger District has a trail map and can advise you on trail options.

From Cove Lake, AR 309 continues the climb up **Mount Magazine.** This flat-topped mountain would be called a mesa in the West. Named by French hunters, the shape of Mount Magazine reminded them of a barn or warehouse—*magasin,* in French. The mountain is composed of layers of sandstone and shale with a very resistant cap of Savannah Formation sandstone that was deposited about 300 million years ago. Steep bluffs circling the top of the mountain form cliffs up to 200 feet tall. Mount Magazine truly has the character of a mountain with its summit sometimes shrouded in low-lying clouds and its temperature averaging 6 and sometimes 25 degrees cooler than the surrounding valleys. Wild and rugged, Mount Magazine has the most confirmed sightings of mountains lions in the Ozark and Ouachita regions combined.

Although the odds of seeing a mountain lion are extremely slim, there are plenty of opportunities to see other kinds of wildlife. Forest inhabitants include deer, bobcats, foxes, raccoons, opossums, skunks, and squirrels. A variety of bird species also inhabit the area, including northern cardinal, whippoorwill, indigo bunting, Carolina chickadee, tufted titmouse, and a variety of woodpeckers. Rare sightings of painted buntings, scarlet and summer tanagers, and rufous-crowned sparrows in open areas along the cliff tops are possible.

One especially noteworthy animal that has found a home on Mount Magazine is the black bear. Sometimes seen at night around the Cameron Bluff campground, black bear sightings are becoming more frequent in the rugged mountains of the Ozarks and the Ouachitas. This has not always been the case. At one time, black bears were common in Arkansas, and until 1923 Arkansas was known as "The Bear State." That year the state's general assembly changed it to "The Wonder State," probably because of the disappearance of the black bear. In 1927 all bear hunting was banned. By 1940 fewer than fifty black bears remained in the state, with most sightings occurring in southeast Arkansas. With the establishment of the Ozark and Ouachita national forests, the black bear's habitat improved, so the Arkansas Game & Fish Commission began restoration. Between 1954 and 1968, 254 black bears were trapped in Minnesota and in Manitoba, Canada, and released on Forest Service land. The restoration effort was first thought to be a failure, for few bears were being sighted. This, however, was probably due to their secretive nature and the remoteness of the rugged mountains into which they had been placed. But by 1973 there were an estimated 700 animals; and now approximately 2,000 black bears are living in Arkansas. As their population increases, the black bear's range is expanding into Missouri and Oklahoma. Although sightings of black bears are considered very rare, when encountered they should be treated with respect and kept at a distance.

A variety of natural features are found on Mount Magazine. Dense forests, glades, bluffs, springs, and streams provide habitat for a variety of plant life. Dry, exposed sandstone cliffs and glades support stunted trees, grasses, and sun-loving wildflowers. Meanwhile, shaded north slopes and ravines provide habitat for orchids, ferns, and spring blossoms. The mountain is rich in plant diversity; more than 600 plant species have been found on its upper elevations alone. Unusual plants growing on the mountain include the maple-leaved oak, a variety of Shumard oak with maple like leaves that is found only on Mount Magazine on shaded north slopes. Growing near the oak, the Rocky Mountain woodsia fern is also found nowhere else between the Rocky Mountains and the Appalachians. Other interesting plants include pipewort, hay-scented fern, and bottle gentian.

Near the top, two pullouts offer impressive views looking east. On top of the mesa be sure to visit the newly constructed **Mount Magazine State Park Visitor Center,** which contains exhibits, an auditorium, a wildlife viewing area, a gift shop, rest rooms, and trail maps. Just past the visitor center, FR 1606 leads to the Cameron Bluff overlook and campground. Be sure to hike the Signal Hill Trail, which is across from the entrance to the campground. The ten-

Views of impressive cliffs and vast expanses are afforded from Mount Magazine, the highest point in the Midwest.

minute hike up the last 200 feet of the mountain ensures that you are standing on the highest point in the Midwest. The Mount Magazine Trail can also be accessed at the campground. The road continues around to the south side of the mountain, where Mount Magazine Lodge once stood. It burned in 1971. Mount Magazine State Park is currently under construction with a new lodge, cabins, and a hotel scheduled for completion by the summer of 2005. Careful consideration is being given to the design of these buildings so that they do not take away from the rugged character of the mountains.

Returning to AR 309, the drive passes a road that goes 16 miles to Spring Lake, an eighty-acre lake built for fishing.

The drive continues, passing the East End Picnic Area, another scenic overlook, and a road that leads to Cedar Piney Lake, about 1 mile away. The seventeen-acre lake has a fishing pier and boat launch. After a long descent down the mountain, the drive ends at **Havana,** located in the Petit Jean River valley.

Hot Springs National Park

HOT SPRINGS, ARKANSAS

GENERAL DESCRIPTION: A 5-mile drive in Hot Springs National Park with scenic views, historic sites, interesting rock outcrops, and hot springs.

SPECIAL ATTRACTIONS: Hot Springs, Bathhouse Row, Hot Springs Mountain Drive, West Mountain Drive, Hot Springs Mountain Tower, and National Park Aquarium; scenic views, hiking, camping, and hot springs bathing.

LOCATION: East-central Ouachitas. The drive begins and ends on Arkansas Highway 7 on the north side of Hot Springs.

DRIVE ROUTE NUMBERS: Arkansas Highway 7.

CAMPING: Gulpha Gorge Campground, located on the east side of Hot Springs National Park, has 43 tent and trailer sites. Water, comfort stations, and a dumping station are provided; however, there are no showers and no water or electrical hookups. There are also campsites at the nearby national forest, U.S. Army Corps of Engineers' Lake Ouachita, and Lake Ouachita State Park.

SERVICES: All services at Hot Springs.

NEARBY ATTRACTIONS: Scenic 7 Byway and Crystal Trail scenic drives, Ouachita National Forest, Lake Ouachita, Mid-America Museum.

THE DRIVE

Hot Springs National Park is located in the middle of a series of mountains called the Zig-Zag Mountains. These long, linear mountains spaced from 1 to 3 miles apart are the result of giant folds produced during the mountain building of the entire region. The angle of these tilted layers of bedrock and the type of rock itself account for the unique occurrence of hot springs in this area. Although hot springs are found in a few locations in the Appalachian Mountains and are much more common in the West in places such as Yellowstone, in the Midwest they occur only at Hot Springs, Arkansas.

Geologists believe the hot springs originate in the valley north of Hot Springs National Park, which is traversed by AR 7, Park Avenue, and Whit-

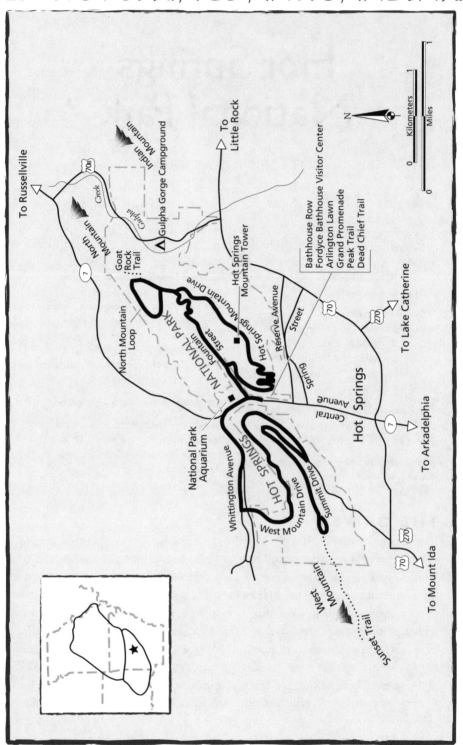

To Russellville

To Little Rock

North Mountain

Indian Mountain

Gulpha Creek

Gulpha Gorge Campground

Goat Rock Trail

7

70B

N

Kilometers
Miles

Bathhouse Row
Fordyce Bathhouse Visitor Center
Arlington Lawn
Grand Promenade
Peak Trail
Dead Chief Trail

North Mountain Loop

NATIONAL PARK

Fountain Street

Hot Springs Mountain Drive

Hot Springs Mountain Tower

Reserve Avenue

Spring Street

70

270

To Lake Catherine

Central Avenue

Hot Springs

National Park Aquarium

Whittington Avenue

HOT SPRINGS

West Mountain Drive

Summit Drive

West Mountain

Sunset Trail

7

To Arkadelphia

270

70

To Mount Ida

tington Avenue. Rainwater is collected in the broad valley and flows downward through extensive cracks and fractures in a hard, brittle rock called Bigfork chert. By using the carbon-14 dating technique on representative water molecules, scientists have estimated that the water, which travels to a depth of from 6,000 to 8,000 feet, takes about 4,000 years to complete that journey. At that depth, the temperature is several degrees hotter than at lesser depths; this heat is produced by the natural radioactive decay of particles in the earth's crust. The heated water, being lighter and under pressure, rises upward through the cracks and fractures in the chert, taking a year to reach the surface. Along the way, the 143-degree-Fahrenheit water dissolves minerals and salts from the surrounding bedrock, giving the water an odorless, yet distinctive taste that was once thought to have curative powers.

For those wanting to try hot spring water, it is available from a fountain located on Reserve Avenue in front of the National Park Service building. Cool refreshing spring water is available from a fountain at the end of Fountain Street. It is common to see local residents and tourists filling containers of water from both of these sources.

BATHHOUSE ROW

The Hot Springs Chamber of Commerce has a visitor center located on Central Avenue and Spring Street, just past the row of bathhouses on Central Avenue. This is a good place to stop for information about things to do and places to stay in Hot Springs. The drive begins at **Hot Springs National Park,** which is located on the north end of Hot Springs. Central Avenue, which is also AR 7, is the principal road. Parking is available along Central Avenue or on the adjoining streets near Bathhouse Row. Finding a space is more difficult on weekends and during the summer tourist season. Arriving early or using the pay lots alleviates the hassle of searching for a parking space in this popular but concentrated area. A visit to the **Fordyce Bathhouse Visitor Center,** located along **Bathhouse Row,** is a good place to get oriented. The visitor center contains exhibits and a film explaining the history of the area and of thermal water bathing. A tour through the restored bathhouse is like stepping back into the 1920s, when the popularity of Bathhouse Row as a travel destination was at its peak. Today traditional thermal baths are available at the Buckstaff Bathhouse on Bathhouse Row and at some of the hotels and medical facilities located near the park. Inquire at the visitor information desk for more details. In back of the Fordyce, a thermal fountain is displayed, one of the few outlets that was not capped to divert water to the bathhouses. Another uncapped hot spring, Maurice Historic Spring, can be seen on the north side of the Maurice Bathhouse, which is next to the Fordyce.

From Fordyce Bathhouse, walk north along Central Avenue and Bathhouse Row to **Arlington Lawn,** just before the corner of Central Avenue and Fountain Street. Against the bluff, hot springwater flows down the Hot Water Cascade into concrete pools in which visitors seem to be compelled to soak their sidewalk-weary feet. To the left of Hot Water Cascade, **DeSoto Rock** marks what some believe to be the site visited by Hernando de Soto and his men in the Spanish Expedition of 1541. The text of his chapter of narratives describing this part of his expedition was lost, but its title was "Hot Rivers and Salt Made from Sand." It is not known whether the conquistadors actually visited the hot springs, which are actually freshwater springs, or one of the several warm, salty seeps that are known elsewhere in the region. Evidence shows that thousands of years before Europeans first set foot in the hot springs, Indians were bathing in the warm, healing waters. The Caddo Indians believed that their people originated in the waters of the hot springs.

The French followed the Spanish into Arkansas. Although there is little written record left from these early trappers and hunters, they were surely aware of the hot springs. In 1803 the United States purchased the Louisiana Territory from France. President Thomas Jefferson, wanting to learn more about these new lands, sent expeditions into the region west of the Mississippi River. One of these parties, led by William Dunbar and Dr. George Hunter, traveled from the Mississippi River up the Red and Black Rivers to the Ouachita River. Navigating up the river, they unloaded their boats at a point where Gulpha Creek enters the Ouachita. Traveling 9 miles overland, they entered the valley of the hot springs and found a deserted cabin and a few shelters. The valley was an impressive site, with springs bellowing up steam along the hillside and issuing from low cones of tufa, a calcareous rock stained various shades of orange and red by traces of iron oxide. Today many of the springs have been capped and the tufa deposits covered up with soil. DeSoto Rock is one such remnant that was made of tufa that broke away from the nearby cliff. Another place to see tufa is Hot Water Cascade, where tufa is still being formed.

Upon returning home, Dunbar and Hunter communicated their findings to President Jefferson; their news generated much interest in the "Hot Springs of the Washita." Visitors began to seek out the soothing springs; some stayed and built cabins. The first hotel was established in 1828. The U.S. government recognized the significance of the area and set aside the hot springs and immediate surroundings as a federal reservation in 1832. In 1921 the area was designated as a national park. Hot Springs slowly began to grow with bathhouses, saloons, doctor's offices, and stores. The first two decades of the twentieth century were a time of rapid growth and change, despite a devastating fire that swept through 50 blocks of residences and businesses in 1913. As the twentieth century progressed, the medical profession increasingly doubted the water's healing powers, which resulted in less interest and visitation by the public. Today Hot Springs is thriving due to the development of its other attractions. However, the historic character of Hot Springs and the Victorian buildings along Bathhouse Row continue to appeal to tourists and those who continue to believe in the water's special healing and therapeutic powers.

The **National Park Aquarium** is located just past the Arlington Hotel on Central Avenue. This building houses both fresh- and saltwater aquaria and more than 250 species of tropical, native, and saltwater fish. Of particular interest is the fifty-year-old, 150-pound alligator snapping turtle that is native to backwater areas in the delta region of Arkansas.

Before leaving Bathhouse Row, take a walk along the **Grand Promenade.** This level, brick-lined pavement cuts across the lower flank of Hot Springs Mountain and parallels Central Avenue and Bathhouse Row. The half-mile promenade can be accessed from either end of Bathhouse Row or from behind Fordyce Bathhouse. It is wheelchair accessible from the north end or from behind the Fordyce. The promenade is a good place to observe birds such as mockingbirds, catbirds, cardinals, and thrushes. A bird checklist for the park is available at the visitor center. It is also the main access for Peak Trail and Dead Chief Trail. The Peak Trail starts midway down the promenade. This half-mile, moderately strenuous trail leads to the summit of Hot Springs Mountain and the Mountain Tower. The Dead Chief Trail is located at the south end of the promenade. This 1.4-mile trail is strenuous (at the start) and leads to Gulpha Gorge Campground. In all, there are twenty trails with a total of 22 miles available for hiking at Hot Springs National Park. Unfortunately, a trail guide book has not yet been developed describing the routes. Two more trails will be discussed later in this drive description.

HOT SPRINGS MOUNTAIN AND WEST MOUNTAIN DRIVES

There are two scenic drives within Hot Springs National Park. The first, **Hot Springs Mountain Drive,** is reached by driving north along Central Avenue and turning right on Fountain Street. Follow the signs to the entrance. The 4.5-mile one-way loop first stops at **Hot Springs Mountain Tower,** a site with a picnic area, water, and rest rooms. This commercially operated, 216-foot observation tower offers an outstanding panoramic view of Hot Springs and

Above Bathhouse Row, one can take a leisurely stroll along the brick-lined Grand Promenade.

the surrounding Ouachita Mountains. The second level of the tower contains exhibits and a glass-protected view. On pleasant days, the third level affords an open-air experience.

A drive to the upper loop, called **North Mountain Loop,** leads to a scenic view and a 0.7-mile hike to Goat Rock, a massive Arkansas novaculite outcrop. Just before reaching Goat Rock, the trail crosses rare grassy openings called novaculite glades, which harbor a diversity of wildflowers and sun-basking lizards.

The second scenic drive, **West Mountain Drive,** can be reached by following Central Avenue north to Whittington Avenue and turning left. After about half a mile, turn left again at the WEST MOUNTAIN DRIVE sign and begin the tour. After about a mile, take the Summit Drive road to the top of West Mountain. There are scenic pullouts along the way. As the road circles the crest, notice the large white rock outcrop in the center just off the parking lot. This is Arkansas novaculite, a dense rock composed of fine silica that is prized around the world for its qualities as a sharpening stone. Indians crafted arrowheads, spearpoints, tools, and implements using this rock. One novaculite pit on Indian Mountain, which can be reached opposite the Gulpha Gorge Campground, measures 150 feet in diameter and 25 feet deep.

This large outcrop at the end of West Mountain Drive is Arkansas novaculite, which is known worldwide for its use as a sharpening stone.

The shaping of arrowpoints was rarely done at the quarry; the rock was carried in blocks back to villages, where it was chipped and flaked into the desired shapes. Arkansas novaculite can be seen in outcrops on the crests and upper slopes of the mountains in and around Hot Springs National Park and along Scenic Drive 27. Rock shops in the Hot Springs area sell the "Arkansas Stone" individually or in gift packages.

Also at the parking lot is the start of the Sunset Trail, an 8.5-mile trail that follows the ridges of West Mountain, Music Mountain, and Sugarloaf Mountain. After 2.2 miles, the trail reaches the top of Music Mountain, which, at 1,450 feet above sea level, is the highest point in the park. There are several great views and interesting rock outcrops along the way.

27

Crystal Trail

HOT SPRINGS TO PAGE, ARKANSAS/OKLAHOMA

GENERAL DESCRIPTION: A 91-mile drive beginning at Hot Springs; traveling westward through the heart of the Ouachita Mountains, where beautiful quartz crystals abound; and ending at Page, Oklahoma.

SPECIAL ATTRACTIONS: Hot Springs, Mount Ida, Ouachita National Forest, Hickory Nut Mountain Recreation Area, Crystal Vista Auto Tour, Big Brushy Recreation Area, Ouachita Trail, Womble Trail, Lake Ouachita, Black Fork Mountain Wilderness, and Mid-America Museum; scenic views, hiking, crystal prospecting, canoeing, camping, fishing, and hunting.

LOCATION: Central Ouachitas. The drive begins on U.S. Highway 270 on the west side of Hot Springs and ends at Page, Oklahoma.

DRIVE ROUTE NUMBERS: U.S. Highway 270, Arkansas Highway 227, and Forest Road 50.

CAMPING: There are 6 national forest campsites, 16 U.S. Army Corps of Engineers' Lake Ouachita campsites, and additional campsites at Lake Ouachita and Queen Wilhelmina state parks.

SERVICES: All services at Hot Springs, Mount Ida, and Mena. Food and gas at Royal and Crystal Springs. Gas at Hurricane Grove and Pencil Bluff.

NEARBY ATTRACTIONS: Hot Springs National Park; Scenic 7 Byway; Little Missouri Falls; Crystal Vista; Heavener Runestone State Park; Talimena Scenic Drive; and Poteau Mountain, Caney Creek, Upper Kiamichi River, Dry Creek, and Flatside wilderness areas.

THE DRIVE

While the Ozarks are flat-topped mountains, the Ouachitas are long, narrow ridges running from east to west. Both mountain regions began forming during the Paleozoic Era, about 300 million years ago, when the continents of South America and Africa collided with the southern end of North America. The Ozarks were uplifted into a high, flat plateau, while the Ouachitas, being closer to the point of collision, were wrinkled and folded into long ridges. This mountain-building process occurred over millions of years and added a couple of inches of height per year, then abruptly stopped. Since then, the mountains have been eroded by rain and wind to their present shape.

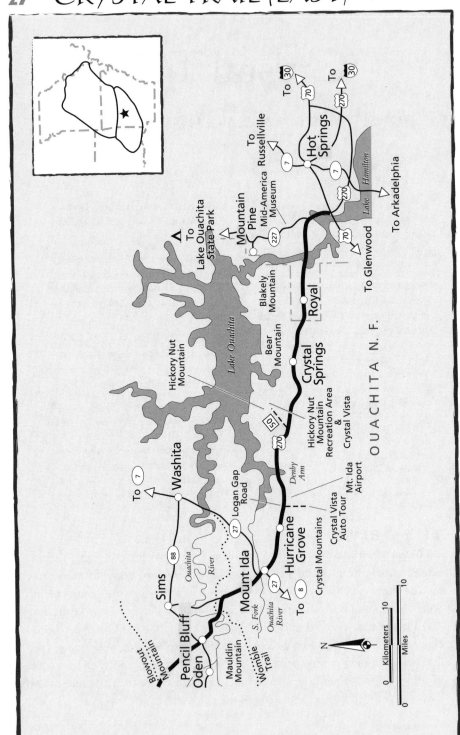

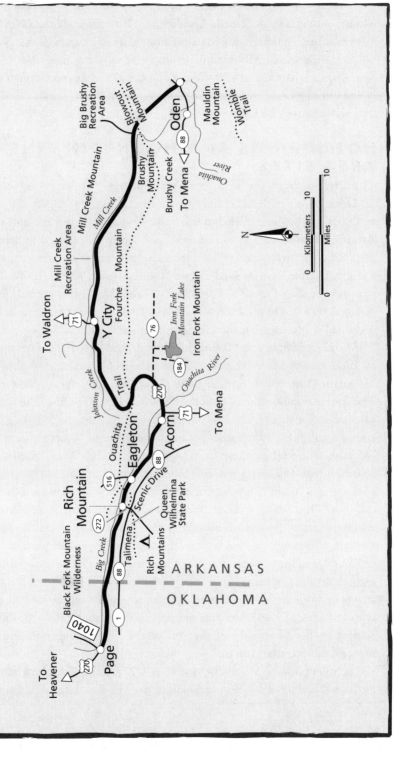

This east-west trending chain of mountains is unique in the United States. Most mountain ranges, like the Appalachians, Rockies, and Sierra Nevada, have a north-south alignment due to past continental collisions from the east (forming the Appalachian Mountains) or from the west (forming the Rocky and Sierra Nevada Mountains). This tour along US 270 takes you through the heart of the Ouachitas and provides excellent opportunities to see the results of this ancient mountain-building process.

HOT SPRINGS AND MOUNTAIN PINE AREA SITES

The drive begins on the west side of **Hot Springs.** For details on Hot Springs, see Drive 26. Where US 270 and AR 227 meet, a side trip on AR 227 takes you to Lake Ouachita and Blakely Dam, Lake Ouachita State Park, and the **Mid-America Museum.** Follow the signs to this privately owned museum. For a small fee your family can explore interactive exhibits about science, nature, and the arts. The museum, nestled in twenty-one acres of forest, also has a restaurant and gift shop. From Memorial Day to Labor Day it is open daily from 9:30 A.M. to 6:00 P.M. The winter hours are 10:00 A.M. to 5:00 P.M., and the museum is closed on Monday. For more information see Appendix A.

AR 227 continues to **Mountain Pine,** a lumber milling town established in 1928. In another mile, you can see Blakely Mountain as well as Blakely Mountain Dam, which formed **Lake Ouachita,** the largest lake in Arkansas. The dam was constructed across the Ouachita River in 1952. The rock exposures on either side of the dam contain layers of sandstone and shale. The layers were originally horizontal, but intensive geologic forces millions of years ago pushed and folded these layers over on themselves. These phenomena are best seen here and along roadcuts along the route. If you are boating on the lake, the U.S. Army Corps of Engineers has developed a unique boating trail, called the Ouachita Geo-Float Trail, which has interpretive stops along a water route explaining geologic features. Ask for it at the Corps' office just beyond the dam. Lake Ouachita was built by the Corps of Engineers for flood control, recreation, and the production of hydroelectric power. At normal pool, the lake extends up the Ouachita River valley a distance of 30 miles and has a surface area of approximately 40,000 acres. Fishing is popular on the lake; its tributary arms are especially good for crappie, largemouth bass, white bass, and catfish. Adding to the popularity of the lake is the surrounding beautiful, heavily forested, mountainous terrain.

Six miles north of Mountain Pine on AR 227, **Lake Ouachita State Park** provides camping, a swimming beach, a marina, and a visitor center with a store, gift shop, and cafe. Interpretive programs and guided hikes are offered, or you may also hike the two trails on your own. The 4-mile Caddo Bend Trail meanders through the forests and along the lakeshore peninsula. The Dogwood Trail is a casual, quarter-mile loop beginning near Camp Area C. Be sure to visit Three Sisters Springs, which has been a popular attraction in the area since the late 1880s. The water welling up from these springs is said to have curative powers for different ailments. An exhibit on the springs is located in the visitor center.

Return to US 270 and proceed west for 3 miles, crossing over the upper end of **Lake Hamilton.** Completed by the Arkansas Power and Light Company in 1931, Hamilton Lake is 24 miles long and covers 9,000 acres. The lake, which impounds the Ouachita River, is privately owned and was built before the U.S. Army Corps of Engineers' lakes, which accounts for the hundreds of private homes, restaurants, and tourist attractions around Lake Hamilton. The main part of the lake lies along the south side of Hot Springs. Many rocky points and sheltered coves provide varied habitats for fish such as crappie, largemouth bass, bream, channel catfish, and, more recently, walleye. Trout are stocked in the upper part of the lake, where cool water is released from Lake Ouachita and the Arkansas Game & Fish Commission maintains a trout hatchery just below the dam.

Along US 270 you will notice several Corps of Engineers public use areas and Forest Service recreation areas. Many offer camping and access to the lake. Maps and brochures can be obtained by writing or visiting their offices, which are listed in Appendix A. This drive leads you to some of the more interesting areas.

CRYSTAL SPRINGS AND MOUNT IDA AREA SITES

Continue on US 270 to **Crystal Springs,** a 1930s recreational area named for a clear spring flowing from the base of Crystal Mountain to the north. From here to Mount Ida, roadside stands selling crystals become more evident. The sandstone in this region of the Ouachitas holds veins of quartz crystals; some of the crystals can be 2 or 3 feet long. Most, however, form porcupinelike clusters up to 6 feet in diameter. Roadside stands sell the crystals for rock gardens and interior ornaments. Smaller pieces are fashioned into costume jewelry.

After another 5 miles on US 270, a side trip on FR 50 leads to a spectacular view of Lake Ouachita and the surrounding mountains. The 4-mile gravel road goes to **Hickory Nut Mountain Recreation Area** and just beyond that

A far-reaching view from Lake Ouachita Vista.

Lake Ouachita Vista. From the overlook, Lake Ouachita can be viewed 800 feet below.

Along US 270 for the next 50 miles or so, there are a series of Forest Service recreation areas that offer camping and some recreational activities. For more information check with the Womble Ranger Station, just before Mount Ida.

Continuing on US 270, proceed west and in 3.5 miles cross the Denby Arm of Lake Ouachita. At the Womble Ranger Station, stop and ask for Forest Service maps and information. Ask about the **Crystal Vista Auto Tour,** which is a self-guided drive featuring the best of the Winona District, including Crystal Vista where you can collect quartz crystals.

Mount Ida was founded in 1836 when Granville Whittington, a Massachusetts immigrant who, a year earlier, had helped to draft a petition requesting Arkansas statehood, built a general store in the area. Mount Ida was incorporated in 1854, and for more than a hundred years it was a center for extensive crystal mining. Today the town is known as the "Quartz Crystal Capital of the World." Taking millions of years to form, these crystals are transparent or translucent six-sided prisms that terminate in six-sided pyramids. They are used for thousands of products ranging from sandpaper to crystal balls. The area has many dig-it-yourself mines and a few mineral museums. An annual event in mid-October, the Quartz, Quilts, and Crafts Festival offers music, food, displays, and a crystal dig. As many as 123 entrants from twenty-seven states plus diggers from Canada have competed in local mines for prizes awarded to those with the best crystals.

Note on the map the town of Washita, about 10 miles north of Mount Ida on AR 27. The town is named with an Indian word meaning "good hunting ground." The French explorers spelled the sound of Washita as "Ouachita," which became the common spelling for the region.

Continuing west on US 270 for about 4 miles, the road crosses the 39.5-mile **Womble Trail,** the third-longest trail in Arkansas. The Womble Trail was once proposed to be a part of the Ouachita National Recreation Trail. However, when it became too difficult to extend the Ouachita Trail west of Gaston Mountain, this trail became the Womble. The Ouachita Trail was relocated north of here. From this access, the Womble Trail goes west, crossing a couple of nice streams, then climbs Mauldin Mountain, passes Gaston Mountain, and ends at Norfork Lake for a total distance of 14.2 miles. East of US 270, the trail goes 25.7 miles, joining the Ouachita Trail toward its end. This stretch of the trail meanders along the scenic shores of Lake Ouachita and offers breathtaking views and lots of large trees along the way.

The highway continues west, crossing over the **Ouachita River.** The Ouachita is the largest and longest river within the Ouachita mountain region. It begins as a mountain stream in the Acorn Basin, northwest of Mena, and meanders eastward through the heart of the Ouachita National Forest to a point just west of Hot Springs, where its flow is checked by three man-made dams. The river then flows southward into Louisiana. There are nine camping areas and landing points along the river above Lake Ouachita that can be reached by Forest Service roads. The river float is not too difficult; the paddler has a chance to experience the remoteness of the area in the upper stretches and a chance to fish in the sections closer to the lake. Information on river floats, access points, and camping areas can be obtained from the local ranger district office or from Forest Service headquarters in Hot Springs.

About 3 miles beyond the Ouachita River crossing, a scenic view on the left (south) side of the road features a couple of interpretive signs and a view of Mauldin Mountain.

PENCIL BLUFF AND ODEN AREA SITES

Continue on US 270 to **Pencil Bluff.** A side trip on AR 88 west for 5 miles will take you to the Oden Ranger Station, where you can obtain maps and information about activities in the Ouachita National Forest. Also ask about hiking the nearby 1-mile Serendipity Loop Interpretive Trail.

Five miles from Pencil Bluff on US 270, the road climbs Blowout Mountain. Ignore a sign on the right at FR 33. It reads BLOWOUT MOUNTAIN SCENIC AREA, which sounds inviting but lacks developed recreational opportunities. In about another mile, the road crosses the Ouachita National Recreation Trail, or **Ouachita Trail.** This 223-mile trail from Talimena State Park in Oklahoma to Pinnacle Mountain State Park near Little Rock, Arkansas, contains many challenges to go along with its beautiful streams, extensive forests, and outstanding vistas. Unlike the Ozark Trail, which goes up and down all day long, the Ouachita Trail will climb a hogback ridge and stay there for hours, following the east-west trending mountains. Just beyond the trail and on the south side of US 270, **Big Brushy Recreation Area** provides access to the Ouachita Trail. In the campground, another trail, the **Brushy Creek Loop Trail,** provides a 6.9-mile hike along scenic Brushy Creek, joins the Ouachita Trail, passes Brushy Mountain (with some great views along the way), and ends back at Big Brushy Recreation Area. Just before reaching the recreation area, a half-mile hike up Brushy Mountain offers nice views during winter, when the trees are bare.

Proceed up Mill Creek valley on US 270; Fourche Mountain is on the south and Mill Creek Mountain is on the north. The road passes **Mill Creek Recreation Area,** which provides camping (including equestrian campsites), swimming in Mill Creek, and a three-quarter-mile interpretive trail to a scenic overlook. Beginning at the recreation area, the Mill Mountain Trail heads south, crosses US 270, and branches out into a network of 28 miles of equestrian/hiking trails. Unfortunately, it appears that the Mill Creek Recreation Area will to be closing soon because of budget constraints and a realignment of the recreation areas in the Ouachita National Forest. Check with the Poteau Ranger District office for the status of the recreational area at (479) 637–4174. A map for the Fourche Mountain Trail is available at the Poteau Ranger District office in Waldron. See Appendix A for the address.

Y CITY TO PAGE

Proceed to **Y City**. Just beyond Y City, on US 270, the road follows Johnson Creek for about 6 miles before turning south as it climbs through a gap in Fourche Mountain and crosses the Ouachita Trail again. If you are interested in hiking this section of the trail, finding the parking lot can be a bit difficult. To locate the trailhead parking area, travel 1.5 miles south along US 270 from the Polk County sign marker. There is an unmarked pulloff on the west side of the highway that is difficult to see. From the parking lot, the trail goes east 26.4

A bridge at Big Brushy Recreation Area offers a view of the tranquil waters of Brushy Creek.

miles to US 70 along a high, dry section (so carry plenty of water). The westward trail goes 16.5 miles to Queen Wilhelmina State Park. A mile-long leisure walk on the trail west from the parking lot passes several waterfalls that flow most of the year.

About 2 miles down US 270, AR 76, to the left, leads another 2 miles to **Iron Fork Mountain Lake.** This is a small fishing lake managed by the Arkansas Game & Fish Commission in cooperation with the city of Mena. No camping facilities or trails are provided.

US 270 continues through the small community of **Acorn,** where the Big Creek and other creeks combine to form the upper reaches of the Ouachita River. Just past Eagleton, the highway crosses the Ouachita Trail again and goes by the **Black Fork Mountain Wilderness Trailhead.** A parking lot is on the north side of the road. The trail south and west up Rich Mountain goes a distance of 5.1 miles to Queen Wilhelmina State Park. The trail north is steep and goes up Black Fork Mountain 1 mile, where the Ouachita Trail breaks east and the Black Fork Mountain Trail heads west. There is an incredible view from the top of Black Fork Mountain. The trail is 11.6 miles round-trip. The hike climbs gradually and passes through an area that burned in 1963. The fire covered about 13,000 acres and was caused by a spark from a passing train. After 2.3 miles, the trail enters the 13,579-acre Black Fork Mountain Wilderness. Along the top of this 15-mile-long mountain, severely stunted post oak, blackjack oak, and black oak trees are usually less than 8 feet tall and resemble large shrubs. This habitat receives maximum exposure to the winds, which distort their branches and cause the thin, rocky soil to dry very quickly. Also of interest are the rock flows or "glaciers." Loose, unstable rocks are continually moving downslope, creating perilous conditions for plants trying to maintain a foothold on life. These rock glaciers are unique to this part of the Ouachita Mountains and to the Midwest. More examples can be seen along the Talimena Drive just south of here (see Drive 29).

Continue on US 270 to the community of Rich Mountain; then a side road, AR 272, goes south and up Rich Mountain to Queen Wilhelmina State Park and connects with Talimena Scenic Drive. US 270 proceeds west, paralleling Big Creek and the Kansas City Southern Railroad, crosses the state line into Oklahoma, and enters **Page,** a small village nestled in the heart of the Ouachita National Forest. The west side of Black Fork Mountain Wilderness can be reached by traveling 2 miles north out of Page on FR 1040 to a parking area that provides space for equestrian trailers. There are no official trails on this side of the wilderness area. Contact the Mena Ranger District Office for access information.

Caddo Gap

GLENWOOD TO LANGLEY, ARKANSAS

GENERAL DESCRIPTION: A 52-mile drive beginning at Glenwood, traveling west through Caddo Gap, and featuring crystal country, scenic overlooks, mountains of Arkansas Stone, and Little Missouri Falls.

SPECIAL ATTRACTIONS: Caddo Gap, Caddo River, Collier Springs, Crystal Recreation Area, Crystal Mountain Scenic Area, Crystal Vista, Little Missouri Falls, Albert Pike Recreation Area, and Ouachita National Forest; hiking, scenic views, camping, canoeing, swimming, fishing, hunting, and crystal prospecting.

LOCATION: Central Ouachitas. The drive begins on Arkansas Highway 8 at Glenwood and travels west, ending at Ouachita National Forest's Albert Pike Recreation Area.

DRIVE ROUTE NUMBERS: Arkansas Highways 8, 27, and 369 and Forest Roads 25, 43, 177, 539, and 2237.

CAMPING: Forest Service campsites are available at Crystal, Albert Pike, Shady Lake, and Bard Springs recreation areas and also at the U.S. Army Corps of Engineers' Lake Greeson, which has 13 campgrounds.

SERVICES: All services at Glenwood. Gas and food at Norman, Black Springs, and nearby Mount Ida.

NEARBY ATTRACTIONS: Lake Greeson, crystal shops at Mount Ida, Caney Creek Wilderness Area, Cossatot River State Park Natural Area, and Daisy and Crater of Diamonds state parks.

THE DRIVE

This region, known as the Central Ouachitas, offers dramatic views of mountains that have been pushed and folded over on themselves, creating narrow ridges, steep slopes, and deep valleys. This drive will explore the Crystal, Caddo, and Cossatot Mountains and their beautiful views, interesting rocks, clear-flowing streams, and unusual plants and animals that are characteristic of this region.

GLENWOOD TO CADDO GAP

The drive begins on the west side of **Glenwood** on AR 8. Glenwood grew up around a sawmill on the Missouri Pacific Railroad. Just south of town along US 70 there is a popular put-in and take-out point for those floating the

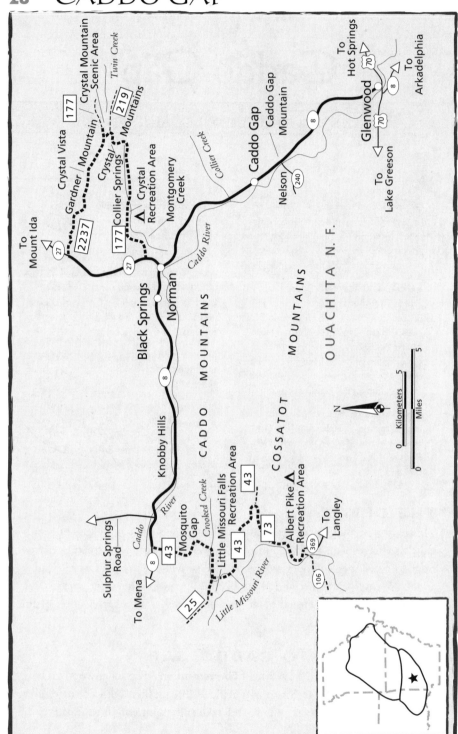

Caddo River. The river parallels AR 8 all the way to its headwaters in the Missouri Mountains, about 23 miles west of here. That stretch of the river is floatable in the spring; below Glenwood the river can be floated most other times. The Caddo eventually flows into DeGray Lake, which was completed in 1972 and impounded the Caddo.

Three miles west of Glenwood on AR 8, you will notice a prominent notch straight ahead in Nelson Mountain. This is **Caddo Gap.** Carved by the Caddo River, the opening now also gives passage to the Missouri Pacific Railroad and AR 8. In about 3 more miles, the road climbs into the gap. Before entering the gap, a side trip on AR 240 affords an opportunity to view the Caddo River while driving across the highway bridge. The river here is broad, clear, and very inviting. Return to AR 8 and drive into Caddo Gap. Notice the roadcut along the highway. It is worth finding a place to park along the shoulder on the outside lane. This is a busy highway, so be careful. The roadcut formations evoke wonderment at what powerful forces there must have been to have pushed these once-horizontal layers of rock to their present vertical positions. If you examine them closely, you will see that some layers are folded back over themselves. This small exposure dramatically illustrates the mountain-building processes that created the Ouachita Mountains. These cream-to-white layers of rock are Arkansas novaculite, or "Arkansas Stone," which is commonly used to sharpen knives, tools, and other instruments. The nearby town of Caddo Gap has a historical marker that explains the local history of the area. It is said that the narrow pass at Caddo Gap marks the de Soto expedition's most westward journey into North America. The historical site bears a monument to the Tula Indians who fiercely fought the uninvited Spanish expedition in 1541, forcing de Soto and his men to retreat down the Caddo and Ouachita Rivers, eventually to Louisiana, where de Soto later died.

NORMAN AND CRYSTAL MOUNTAIN SITES

Proceed on AR 8 for 5 miles to the town of **Norman.** Turn north onto AR 27 and go 0.6 mile. Then turn east onto FR 177 and go 3 miles to the **Crystal Recreation Area.** This attractive wooded setting along Montgomery Creek offers camping, picnicking, sanitary facilities, drinking water, swimming, and a hiking trail. The trail is a 0.7-mile loop that begins just opposite campsite #5; it leads to a creek and a spring. The trail continues through stately old trees and along a steep hillside lush with ferns and mosses. Watch for a small waterfall where the trail crosses the creek again on the way back to the parking lot.

Continue on FR 177 for 3 miles to **Collier Springs,** a Forest Service picnic area that features a small, clear-flowing spring. Stay on FR 177 for 1.4

miles, passing FR 177K and, at the intersection of FR 2237, bear right on FR 177 another 0.1 mile. Look for the **Crystal Mountain Scenic Area** sign on the right, and park. To the left of the sign, a half-mile trail passes through giant shortleaf pine trees more than 300 years old, a rare sight today. Pine trees this size are critical for the red-cockaded woodpecker, which prefers a large diameter pine in which to hollow out a nest cavity. Because of a lack of old-growth pine forests, caused by extensive logging, the red-cockaded woodpecker is now on the federal endangered species list. Leaving some areas of old-growth forest will help this woodpecker and other species that are dependent on these kinds of conditions to survive. The trail also passes by a scenic sandstone bluff and crosses Twin Creek before heading back to the trailhead.

Turn around on FR 177 and head west. Then take FR 2237 east to **Crystal Vista,** about 1.9 miles. From the parking lot, a 1-mile hike up a steep trail leads to the top of Gardner Mountain. A four-acre opening marks the remnants of a former crystal mine that is now open for public rock collecting. Quartz crystals can be collected for personal use but not for resale. Only hand tools such as trowels and rock hammers are permitted. The rock before you is Crystal Mountain sandstone. Deposited about 500 million years ago, it is the oldest exposed rock in the Ouachita Mountains. Between the layers of sandstone, quartz crystals slowly grew forming clusters up to 6 feet in diameter. These larger crystals make popular lawn ornaments; smaller pieces are fashioned into

Large leaves of the aptly named umbrella magnolia shade the trail to Little Missouri Falls.

costume jewelry. Called "Arkansas Diamonds," some of the finest crystals, when first cut and polished, closely resemble diamonds; unfortunately, their luster is not as permanent. Continue north past the opening to the top of the ridge for a spectacular view of Lake Ouachita and the surrounding landscape.

From Crystal Vista, FR 2237 continues 4.1 miles to AR 27. If you have the time, a side trip to the Womble Ranger Station on US 270 just east of Mount Ida is worth the effort. The staff there has Forest Service books and maps and a self-guided brochure of the Crystal Vista Auto Tour. The tour route begins 4.5 miles east of the ranger station and provides a more complete tour across the Crystal Mountains, interpreting historic sites and natural features.

Back on AR 27, return to Norman and turn west onto AR 8. After about 7 miles, notice the **Knobby Hills** along the north side of the road. This unusual array of eroded small hills, composed of Polk Creek shale, creates an interesting contrast in sizes and shapes compared to the more resistant sandstones in the surrounding mountains. The road crosses the upper reaches of the Caddo River twice and shortly comes upon FR 43 on the south side of the road.

Turn on FR 43; after about 2.5 miles, the road crosses over the Caddo Mountains through Mosquito Gap. Notice the outcrops of Arkansas novaculite, or Arkansas stone. Novaculite is made up of an extremely hard material called chert, which is mostly silica, the same substance found in sand. Chert was prized by Native Americans for making arrowheads and cutting tools. Today Arkansas novaculite has an international reputation as a sharpening stone for tools and instruments.

LITTLE MISSOURI FALLS AND ALBERT PIKE RECREATION AREAS

At the intersection of FR 43 and 25, go west on FR 25 for a mile to entrance road FR 539 and then another 0.7 mile to **Little Missouri Falls Recreation Area.** A short trail leads to the falls and loops back to the parking area. Along the trail, large American beech trees with smooth white bark spread their broad limbs into the forest canopy. Also along the trail, look for hop hornbeam, white ash, sweet gum, eastern red cedar, and umbrella magnolia. The Little Missouri River cuts through dense novaculite mountains, confining itself to a narrow gorge. In Missouri such a formation would be called a "shut-in." The Little Missouri River, because of its exceptional condition, is designated as a National Wild and Scenic River. Rising in the Missouri Mountains just west of here, the headwaters area is notable for its spectacular pine-forested ridges and valleys. The river cascades through a series of difficult white-water gorges, including the extraordinary Little Missouri Falls in its upper reaches, before leveling off for a more leisurely journey into Lake Greeson. It is best for floaters to put in downstream from here at the Albert Pike Recreation Area. The 11.6-mile Little Missouri Trail can be accessed at the parking lot and follows the river downstream with five crossings that can be traversed at normal flow rates. The trail ends by way of FR 10105.

Return to FR 43 and continue 8 miles to the **Albert Pike Recreation Area.** A crystal-clear pool on the Little Missouri River is the major attraction here. In addition to camping, swimming is allowed and there is a 1-mile inter- pretive trail. Trailheads also begin here for the 16-mile one-way Little Missouri Trail, the 26.8-mile Eagle Rock Loop Trail, and the 26-mile Viles Branch Trail. Information on these trails is available at the Albert Pike Recreation Area or from the Caddo Ranger District office in Glenwood. See Appendix A for their addresses and phone numbers. This is a popular put-in for canoeists wanting to float the 8.5 miles to the AR 84 bridge or beyond to the US 70 bridge. The floating conditions are highly dependent upon suitable amounts of rainfall. Rated up to Class IV, the twisting drops, rapids, and standing waves are best reserved for the experienced paddler. As you leave the recreation area on AR 369 and drive toward Langley, notice the vertical rock strata as the road climbs out of the Little Missouri River valley. This spectacular example of mountain folding is one of the best in the Ouachitas.

The scenic Little Missouri River cascades over resistant Arkansas novaculite at Little Missouri Falls Recreation Area.

Talimena Scenic Drive

MENA TO U.S. HIGHWAY 271, ARKANSAS/OKLAHOMA

GENERAL DESCRIPTION: A 54-mile drive beginning at Mena, Arkansas, and winding along mountain ridges with spectacular views.

SPECIAL ATTRACTIONS: Queen Wilhelmina State Park and Lodge, Robert S. Kerr Memorial Arboretum and Nature Center, Ouachita Trail, Winding Stair Mountain National Recreation Area, and Ouachita National Forest; fall colors, scenic/interpretive vistas, "dwarf" or "elfin" forests, rock glaciers, hiking, camping, horseback riding, historical sites, and hunting.

LOCATION: Western Ouachitas. The drive begins on Arkansas Highway 88 at Mena and continues to the state line, where it becomes Oklahoma Highway 1 and continues to the intersection with U.S. Highway 271.

DRIVE ROUTE NUMBERS: Arkansas Highway 88 and Oklahoma Highway 1.

CAMPING: Queen Wilhelmina State Park has a lodge offering 36 guest rooms, a restaurant, a private meeting room for up to 50 people, 35 campsites with water, electrical hookups, showers, and 5 tent sites. Talimena State Park has picnic sites, 7 RV sites, 15 unimproved campsites, and a comfort station with shower. The Forest Service's Winding Stair Campground has 27 campsites, water, and flush toilets.

SERVICES: All services at Mena and nearby Talihina.

NEARBY ATTRACTIONS: Black Fork Mountain Wilderness, Kiamichi River Wilderness; Heavener Runestone State Park; Three Sticks Monument; John F. Kennedy Memorial; Little Missouri Falls; Crystal Trail, Heavener, Runestone, and Caddo Gap scenic drives; and Cossatot River State Park Natural Area.

THE DRIVE

Talimena Scenic Drive is perhaps the most impressively scenic of all the drives in both the Ozarks and the Ouachita Mountains. This highway was intentionally built as a scenic drive across the long and narrow Rich and Winding Stair Mountains because of the dramatic and far-ranging views afforded in all directions. (WARNING: Low-lying clouds and morning fog can obscure views anytime. Ice can form on the roads in winter.) The name "Talimena" is derived from blending the names of the towns at either end of the drive, Talihina and Mena. Construction began in June 1964 and was completed in April 1970.

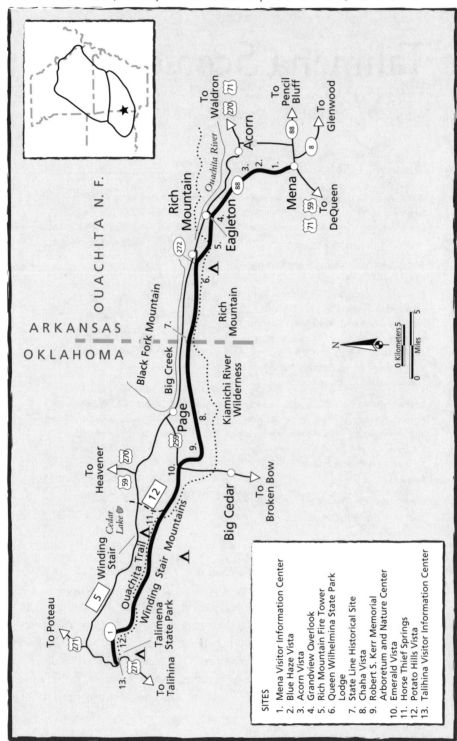

SITES

1. Mena Visitor Information Center
2. Blue Haze Vista
3. Acorn Vista
4. Grandview Overlook
5. Rich Mountain Fire Tower
6. Queen Wilhelmina State Park Lodge
7. State Line Historical Site
8. Chaha Vista
9. Robert S. Kerr Memorial Arboretum and Nature Center
10. Emerald Vista
11. Horse Thief Springs
12. Potato Hills Vista
13. Talihina Visitor Information Center

Because of its narrow ridges, steep slopes, fog, and ice storms, the construction of the road, according to one highway worker, was challenging and sometimes dangerous. In February 1989 the Talimena Scenic Drive was one of the first scenic highways to be designated a National Forest Scenic Byway.

To gain a true appreciation for the ruggedness of this part of the Ouachitas, visit this drive in early May. In the deep valleys the leaves are fully out and spring is at its peak. But 2,000 feet above, on top of the Rich, Black Fork, and Winding Stair Mountains, the leaf buds on the oak and hickory trees are just beginning to open. In a five-minute drive you can pass from early to late spring, just by changing altitude. This interesting response of nature to altitude and temperature differences is commonly seen in the Rockies, the Sierras, and the Appalachians; but in the Midwest, it is uniquely found only in this part of the Ouachitas.

MENA TO RICH MOUNTAIN

The drive begins at **Mena,** which, with 5,475 inhabitants, is one of the larger towns in western Arkansas. The town of Mena was born with the construction of a new railroad line. Turned down by United States investors in 1896 because of a depression, the railroad builder for the Kansas City Southern, Arthur Stilwell, looked to Holland for the three million dollars needed to finish the proposed line from Siloam Springs, Arkansas, to Shreveport, Louisiana. With the word that several Dutchmen would contribute the money to complete this first railroad through the mountains, a tent city of more than 1,000 was created in fewer than forty days. The *Mena Star* newspaper is one business that has operated ever since that first day. The town itself is named for Mena DeGoiejen, the wife of one of the Dutch investors, John DeGoiejen.

There are several historic buildings to see in Mena; information is available from the Mena Depot Center, located in the center of town along the Kansas City Southern railroad. Maintained by the Mena–Polk County Chamber of Commerce, the depot also contains historic displays, railroad memorabilia, and art exhibits. For information on the Ouachita National Forest, the Mena Ranger District office is located in town along US 71 north.

In Mena follow AR 88 west and you will begin to ascend Rich Mountain, named by early settlers for the very productive soils found on the north slope of the mountain. Leaving town and on the right, the Forest Service's **Mena Visitor Information Center,** which is open daily from April to November, is a good place to obtain maps, brochures, guidebooks, and information on activities from Forest Service volunteers. There are twenty-three vistas and fifteen historic sites along this drive, with most displaying interpretive signs. Only

High cirrus clouds provide a dramatic backdrop to the attractive Talimena Scenic Drive sign that marks the boundary between Arkansas and Oklahoma.

selected stops will be discussed here. However, all the stops are worth a visit, and a more complete guide on this special drive can be purchased at the visitor centers at either end. There are two trails at the Mena visitor center. The first is the Mountain Settler Interpretative Trail, which is a short, easy loop. The second is Earthquake Ridge Loop, named for a rock formation found not far off the trail. This is a more vigorous, 2.1-mile hike that parallels AR 88 up and down the east flank of Rich Mountain. There are some great views, large trees, a small spring, and several rock formations along the way. Leaving the visitor center, the road continues to climb, and after 2 miles, it reaches the **Blue Haze Vista,** which overlooks the Ouachita River valley. In another 0.6 mile, **Acorn Vista** offers a view of the community of Acorn. The town's original name, "Gourd Neck," was descriptive of the shape of the valley, with the "handle" of the gourd lying between Fourche and Rich Mountains. This is a good overlook for viewing sunrises across the Ouachita River valley. For the next half mile of the drive, the road snakes along an exposed section of the Jackfork Group, showing layers of sandstone and shale in an interesting pattern.

Six miles from the beginning of the drive, **Grandview Overlook** provides a commanding view of the south slope of Rich Mountain and a large portion of the Mountain Fork River basin; to the west are the Kiamichi and Winding Stair Mountains in Oklahoma. From this point, spectacular sunsets that backlight rows of mountains can capture the photographer's eye. Above the roadcut at the parking lot, a very good example of a "dwarf," or "elfin," forest can be viewed. Here post oak and blackjack oak trees take on a stunted appearance due to their environmental conditions. Located on the narrow crest of a tall mountain, these trees are exposed to extremes in heat and cold. The shallow, poor-quality soils, coupled with the trees' exposure to high winds, ice storms, severe winter temperatures, and summer drought, greatly slow their growth. A hundred-year-old tree could be only 8 feet tall.

In about 3.5 miles, a steep road leads to the **Rich Mountain Fire Tower.** The Forest Service began operating this tower in 1907, though it is no longer used. Air patrols now take the place of fire spotters. The altitude here is 2,681 feet. This is only 72 feet below the peak of Mount Magazine, the highest point in the Midwest. The tower is open during the summer months at selected hours.

QUEEN WILHELMINA STATE PARK

Continue to **Queen Wilhelmina State Park.** The original lodge was built in 1896 by investors in the Kansas City Southern Railway as an unusual resort retreat for passengers on the line. The three-story lodge became known as the "castle in the sky." Since the railroad was largely financed by Dutch interests, the new resort was named in honor of Holland's Queen Wilhelmina, who is reputed to have had some of her personal funds invested in the project. Unfortunately, because of its remoteness, the lodge closed after three years and fell into disrepair. It was not until the 1960s, after the area became a state park, that the lodge was reconstructed. It was destroyed by fire in 1973 and rebuilt as a modern lodge in the same basic style, using much of the original stone.

On the east side of the Queen Wilhelmina Lodge, the Lover's Leap Trail winds its way through woods and rock outcrops to a large, exposed cliff at the head of a steep ravine, a hiking distance of 0.3 mile. Beyond this great view, the trail becomes strenuous at times and ends back at the lodge after a total of 1.1 miles. The first section of this trail is part of the **Ouachita Trail,** which originates 51 miles west in Oklahoma and ends 171 miles east at Pinnacle Mountain State Park, this side of Little Rock. The Ouachita Trail breaks off just beyond the Lover's Leap Trail, crosses over the scenic drive, and drops down the north side of Rich Mountain. It then crosses over the Ouachita River and heads up the east end of Black Fork Mountain. After dropping down to Eagle Gap, it then goes up and along Fourche Mountain eventually to US 71, a distance of 16.5 miles. West of Queen Wilhelmina State Park, this section of the Ouachita Trail crosses the length of Rich Mountain and part of Winding Stair Mountain for 27.9 miles, the longest section along the Ouachita Trail.

Looking north from the lodge to Black Fork Mountain, notice several white streaks running down the upper flanks of the mountain. They are called "rock glaciers." Their unusual occurrence in this part of the Ouachitas is discussed below, at Chaha Point.

Continue west 5 miles down AR 88, passing several old homestead sites to the **State Line Historical Site.** A path leads from the parking area to a 1877 survey marker of the 48th mile of the line between Arkansas and the Choctaw Nation. The original survey line, established in 1825, was found to diverge to the west, depriving the relocated Choctaws of some of their new land. The original home of the Choctaw Indians was central and northern Mississippi. Having been influenced by the Spanish and the French for several years, they were adapting to living with the white settlers until the latter's greed for more land forced the Choctaws to move westward. Today they still make up a large part of the citizenry of southeastern Oklahoma; the Choctaw Nation headquarters is located in Tuskahoma.

TALIMENA VISTAS

In another 8 miles, the **Chaha Vista** (*Chaha* is Choctaw for "mountain higher than others") offers a view of Kiamichi Mountain and the Kiamichi River valley below. East of the parking lot, notice, on the upper slope, an opening in the forest covered with rocks. This is a rock glacier, named for its tendency to move downhill much like an ordinary ice glacier. These rocks, composed of Jackfork sandstone, are prominent features on the Rich and Black Fork Mountains. Because of their unstable nature, plants and soils are not able to establish on these exposed rock surfaces.

In 5.7 miles, the **Robert S. Kerr Memorial Arboretum and Nature Center** offers the opportunity to see interpretive displays and walk self-guided trails emphasizing the natural world of the forest. Each trail is less than a mile long; one trail focuses on soil formation, another identifies various plants including trees, while the third explains plant succession and communities.

The road continues west, leaving Rich Mountain, and crosses US 259, which is part of Drive 30. The ascent of Winding Stair Mountain begins with numerous opportunities for far-reaching views, and long, swooping stretches of highway make this section possibly the most exciting of all the scenic drives.

The first overlook, **Emerald Vista,** offers a view north to Cedar Lake, Lake Wister, Poteau Mountain, the town of Heavener, and the Poteau River valley. On the horizon, Cavanal Hill, towering above the City of Poteau, is visible some 12 miles away.

Far-reaching views and long, swooping stretches of highway along Winding Stair Mountain make this perhaps the most exciting of all the scenic drives.

Continuing past Winding Stair Campground, several more pullouts offer tremendous views of the surrounding mountains and valleys. To the right, Cedar Lake Road, or FR 12, leads to Holson Valley and the Cedar Lake Recreation Area. This area contains an eighty-four-acre lake, with camping, showers, boating, picnicking, and hiking trails.

Another 1.7 miles will bring you to the historic **Horse Thief Springs,** a crossing for people moving horses from Texas to market in Missouri. Horse thieves were common along the route; the last group of outlaws were captured near the spring in the early 1900s. A 5-mile trail called Horse Thief Springs Trail starts here and descends Winding Stair Mountain to Cedar Lake.

The **Potato Hills Vista** provides an opportunity to see the Potato Hills, which were named for their likeness to the "hills," or mounds, in which potatoes are planted.

The end of the drive is marked by the Forest Service's **Talihina Visitor Information Center.** The center features displays, maps, brochures, and books relating to the region. Knowledgeable volunteers are there to answer questions you may have about activities and weather conditions. The road also intersects with US 271, which is part of Drive 31.

Heavener Runestone

POTEAU TO THREE STICKS MONUMENT, OKLAHOMA

GENERAL DESCRIPTION: A 35-mile drive starting at Poteau and heading south through the valley of the Viking explorers and over the Winding Stair Mountains to Big Cedar.

SPECIAL ATTRACTIONS: Cavanal Mountain, Robert S. Kerr Historical Museum, Heavener Runestone State Park, Peter Conser Home, Cedar Lake Recreation Area, Ouachita National Forest, Winding Stair Mountains, Ouachita Trail, John F. Kennedy Memorial, Kiamichi River, Kiamichi Mountains, and Three Sticks Monument; scenic views, hiking, equestrian trails, camping, swimming, fishing, and hunting.

LOCATION: West-central Ouachitas. The drive begins on U.S. Highway 59 at Poteau, travels south to U.S. Highway 259, and ends at Three Sticks Monument.

DRIVE ROUTE NUMBERS: U.S. Highways 59 and 259.

CAMPING: Lake Wister State Park has 5 campgrounds with 172 sites; most offer showers, water, electricity, and RV hookups. Heavener Runestone State Park has day use only. Cedar Lake Recreation Area has 88 campsites. Winding Stair Recreation Area has 27 campsites. Primitive camping is allowed in the Ouachita National Forest.

SERVICES: All services at Poteau and Heavener. Gas and food at Howe and Hodgen.

NEARBY ATTRACTIONS: Black Fork Mountain and Upper Kiamichi River wilderness areas; Talimena Scenic Drive; Three Creeks National Scenic Area; and Indian Nations National Scenic and Wildlife Area.

THE DRIVE

The northern part of the drive lies in the Arkansas River valley region of the Ouachitas. Although the Arkansas River is 15 miles to the north, its meandering and flooding over hundreds of thousands of years have influenced the character of the surrounding landscape. Broad, forested floodplains with prairie openings were once common near the river and along its major tributaries such as the Poteau River. On higher ground, rolling hills with scattered trees and a prairie understory provided habitat for elk, bison, and other animals of the open range. Land use changes and overhunting of the animals that once roamed the prairie have destroyed the former ecology.

The southern part of the drive enters the west-central region of the Ouachita Mountains. The mountains, with steep slopes and narrow valleys, are still forested today. They provide habitat for a wide variety of plants and animals— some of which are found only in this unique and fascinating landscape. Because the mountains trend to the east and west, there are a number of impressive views as the road climbs up and down its flanks winding its way south.

POTEAU

The drive begins in **Poteau.** For information about activities in the area, visit the Poteau Chamber of Commerce located at 201 South Broadway, which is the main road through town. Poteau was founded in 1887. Its name, from the French word for "post," was taken from the nearby Poteau River. A post, or stake, was used to mark trade areas in Indian territory. Poteau is nestled in a picturesque valley, with the Sugar Loaf Mountains (2,600 feet in elevation) to the east and the overshadowing **Cavanal Mountain** (2,369 feet in elevation) on the west. The word "Cavanal" is derived from a French word meaning "cave." The mountain is called the "world's highest hill," because geologists use the term "mountain" only on landforms that rise a minimum of 2,000 feet above the surrounding landscape. Cavanal Mountain happens to rise 1,999 feet above Poteau, technically classifying it as a hill. A 6-mile scenic road to the top of Cavanal Mountain can be reached from US 59 in Poteau beginning at Broadway and Stadium Drive. Turn west on Stadium Drive, which becomes Witteville Drive in 2 blocks. Continue on Witteville Drive, passing under the city bypass bridge, and stay on this narrow drive until you come to a Y in the road. Take the left road, not the right road, which is Caldwell Drive. Follow the road to the top of Cavanal.

Return to US 59 in Poteau and proceed south and in a few miles you will see a **Robert S. Kerr Historical Museum** sign on the right. A side trip on Ridge Road, which shortly intersects Kerr Mansion Road, leads to the museum, a distance of 2.5 miles. The museum is part of a complex that includes the Kerr Mansion and Conference Center. The mansion contains overnight accommodations, meeting rooms, and a dining room to seat up to a hundred people. The late Robert S. Kerr was a very influential governor and then senator of the State of Oklahoma. The museum contains furniture, pictures, and mementos of the senator. Other displays highlight the daily lives of early settlers in Eastern Oklahoma, LeFlore County. The museum also houses five cases of original artifacts taken from the Spiro Mounds, a place that is discussed in Drive 31. In addition, two runestones, discussed below, are on display. The museum hours are Monday through Friday 9:00 A.M. to 5:00 P.M. and Saturday and Sunday 1:00 to 5:00 P.M.; it's closed on major holidays.

HEAVENER AND HODGEN AREA SITES

Proceed on US 59 south to **Heavener.** Notice the commanding mountain northeast of Heavener. This is Poteau Mountain, a 1,200-foot, flat-topped mountain composed of sandstone, shale, and coal seams, which extends for 28 miles eastward with 23 of those miles in Arkansas. The town of Heavener was built in 1896 along the newly laid tracks of the Kansas City, Pittsburg, and Gulf Railway (now the Kansas City Southern Railway).

In Heavener, follow the signs to **Heavener Runestone State Park,** which is situated high up on Poteau Mountain, about 2 miles from US 59. The park was dedicated in 1970 to protect and display ancient Viking inscriptions on a large slab of Savannah sandstone. A rune is any of the characters of an alphabet used by the ancient Scandinavian and other Germanic peoples. Such rock carvings are known as "runestones." These inscriptions have been dated as early as A.D. 600 and not later than A.D. 900, based on the type of characters used. Similar inscriptions have been found in New England at a settlement on the Atlantic coast by pre-Columbian Norsemen or Vikings. These Scandinavians traveled from their homeland to Iceland, then to Greenland, across Baffin Bay to Canada, and south to New England, where they established a settlement. From there it is speculated that they went down the Atlantic coast, around

This ancient Viking inscription at Heavener Runestone State Park is said to have been carved in sandstone more than 1,300 years ago.

Florida, and up the Gulf coast to the Mississippi River. Apparently they then traveled up the Mississippi River to the Arkansas River and from there to the Poteau River, which leads to within a mile of the runestone.

The Heavener Runestone inscription reads *Glome Dal,* which translates as "valley owned by Glome," indicating that this might have been a boundary marker or land claim. Two other runestones, which were found nearby in 1969, help support the theory of the early Vikings' presence. Replicas of these inscriptions are on display at the state park. Unfortunately, it is reported that additional runestones existed but were destroyed in the 1940s by treasure hunters.

In addition to a visitor center, Heavener Runestone State Park offers a winding, scenic trail that leads to a cove containing huge sandstone slabs that have broken away from the bluff face. The large sandstone rock with the runic inscription is housed in a small display building to protect it from further deterioration and potential vandals. A drive past the visitor center leads to a picnic area and a spectacular view of the Poteau River valley and the town of Heavener. The state park also has a 1-mile nature trail and two shorter trails that follow the bluff line.

Return to Heavener and head south on US 59. At the town of Hodgen, a highway sign marks the way to the **Peter Conser Home** by directing you to turn west on an unmarked road. After 3 miles you can see a white, two-story, wood-frame house. Tours of the 1894 home built by Peter Conser are available Wednesday through Sunday. Conser, whose mother was Choctaw, became deputy sheriff in 1877 at the age of twenty-five; later he was a captain of the Choctaw Lighthorse, a mounted police force of the Five Civilized Tribes. They were an effective peacekeeping force in the region. He also served as a representative and senator to the Choctaw Council. He died in 1934, with wealth and social prestige. The Oklahoma Historical Society has renovated the house, returning it to its appearance during the Indian Territory period.

After returning to US 59, notice the mountain range rising to the south, the Winding Stair Mountains. An east-west range typical of the Ouachitas, it features some of the highest and grandest mountains in the region. This drive will soon lead into the midst of these mountains.

Ten miles south of Heavener a road to the right, called Holson Valley Road, goes 2.7 miles to the **Cedar Lake Recreation Area.** This Forest Service area contains an eighty-six-acre lake, swimming beaches, and a fishing pier. In addition to camping, more than 70 miles of marked equestrian trails wind over hills and mountains and through rich river bottoms. These trails are also open to hikers and mountain bikers. One 5-mile trail, Horsethief Springs Trail, begins in the recreation area and climbs up the Winding Stair Mountains to Talimena Scenic Drive.

WINDING STAIR MOUNTAINS AND BIG CEDAR

In another half mile south on US 59 from Holson Valley Road and on the right you'll find the Choctaw Visitor's Center of the Choctaw Ranger District, Ouachita National Forest. There you can obtain information on places to visit, trails to hike, maps, and souvenirs. Continuing on US 59, in 4 miles, take US 259 south and begin the climb up **Winding Stair Mountain.** In about 4 miles, the road crosses Talimena Scenic Drive. For more details see Drive 29. In another 1.3 miles is the **Pipe Spring Picnic Ground** (five units).

After a little over 2 miles, the highway crosses the **Ouachita Trail.** Parking is on the west side of the road. The trail east crosses a short stretch of the Indian Nations National Scenic and Wildlife Area, runs down the middle of the Upper Kiamichi Wilderness Area, then crosses into Arkansas and ends at Queen Wilhelmina State Park, a total distance of 27.9 miles. The trail west follows the Winding Stair Mountains to the beginning of the Ouachita Trail at Talimena State Park, a total length of 23.7 miles. The entire distance offers beautiful views, steep mountains, lush vegetation, and lots of rocks. The Ouachita National Recreation Trail is the longest trail in Arkansas, extending 225 miles from Talimena State Park to Pinnacle Mountain State Park, just west of Little Rock, Arkansas.

After another mile on US 259, a side trip on FR 6032 leads 3 miles east to the 9,371-acre Upper Kiamichi River Wilderness Area. The Ouachita Trail can also be accessed at the boundary of the wilderness area.

In 0.7 mile on US 259, **Big Cedar,** now a ghost town, once boasted a population of about fifty people in 1910. On the south side of the intersection of US 259 and Oklahoma 63, a **monument** commemorates **President John F. Kennedy**'s visit to Big Cedar on October 29, 1961, to speak at the dedication of US 259.

Continuing south on US 259, notice the impressive Kiamichi Mountain range ahead. Just 0.6 mile south, the road crosses the **Kiamichi River,** the most popular float stream in the Oklahoma Ouachitas. It originates on the south slope of Rich Mountain, northwest of Mena, Arkansas, near the Ouachita River. The Kiamichi flows west before turning south to eventually join the Red River. The best floating opportunities occur in the spring and fall at higher water levels. Due to several white-water hazards, it is not recommended for the inexperienced floater.

This monument commemorates the dedication of U.S. Highway 259 by President John F. Kennedy in 1961.

In 4 miles the road climbs to the summit of the **Kiamichi Mountains.** Kiamichi is derived from the French word *kamichi,* which means "horned screamer," a species of bird. It might have referred to the now-extinct Carolina parakeet, whose call consisted of much yelling and screeching. An observation pullout provides an opportunity to see **Three Sticks Monument,** which honors several political leaders who were credited with the rapid development of the State of Oklahoma. Their names are inscribed on a plaque at the base of the monument.

31

Spiro Mounds

FORT SMITH TO TALIHINA, ARKANSAS/OKLAHOMA

GENERAL DESCRIPTION: A 58-mile drive beginning in Fort Smith, then generally heading south to the Spiro Indian Mounds and ending just beyond the Winding Stair Mountains at Talihina.

SPECIAL ATTRACTIONS: Fort Smith Historic District, Spiro Indian Mounds, Cavanal Mountain, Ouachita National Forest, Winding Stair Mountains, Ouachita Trail, and Talimena State Park; scenic views, fall colors, hiking, camping, swimming, fishing, and hunting.

LOCATION: Western Ouachitas. The drive is on U.S. Highway 271 from Fort Smith to Talihina.

DRIVE ROUTE NUMBERS: U.S. Highway 271.

CAMPING: Lake Wister State Park has 5 campgrounds with 172 sites; most offer showers, water, electricity, and RV hookups. Talimena State Park has picnic sites, 7 RV sites, 15 unimproved campsites, and a comfort station with shower. Primitive camping is allowed in the Ouachita National Forest.

SERVICES: All services at Fort Smith, Spiro, Poteau, and Talihina. Gas and food at Panama and Wister.

NEARBY ATTRACTIONS: Robbers Cave State Park, Talimena and Heavener Runestone scenic drives, and Sardis Lake.

THE DRIVE

Heading south out of the Arkansas River valley, this drive climbs over the Winding Stair Mountains and comes within sight of the Kiamichi Mountains. Both of these east-west trending mountain chains are located in the western part of the Ouachita Mountains. In the Fort Smith area, the relatively flat to rolling Arkansas River valley was once characterized by prairie and bottomland hardwood forests. Today it is primarily pasture and cultivated land. The Ouachita Mountains, because of their rugged nature, still contain extensive forests of pine and hardwoods.

FORT SMITH

The drive begins in **Fort Smith,** the second-largest city in Arkansas. The development of Fort Smith can be traced back to the early 1800s, when the

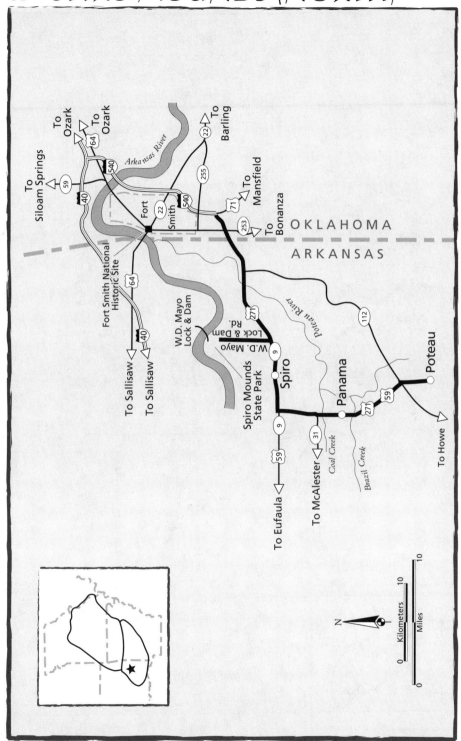

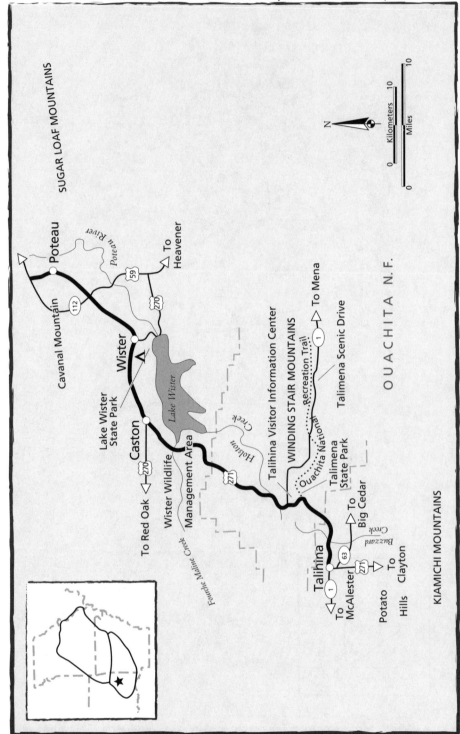

Cherokee Indians were forced to move west from their Appalachian homelands. In 1818 the U.S. government gave the Cherokees a large tract in northern Arkansas; however, it was not long before the Cherokees were having trouble with the resident Osage Indians, white hunters, and white squatters trying to settle in Indian territory. In 1817, on orders from Secretary of War Joel R. Poinsett, General Thomas A. Smith detailed Major William Bradford to establish a fort to keep peace. After arriving from Bellefontaine, on the Missouri River north of St. Louis, his small contingent of sixty-four men began work on a military outpost. Five years later the fort was completed and named Fort Smith after Bradford's commanding officer. However, the presence of the fort did not squelch the conflicts among the Indian tribes and the white hunters and squatters, so the original garrison was moved northwest to Fort Gibson in 1824, closer to the frontier.

Although the initial fort never fulfilled its original mission, it did stimulate the development of the town. In 1841, after much political pressure, a new fort (now a national historic site) was built near the site of the original post to serve as a supply depot for other frontier forts. Two years later the town of Fort Smith was incorporated. The town quickly grew when gold was discovered on the West Coast in 1848; Fort Smith served as a major supplier for the miners heading to California. The arrival of the first Butterfield stagecoach in 1858 caused

Once a federal courthouse, this building now houses a gift shop and exhibits depicting events surrounding the establishment of Fort Smith.

Spiro Mounds

more people who were traveling from St. Louis to California to pass through Fort Smith, bringing more business to the town.

The arrival of the railroads in 1879 also contributed significantly to the development of Fort Smith. These railroads stimulated coal mining in the region, provided cheap transportation for agricultural products, and encouraged industries to locate in Fort Smith.

Today Fort Smith provides conveniences and services customarily found in larger cities. Overnight lodging, restaurants, numerous historical and cultural attractions, and shopping opportunities contribute to the city's prosperity. For information on activities in Fort Smith, contact the Fort Smith Convention and Visitors Bureau (see Appendix A). Be sure to visit the Fort Smith Historic District, which includes the **Fort Smith National Historic Site.** It can be reached by following AR 22, which is Rogers Avenue, to the west end of the city. When AR 22 turns right onto Garrison Avenue, stay left on Rogers Avenue, which leads to the historic site. Parking is available at the south end of the site. The principal building, a former federal courthouse, contains a visitor center with exhibits and items for sale. A paved river trail is located on the southwest side of the grounds. It goes an eighth of a mile to a Trail of Tears Overlook where an exhibit explains the relocation of the Cherokee Nation, Chickasaw Nation, Choctaw Nation, Muscogee (Creek) Nation, and Seminole Nation and their crossing along this stretch of the Arkansas River to reservations in Oklahoma. The trail continues along the river for half a mile to a city park and nearby Miss Laura's, which was once called the Riverfront Hotel. Now the city's visitor center, it is the only former bordello listed on the National Register of Historic Places. The visitor center is located on North Second and B Street. If you stop at the visitor center, be sure to pick up a very informative brochure with map that showcases historic buildings, restaurants, accommodations, and annual events.

Just east of the Fort Smith National Historic Site, at Fourth and Rogers Street, the Fort Smith Museum of History contains exhibits on the city's history beginning with the first fort in 1817, through the westward expansion, the Civil War, and the gay nineties. An old-fashioned soda fountain is also in operation, along with a gift shop and bookstore.

SPIRO MOUNDS

To continue the drive, proceed south from Fort Smith joining US 271 from I–540. US 271 crosses over the Poteau River and, in 4 miles, intersects with a road and a sign indicating the direction to **Spiro Mounds State Park.** Follow the road for another 4 miles to the park. Located on 140 acres, the park is

*Brush-covered Craig Mound is one of several important archaeological sites
at Spiro Mounds State Park.*

the site of an Indian mound-building culture that occupied the area from A.D. 850 to A.D. 1450. Named for the nearby town of Spiro, the mounds are considered one of the most important archaeological sites in the United States. The museum and interpretive center contains fascinating and elegant displays of stone effigy pipes in human and animal forms, shell beads, pottery, copper plaques, basketry, engraved conch shell bowls, and other artifacts. An interpretive trail behind the center leads to twelve mounds that were built for religious and political ceremonies and burial sites for prominent leaders.

Located on a bend of the Arkansas River, the site was a natural gateway between Indian societies in the southeastern United States and those living in the Great Plains to the west. For several centuries the Spiro culture exerted much political, religious, and economic influence with mound construction, political and religious leadership, horticulture, craftsmanship, and trading practices.

Despite its complex and advanced society, the Spiro culture mysteriously disappeared around A.D. 1450. Reasons for abandonment of the Spiro site are unknown, and archaeologists speculate any number of causes, including a long period of drought, warfare, internal strife, disease, or a combination of factors.

Although it was known locally as a prehistoric Indian site as early as the late nineteenth century, it was not until 1933 that the Spiro Mounds attracted national and worldwide attention. That year a group of treasure hunters calling themselves the Pocola Mining Company leased the land containing the mounds and began digging at Craig Mound, which was the largest of the mounds. Unfortunately, thousands of artifacts were either carelessly destroyed or sold indiscriminately to onlookers or private collectors. Although some of these artifacts did find their way into museums, there was little or no description as to their significance or the context in which they were found. Fortunately, when the mining company's lease ran out in 1935, federal and state agencies and institutions took over and conducted a systematic excavation of the remainder of the Spiro Mounds. Today the Oklahoma Archaeological Survey carries out excavations at the park and publishes scientific findings and interpretations.

Spiro Mounds State Park is closed every Monday, and Tuesday from November to April. Daytime hours are 9:00 A.M. to 5:00 P.M., except for Sunday, when the hours are noon to 5:00 P.M. Other artifacts from the Spiro Mounds are on display at the University of Oklahoma in Norman, the Oklahoma Historical Museum in Oklahoma City, and the Philbrook Museum in Tulsa.

Return to US 271 and proceed to **Spiro.** Founded in 1895 when the Kansas City Southern Railroad was extended through the region, Spiro is primarily a service and trade center for the surrounding villages, farms, and ranches.

PANAMA TO TALIHINA

Continue on US 271 for 4 miles to **Panama.** Named for the Panama Canal, which was under construction at the time, the town was established as a coal-shipping point when the Kansas City Southern Railway expanded south through the Ouachitas. Many of the homes date back to the turn-of-the-century coal-mining era when the town prospered. The view to the south reveals a prominent landmark, **Cavanal Mountain,** which marks the location of the town of Poteau. The road crosses Coal Creek just before the creek empties into Poteau River to the east.

After another 5 miles, US 271 enters **Poteau,** seat of Le Flore County. For details on Poteau and Cavanal Mountain, see Drive 30. You can elect to bypass Poteau here by taking the new highway around the west side of town.

Leaving Poteau, continue on US 271 for 9 miles to **Wister.** This town began in 1890 when the Arkansas and Choctaw Railroad came westward into Oklahoma and formed a junction with the St. Louis and San Francisco Railroad's Texas branch. Today, due to its strategic location at the junction of US 270 and US 271, Wister is experiencing modest growth and serves as a center for hunters, fishermen, and tourists. Two miles south of Wister on US 270, Lake

Wister and **Lake Wister State Park** provide camping, boating, fishing, and camping. Hiking is also available on the Lone Star Interpretive Trail. The area has a variety of habitats including oak and pine uplands and grassy glades. Waterfowl and bald eagles can be seen in fall and winter, and a variety of songbirds and raptors are present the rest of the year. Otters are occasionally sighted in nearby streams.

Passing through the nearly abandoned community of **Caston,** the road heads south towards the majestic Winding Stair Mountains, some of the highest and grandest in the region. In a couple of miles the road crosses Fourche Maline Creek, which in French designates that it is a sharply branching creek. The creek is dammed east of here to form Lake Wister, a 4,000-acre lake surrounded by 33,428 acres set aside as a wildlife management area. The road passes through this special area, which is called **Wister Wildlife Management Area.**

In a little over 3 miles, the road begins to climb the north slope of the **Winding Stair Mountains.** About a mile later, the boundary of the **Ouachita National Forest** begins. US 271 skirts the western edge of the national forest, which extends eastward to near Little Rock, Arkansas. The 1,276,973-acre national forest provides 33 developed recreation areas, 7 scenic areas, 7 wilderness areas, and 480 miles of trails. Information on activities can be obtained at the supervisor's office in Hot Springs or from any of the twelve district offices.

There are 7 miles of loops and switchbacks as the road climbs to the summit of the Winding Stair Mountains, 1,289 feet above sea level. US 271 then intersects with Oklahoma Highway 1, **Talimena Scenic Drive** (see Drive 29 for more details), and Talihena Visitor Information Center. Publications and information on activities in the area are available at the center.

About a mile beyond the visitor center, **Talimena State Park** provides camping and access to the **Ouachita Trail.** The trailhead initiates a 222.5-mile-long journey eastward to Pinnacle Mountain State Park, just west of Little Rock, Arkansas. The trail was constructed from 1971 to 1981 by Forest Service and state park personnel and groups of volunteers. Although the trail has had a bad reputation in the past for poor design and development, recent improvements and a stronger commitment by the Forest Service have greatly improved the trail. This stretch of the trail goes 23.7 miles to the Winding Stair Campground and is considered the most difficult section of the Ouachita Trail to hike.

US 271 descends the Winding Stair Mountains and in 7 miles enters **Talihina.** Settled in 1888, the town's name is derived from a Choctaw Indian word for "the great iron road," signifying the arrival of the St. Louis and San Francisco Railroad, which laid its tracks through the Winding Stair Mountains. The town, having grown up around the railroad, still remained fairly isolated until 1919 when a reliable road was built through the forest by convict labor. Nestled in the valley of the Kiamichi River, impressive views are offered of the Winding Stair range to the north and east, the towering Kiamichi Mountains to the south, and the knobby Potato Hills to the east.

Cherokee Nation

SALLISAW TO TAHLEQUAH, OKLAHOMA

GENERAL DESCRIPTION: A 58-mile drive beginning at Sallisaw in the Arkansas River valley and traveling west and then north into the Ozarks to the heart of the Cherokee Nation at Tahlequah.

SPECIAL ATTRACTIONS: Sequoyah's Home Site, Sequoyah National Wildlife Refuge, Robert S. Kerr Lake, Lake Tenkiller, Cherokee Courthouse Historic Site, Murrell Home, Cherokee National Museum, and Cherokee Capitol Building; scenic views, hiking, camping, swimming, fishing (including trout), and hunting.

LOCATION: Arkansas River valley and southwestern edge of the Ozarks. The drive is from Sallisaw to Tahlequah.

DRIVE ROUTE NUMBERS: U.S. Highways 59 and 64 and Oklahoma Highways 82 and 100.

CAMPING: Tenkiller State Park has 40 native stone and timber cabins for rent

plus 10 camping areas with a total of 221 campsites. These vary from primitive sites to modern ones with electricity, water, showers, and rest rooms. Cherokee Landing State Park has 100 campsites with 59 electric hookups, water, showers, and rest rooms. On Lake Tenkiller, the U.S. Army Corps of Engineers has 18 recreation areas, 15 of which have campsites. Rest rooms, electrical hookups, showers, and water are provided depending on recreation area. On Robert S. Kerr Lake, the Corps offers 13 recreation areas, 8 of which have designated camping. Facilities vary according to camping area.

SERVICES: All services at Sallisaw, Vian, Gore, and Tahlequah. Food and gas at Cookson and Keys.

NEARBY ATTRACTIONS: Sallisaw State Park, Fort Smith, Spiro Mounds Scenic Drive, and the Illinois River.

THE DRIVE

The drive begins in the Arkansas River valley in what is known as the Arkoma Basin, which separates the Ozarks from the Ouachita Mountains. Mountain remnants viewed to the south were isolated from the main Ouachitas by basin settling and the erosive action of rivers over millions of years. The Arkansas River valley was once primarily a mixture of prairie and bottomland hardwood forest, with some marshes and sloughs left behind by the meandering Arkansas River. Today the deep, fertile soil produces crops and provides pastures

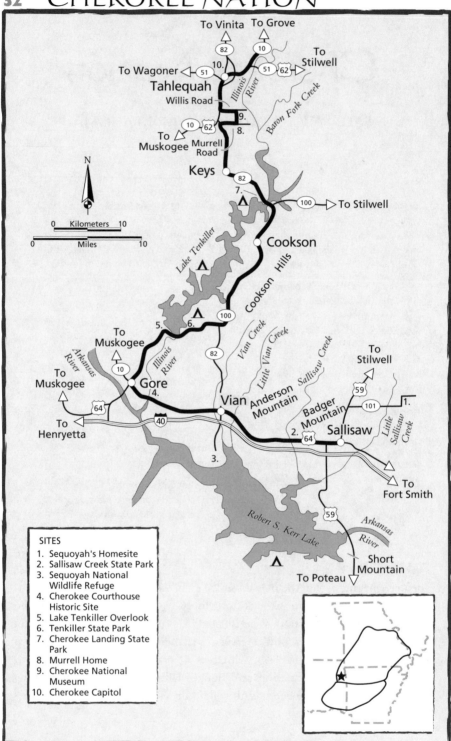

SITES
1. Sequoyah's Homesite
2. Sallisaw Creek State Park
3. Sequoyah National Wildlife Refuge
4. Cherokee Courthouse Historic Site
5. Lake Tenkiller Overlook
6. Tenkiller State Park
7. Cherokee Landing State Park
8. Murrell Home
9. Cherokee National Museum
10. Cherokee Capitol

for cattle. The northern part of the drive enters the Cookson Hills on the western edge of the Ozarks. The terrain is less mountainous, being characterized instead by large, rolling hills covered with upland hardwood forests of oak and hickory. In some parts of this region the forests were more like woodlands or savannas with scattered trees and an understory of prairie grasses and forbs (wildflowers). Elk and bison once roamed this land, as did the Caddo and then the Osage Indians, long before the time of European settlement and the displacement of eastern Indian nations to this part of Oklahoma.

SALLISAW AREA SITES

Easy access to **Sallisaw** is provided off I–40, but the rest of the drive will take advantage of two-lane roads that offer the opportunity to sightsee at a much slower pace. Sallisaw's name originated with French trappers who called the place *Salaisiau*, meaning "salt provision." Indians, early settlers, explorers, and trappers were familiar with the natural salt deposits found along many nearby streams. John Steinbeck, author of *The Grapes of Wrath*, used Sallisaw as the starting point for the novel's "Okies" fleeing to California to escape the dust bowl of the 1930s. Actually it was in western Oklahoma that blowing winds created dust clouds from the dry, flat land that suffered from poor farming practices.

From Sallisaw, a side trip north on US 59 offers an opportunity to see **Sequoyah's homesite.** Take US 59 for 3 miles north to OK 101 and go 6.7 miles east to the homesite. This wooded, ten-acre site features Sequoyah's log cabin housed in a Works Progress Administration (WPA) cover building. There are also walking paths, a visitor center and gift shop, and a daytime picnic area. Sequoyah was perhaps the best educated of the Cherokee statesmen and is credited with devising the written alphabet of the Cherokee language. He was born in the lower Appalachian region of Tennessee in about 1770. His mother was Cherokee; his non-Indian father left the family when Sequoyah was very young. As an adult, he became known as a skilled blacksmith and silversmith and for his drawings and paintings. In 1809 he began experimenting with a written alphabet for the Cherokee language. After years of experimenting, he found that developing an alphabet of letters would not work. Instead he devised different symbols for each word of his language. Although the alphabet was not accepted at first, tribal members eventually were won over, and Sequoyah was recognized as a knowledgeable and respected man. He moved his family to Oklahoma and shortly after built a one-room log cabin. This 1829 structure was designated in 1966 as a National Historic Landmark by the Secretary of the Interior.

Sequoyah became famous worldwide as the inventor of a nation's written language. He was selected as one of Oklahoma's two greatest men in the

A dramatic portrayal of Sequoyah, the father of the Cherokee alphabet, can be seen at Sequoyah's homesite.

National Statuary Hall of Washington D.C. Also, California's giant redwood tree, the Sequoia, was named after him.

Returning to Sallisaw, another side trip is recommended, especially in the fall and winter. The **Robert S. Kerr Lake** is located 8 miles south of Sallisaw. A U.S. Army Corps of Engineers lake on the Arkansas River, the area below the dam offers outstanding opportunities to view bald eagles in fall and winter. Waterfowl, white pelicans, and shorebirds are also seen during migration in the fall and spring. A visitor center with observation decks overlooks the lock and dam. The 5.4-mile Short Mountain Hiking Trail is located near the lock and dam. With steep climbs at either end, the trail eventually reaches the top of Short Mountain for a commanding view. For those who want to take a swim, Kerr Beach is the largest sand beach in Oklahoma.

Return to Sallisaw and proceed west on US 64. On the west side of town you will pass Blue Ribbon Downs, Oklahoma's oldest racing facility and first pari-mutuel racetrack. Beyond the racetrack and for the next several miles, the countryside is carpeted with pastures containing quarter horses, thoroughbreds, Appaloosas, and paint horses being bred and trained for racing at Blue Ribbon Downs. In 2.8 miles, **Sallisaw Creek State Park** offers picnicking and fishing on Brushy Creek Lake. Shortly after Sallisaw Creek, the road crosses the extreme lower edge of the Ozarks. The rest of the drive west and north will explore deeper into the Oklahoma Ozarks.

VIAN AREA SITES

Continue to the town of **Vian.** In this small community, turn south onto OK 82, and follow the signs for 3.5 miles to the entrance of **Sequoyah National Wildlife Refuge.** Established in 1970 to provide habitat for waterfowl and other migratory birds, the refuge contains 20,800 acres, half of them in Kerr Lake. A visitor center is located at the refuge headquarters, and a 6-mile auto tour winds through woodlands, marshes, and along the lakeshore. Much of the rich bottomland is planted in winter wheat, soybeans, milo, and corn. This is cost-shared with local farmers who plant and harvest the crops, leaving a portion for wildlife. In the winter the refuge hosts between 15,000 to 20,000 snow geese, making it home to the largest concentration of snow geese in the state. Bald eagles and white pelicans can also be seen during migration and in winter. The best viewing is from the half-mile hiking trail that goes to an observation platform. Other wildlife, such as bobcats and river otters, can also be seen.

Returning to Vian, turn west and continue on US 64 for 6 miles to the **Cherokee Courthouse Historic Site.** The buildings here served as the original western capital of the Cherokee nation from 1829 to 1839, when a portion of the eastern nation migrated to the Oklahoma Territory after the Treaty of 1817. It was here that Chief John Jolly established a settlement and capital, called Tahlanteeskee, with a National Council House and Courthouse, near the Illinois River. When the eastern Cherokee nation was driven from its homeland on the "Trail of Tears" in 1838–39, the two nations were reunited and the capital reestablished at Tahlequah. A visitor center and gift shop occupies one of the restored log cabins.

Leaving the historic site, US 64 crosses over the Illinois River. The river begins near Hogeye, Arkansas, and flows north and west through the Ozark National Forest and south into Oklahoma to empty into the Arkansas River. The upper reaches, to the point where the river enters Tenkiller Lake, are very popular for canoeing. A section above Tahlequah has been designated an Oklahoma Scenic River. (See the last page of this drive for more information about the Illinois River.)

GORE TO THE CHEROKEE HERITAGE CENTER

After crossing the Illinois River, continue to **Gore.** Originally named "Campbell" and then "Illinois" (after the nearby river), it was renamed "Gore" when statehood was achieved, in honor of Senator Thomas P. Gore. Located 7 miles south of Tenkiller Lake, the town serves as the gateway to the lake area for visitors arriving from the south and west. It is known as the "Trout Capital of Oklahoma," as it is located within a mile of the lower Illinois River, which offers year-round trout fishing. The water temperature, 48 degrees Fahrenheit, is caused by its being released from the bottom of the dam at Lake Tenkiller; this is the ideal temperature for trout.

In Gore take OK 100 north 6 miles to the **Lake Tenkiller dam overlook.** Before the dam was built, there was a ferry crossing in this area operated by a Cherokee Indian family named Tenkiller. The family sold the land to the U.S. Army Corps of Engineers for the lake's development. At the overlook, the Island View Nature Trail edges along the lake for 2 miles to Strayhorn Landing. The first half mile is developed, with bridges and a gravel base. The rest of the trail is more strenuous. From seventy to one hundred bald eagles can be seen in the fall and winter as they fish along the surface of this exceptionally clear lake.

Stay on OK 100, crossing the dam with Tenkiller State Park on the left. This is a popular, sometimes overcrowded state park during the summer. It might be best to visit this state park during the off season, or else choose one of the Corps of Engineers' park areas during the busier times.

Continue to the intersection with OK 82. This is the principal road leading to Tahlequah. The road turns north and crosses the Cookson Hills, offering a rugged, scenic drive over steep wooded hills, sandstone outcrops, and crystal-clear streams. Because of its rugged and inaccessible landscape, Charles "Pretty Boy" Floyd and other notorious outlaws used the Cookson Hills as a hideout during the 1930s.

In 13 miles, OK 82 crosses over the upper end of Lake Tenkiller and passes **Cherokee Landing State Park.** After another 8.4 miles and just before the intersection of OK 62, OK 10, and OK 82, turn right on Murrell Road. Follow the road 1 mile to **Murrell Home.** Built by George Michael Murrell in 1843, the home was the center for many social and political activities among the Cherokee. The mansion is now operated by the Oklahoma State Historical Society and is open Wednesday to Saturday from 10:00 A.M. to 5:00 P.M. and Sunday from 1:00 to 5:00 P.M.; it's closed on Monday and Tuesday.

Opposite the Murrell Home follow the road north 0.7 mile to the **Cherokee Heritage Center.** Established in 1963 by the Cherokee National Historical Society, a private, nonprofit corporation, it was designed to preserve the history and culture of the Cherokee people. The center is on the site of the Park Hill Mission, established in 1836 by Presbyterians as a religious and educational center for the Cherokees. The mission included homes for missionar-

A young Cherokee woman provides a guided tour through the Ancient Village at Tsa-La-Gi.

ies and teachers, a boarding hall for students, a gristmill, shops, stables, and a printing office and book bindery. Thousands of schoolbooks and extracts from the Bible were published, many in the Cherokee alphabet developed by Sequoyah. In 1851 a Cherokee Female Seminary was built and dedicated to the perpetuation of the Cherokee heritage in the resources of its young women. Fire destroyed the structure in 1887; only three of its brick columns still stand today.

The **Cherokee National Museum** opened in 1975 and displays more than 4,300 artifacts related to Cherokee history and culture, as well as valuable art objects. The 24,000-square-foot building also houses the Cherokee National Archives and a library with more than 4,100 volumes related to Cherokee history and culture. A gift shop at the entrance of the museum displays handcrafted items designed by Native American craftspeople.

Be sure to take the guided tour of the **Ancient Village at Tsa-La-Gi.** Completed in 1967, the Ancient Village re-creates the lifestyle of the Cherokees during the sixteenth century, prior to European contact. It has been rated as one of America's finest living museums. The tours are available from May through late August. From early June to late August, every night except Sunday, the amphitheater at Tsa-La-Gi provides the setting for the "Trail of Tears" drama. Beginning with the removal of the Cherokees from their ancestral homeland in 1838, when 4,000 of the 16,000 tribal members died in a forced march, through the statehood of Oklahoma in 1907, the historic drama captures the life of the Cherokee people and the struggles that they overcame after reaching Indian territory.

TAHLEQUAH

Leaving the Cherokee Heritage Center, turn right and then left onto Willis Road. Follow the road to the intersection of OK 10, OK 62, and OK 82, turn right and proceed 2 miles to **Tahlequah.** With a population of 10,400, it is the largest city in the Oklahoma Ozarks. Tahlequah became the permanent capital of the Cherokee nation on September 6, 1839, when the eastern and the western Cherokees met on the site of the present square to sign a new constitution. The **Cherokee Capitol,** completed in 1870, stands on that square today. It now houses the Tahlequah Area Chamber of Commerce and the Cherokee Gift Shop. Follow Muskogee Avenue to the downtown square to see the capitol. Today Tahlequah is primarily a service center and college town, being the home of Northeastern State University. According to the chamber of commerce, for the past eight years the town has been ranked as the fourth-best retirement location in America, based on a study of climate, health care, personal safety, housing, cost of living, and leisure activities.

A side trip east of town on OK 10 provides an opportunity to see the natural flow of the **Illinois River** before it enters into Tenkiller Lake. The river was named after the Illinois Indians, once an important Algonquin tribe. The Illinois River is a favorite recreational waterway, being the only stream in Oklahoma that can accommodate float trips of up to several days in length. Tourist information is available at the Oklahoma Scenic Rivers Commission Headquarters, located just a few miles north on OK 10. Approximately 15 miles from the intersection of US 62 and OK 51, OK 10 goes under some impressive overhanging cliffs that were formed by erosion from the river. This state-designated scenic river is worth spending some time on, or at least viewing from the several accesses along the river's course.

Gateway to the West

LEWIS AND CLARK TO SHAW NATURE RESERVE

GENERAL DESCRIPTION: An 85-mile drive beginning at the Lewis and Clark State Historic Site in Illinois and crossing into Missouri to visit more historical, cultural, and recreational sites and ending at the Shaw Nature Reserve.

SPECIAL ATTRACTIONS: Lewis and Clark State Historic Site, Cahokia Mounds, Columbia Bottom Conservation Area, Old Chain of Rocks Bridge, Laclede's Landing, Eads Bridge, Gateway Arch, Old Cathedral, Old Courthouse, Soulard, Anheuser-Busch Brewery, Tower Grove Park, Missouri Botanical Garden, The Hill, Laumeier Sculpture Park and Museum, Powder Valley Nature Center, Lone Elk Park, World Bird Sanctuary, Wild Candid Survival and Research Center, Route 66 State Park, West Tyson Park, Rockwoods Reservation, Babler State Park, Pacific Palisades Conservation Area, and Shaw Nature Reserve; scenic views, hiking, biking, and wildlife viewing.

LOCATION: Northeastern Ozarks. The drive begins at the junction of Interstate 270 and Illinois Highway 3.

DRIVE ROUTE NUMBERS: Interstates 270, 255, 55, and 44; Illinois Highways 3 and III; Missouri Highways 141, 100, 61, 67, and 109; Business Loop 44; Old Route 66; and County Roads N and OO.

CAMPING: Horseshoe Lake State Park, Illinois, has 48 basic sites with water, pit toilets, and dump station. Babler State Park, Missouri, has 40 sites with electric hookups, 32 basic sites, group camping, and special-use camping areas; water, rest rooms, a shower house, vault toilets, and a dump station are also provided.

SERVICES: All services are available along this urban drive.

NEARBY ATTRACTIONS: Forest Park, St. Louis Zoo, St. Louis Science Center, The Living World, Katy Trail State Park, Grant's Farm, Purina Farms, Jefferson Barracks Historical Park, Riverlands, and St. Louis Art Museum.

THE DRIVE

St. Louis and the surrounding region offer a wide variety of entertainment and cultural and historical features that have provided many authors with an array of book-filling descriptions of activities. This chapter highlights several of those activities that give visitors a sense of the region's deep-seated history combined with opportunities to see nature in an urban environment.

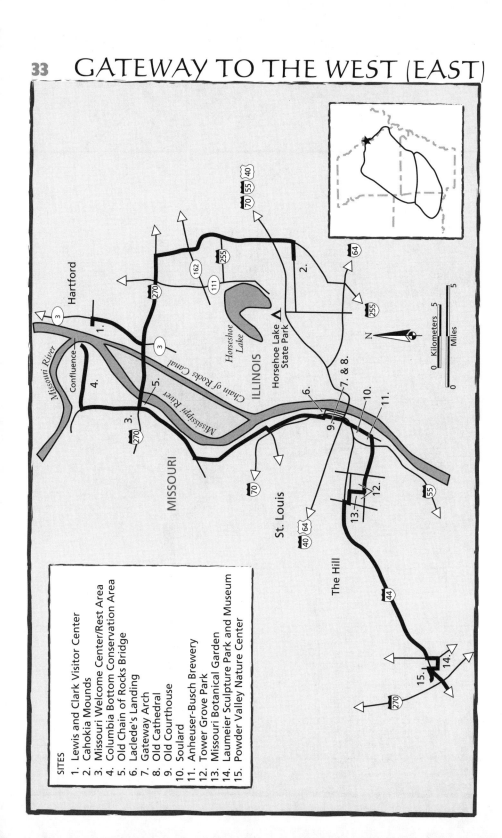

SITES

1. Lewis and Clark Visitor Center
2. Cahokia Mounds
3. Missouri Welcome Center/Rest Area
4. Columbia Bottom Conservation Area
5. Old Chain of Rocks Bridge
6. Laclede's Landing
7. Gateway Arch
8. Old Cathedral
9. Old Courthouse
10. Soulard
11. Anheuser-Busch Brewery
12. Tower Grove Park
13. Missouri Botanical Garden
14. Laumeier Sculpture Park and Museum
15. Powder Valley Nature Center

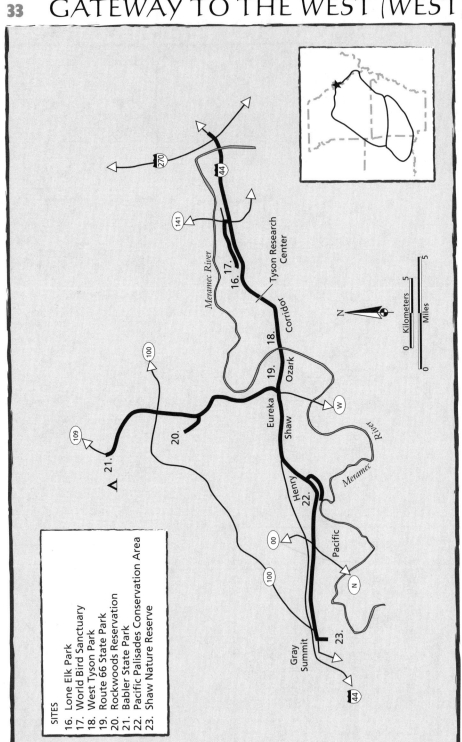

SITES

16. Lone Elk Park
17. World Bird Sanctuary
18. West Tyson Park
19. Route 66 State Park
20. Rockwoods Reservation
21. Babler State Park
22. Pacific Palisades Conservation Area
23. Shaw Nature Reserve

Early inhabitants arrived in the area more than 20,000 years ago. They lived off the abundant plant and animal life and, later, cultivated crops grown in the rich bottomland of the Mississippi River valley. As early Native American culture advanced, these people developed a complex community with a highly specialized social, political, and religious structure. This regional center and its surrounding communities became known as Cahokia, supporting from 10,000 to 20,000 residents that reached peak numbers around A.D. 1200. Europeans did not arrive in this area until the mid-1500s, when the French explorer La Salle traveled down the Mississippi River from Canada to the Gulf of Mexico and named the land west of the river the territory of Louisiana for King Louis XIV of France.

In 1763 Pierre Laclede established a successful fur-trading center in the area now known as Laclede's Landing and soon began working to develop a town. Laclede named the settlement St. Louis, after Crusader King Saint Louis IX, the patron saint of King Louis XV—the reigning French monarch. St. Louis prospered and grew. In 1804, as a result of the Louisiana Purchase, it became part of the United States. With this new development, adventurers, gold seekers, and settlers began streaming through the area, and the term "Gateway to the West" was coined.

ILLINOIS SITES

The drive begins at exit 3B, which is the intersection of I–270B and IL 3. Proceed north on IL 3 for 2.8 miles to New Poag Road and turn left. Follow the sign to the **Lewis and Clark State Historic Site,** a newly completed building with exhibits that commemorate the point of departure for the Lewis and Clark expedition. (NOTE: The building is open Wednesday through Sunday.) The purpose of the expedition was to find a practical transportation link starting at the confluence of the Mississippi and Missouri Rivers and ending at the Pacific Ocean. Take time to explore the detailed exhibits, which are highlighted by the *Corps of Discovery,* a life-size replica of the 55-foot keelboat with a 30-foot mast that they used to journey up the Missouri River. Log buildings outside replicate the five-month base camp, which was located at the nearby Camp River Dubois, where they trained and gathered supplies before beginning their journey on May 14, 1804. Be sure to see the fifteen-minute, high-definition film, *At the Journey's Edge,* which tells the story of the Lewis and Clark Expedition at Camp River Dubois. A road to view the confluence of the two great rivers is located just opposite the entrance to the historic site and is worth the short trip to visit the memorial.

Just before you entered the historic site grounds, you may have noticed a bike trail. It is part of a series of multiuse trails and greenways being developed in the St. Louis metropolitan area by Trailnet, a not-for-profit organization that began in 1988. The goal of Trailnet is twofold: to encourage bicycle transportation to reduce traffic congestion and pollution and to conserve open space for public benefit in the form of greenways, linear parks, and natural areas, often along streams, rivers, and abandoned rail corridors. For more information on trails, events, and volunteering, visit www.trailnet.org or call (314) 416–9930 in Missouri, (618) 874–8554 in Illinois.

Also of interest and just a few miles north on IL 3, the town of **Hartford** is constructing an enclosed multistory tower with elevator that will enable you to view the confluence and surrounding area. It is on schedule for completion in early 2004.

Return to the intersection of I–270 and IL 3. You have an option here of taking a side trip to **Cahokia Mounds,** a State Historic Site and World Heritage Site. This 2,200-acre area preserves the central section of the largest prehistoric Indian city north of Mexico with its sixty-nine remaining man-made earthen mounds, wooden sun calendar, and world-class interpretive center. If you have the time, it is well worth the visit. Take I–270 east 4.4 miles to I–255, exit 30; proceed south on I–255 for about 6.5 miles and turn west at exit 24 onto Collinsville Road. Follow the signs to the interpretive center, which is open Wednesday through Sunday. For site information visit www.cahokiamounds.com or call (618) 346–5160.

ST. LOUIS AREA SITES

Beginning again at the intersection of I–270 and IL 3, proceed west, crossing the Chain of Rocks Canal, which was built to carry barge traffic around the shallow water and rapids in the Mississippi River, a natural water hazard that can be viewed just downstream while crossing the bridge to Missouri. Note also the Historic Illinois Route 66 sign, which designates the famous highway built in the late 1920s to connect Chicago to Los Angeles. After crossing the bridge, immediately take the exit to Riverview Drive, turn right, and notice the **Missouri Welcome Center/Rest Area** on the left side of the road. This is a good opportunity to get a Missouri highway map, as well as other maps and brochures featuring points of interest, places to eat and stay, and activities in the St. Louis area.

Continue north on Riverside Drive for 3 miles to **Columbia Bottom Conservation Area.** This 4,318-acre tract was purchased in 1997 to create an urban conservation area. Take the asphalt road that winds through the area to an impressive, wheelchair-accessible viewing platform that overlooks the confluence of the Missouri and Mississippi Rivers. Wetland habitat is currently being constructed that will allow a wide variety of resident and migratory wildlife viewing opportunities. Just beyond the entrance road to Columbia Bottom, a newly constructed visitor center provides information and exhibits relating to the area.

Return to Riverside Drive and proceed south, passing under I–270, and on the left notice an entrance road to the **Old Chain of Rocks Bridge.** Completed in 1929 at a cost of more than $2 million, the 5,353-foot-long bridge remains one of the longest continuous truss bridges in the country. Once a key link of Route 66, it is now open to pedestrians and bicyclists only. It is a great opportunity to view the mighty Mississippi River at a relaxing pace from border to border. The north end of the St. Louis Riverfront Trail can also be accessed here.

Continuing on Riverside Drive south, in 1.6 miles you will pass an entrance road on the left that leads to a parking lot and access to the **St. Louis Riverfront Trail.** This bicycle/hiking trail connects the Old Chain of Rocks Bridge to the Gateway Arch in downtown St. Louis, a distance of 12 miles.

After another 3.6 miles on Riverfront Drive, veer left onto the beginning of Hall Street and proceed 4.1 miles to Grand Street. Turn right and continue 2 blocks, crossing over railroad tracks, and turn left onto Broadway. In 3.2 miles, turn left on Washington Avenue and go to Fourth and Washington. On the right corner, the **St. Louis Visitor Center,** open from 9:30 A.M. to 4:30 P.M. daily, offers a wealth of information and knowledgeable volunteers to assist you in your travels. You can park immediately around the corner at metered parking or proceed across the intersection, while steering to the right and following the Arch Riverfront/Cassinos/Laclede's Landing sign. The road leads to a fee-parking garage that is recommended to access Laclede's Landing and the Gateway Arch.

Laclede's Landing, immediately north of the parking garage, is accessed by crossing under **Eads Bridge.** Opened in May 1874, it was the world's first steel truss bridge. Built by James Buchanan Eads, a cousin to President James Buchanan, it was the first bridge in St. Louis to cross the Mississippi River, and it remains the oldest bridge still in use spanning the river. Laclede's Landing is part of St. Louis's oldest settlement, which began with a trading post in 1763. The 1850s warehouses and cobblestone streets are all that remain of the city's oldest area after the earliest buildings and streets were cleared to make room for the Gateway Arch Park. Laclede's Landing features a variety of special attractions including restaurants, live music, museums, historical buildings, and carriage rides.

You can access the **Gateway Arch** from the upper level of the parking garage. The park is officially called the Jefferson National Expansion Memorial, but Gateway Arch is the more commonly used title. This impressive 630-foot, stainless steel monument dedicated in 1968 was designed to represent the spirit of western pioneers. Located beneath the arch, an underground visitor center contains the Museum of Westward Expansion; a tram to the top of the arch; a theater showing *Monument to the Dream,* a film on how workers built the Gateway Arch; a giant screen showing of *The Great American West;* and a gift shop. Outside you can take a riverboat tour on the ol' Mississippi, just like Mark Twain. The Gateway Arch is open year-round except for Thanksgiving, Christmas, and New Year's Day. Fees are charged for the tram, movie, and riverboat tour.

Just west of the Gateway Arch, on the same park grounds, the **Old Cathedral,** known officially as the Basilica of St. Louis the King, is one of the world's most honored churches. A museum is located on the west side of the building and contains the tomb of Bishop Rosati, builder of the Old Cathedral; the original bell; a bullet-pierced crucifix; paintings dating back to the late 1700s; a dramatic series of photos; and a souvenir shop.

In addition to the Gateway Arch, the National Park Service also administers the **Old Courthouse,** dating back to the 1820s; it is one of the downtown's oldest buildings. Within, exhibit rooms trace the history of St. Louis from its origins in the eighteenth century to its metropolitan status. There is also an observation area around the rotunda, four stories up. The Old Courthouse is within easy walking distance from the Gateway Arch. Find Market Street, just north of the Old Cathedral, walk west on Market Street, crossing Memorial Drive, and after 1 block you will see the courthouse building. Admission is free.

Leaving the Gateway Arch from the parking garage, turn right and take a drive along Sullivan Boulevard, which parallels the river and offers views of the various boats anchored along the shore, including the **Casino Queen.** The road swings around to Memorial Drive, where you gradually steer your vehicle to the left lane and turn left at the stoplight at Walnut Street. Go 2 blocks west and turn left onto Broadway Street. Proceed south down Broadway for about 1 mile, merging onto Seventh Street. You are entering Soulard with **Soulard Market** located on the right. The market, which has been in operation since 1779, is open Wednesday through Saturday and contains a cornucopia of fruits and vegetables, an array of beautiful cut flowers, fresh and prepared meats, bags of pungent spices and aromatic coffees, fresh donuts, live chickens, and vendors eager to sell you goods at reasonable prices.

Soulard Market was named for Julia Soulard, wife of Antoine Soulard, surveyor general of Upper Louisiana who was given the land in the 1790s by the

The 630-foot Gateway Arch towers over the Jefferson National Expansion Memorial Park.

Spanish governor as payment for his services. In Julia's will, she stipulated that 2 city blocks be given to the City of St. Louis for use as a public market. In addition to the market, a stroll down side streets reveals nineteenth-century architecture, much of it restored to provide living quarters, great restaurants, and live music.

From the Soulard Market continue down Seventh Street for about 1 mile and you will see the large buildings that house the **Anheuser-Busch Brewery.** If you care to take a free tour of the flagship brewery, you will find parking and an entrance along Seventh Street. The tour and gift shop are in operation generally from 9:00 A.M. to 4:00 P.M. Monday through Saturday and from 11:30 A.M. to 4:00 P.M. Sunday. Each tour takes about ninety minutes. The telephone number is (314) 577–2626.

Coming to the next city block, turn right on Arsenal Street and proceed toward I–55. Here you have a choice: You can turn right on I–55 to I–44 and west on I–44 to Grand Boulevard, then left on Grand Boulevard for 1 block to Shaw Boulevard, then right to reach the Missouri Botanical Garden and Tower Grove Park. Or you can continue on Arsenal Street to Tower Grove Park and the Missouri Botanical Garden through residential areas for about 2.6 miles.

The Old Courthouse, dating back to the 1820s, is one of downtown St. Louis's oldest buildings.

If you continue on Arsenal Street, in about half a mile, Benton Park Lake appears on the left. The surrounding Benton Park community was declared a Federal Historic District in 1985 and is continually undergoing restoration of the rich detailing, sturdiness, and flair of the nineteenth-century homes and commercial buildings. In about another 2 miles, turn right on Center Cross Drive and enter **Tower Grove Park.** This 289-acre park is one of only four urban parks in the United States to be declared a National Historic Landmark. It is also one of the world's few remaining Victorian urban parks, with its interesting architectural details, original statuary, fountains, ponds, brightly colored pavilions, shelters, bridges, and music stand. The park, donated to St. Louis in 1868 by Henry Shaw, founder of the Missouri Botanical Garden, provides wonderful opportunities to drive, stroll, or recreate within a charming setting of more than 8,000 trees and shrubs representing 325 species. Admission is free, and special tours can be arranged though the park office. Call (314) 771–2679.

Proceed north through Tower Grove Park on Center Cross Drive, which becomes Tower Grove Avenue after leaving the park. As you travel north, the rock wall along the left side of the street marks the east boundary of the **Missouri Botanical Garden.** Turn left onto Shaw Boulevard and proceed to the entrance of the garden on the south side of the boulevard. There is plenty of parking on either side of the entrance road. Enter the Ridgway Center, which has a restaurant, gift shop, rest rooms, and special exhibits. There is an entrance fee, but it is well worth the price: The Missouri Botanical Garden is a world-class arboretum and the oldest botanical garden in the United States. In 1850 Henry Shaw conceived, designed, and directed these impressive botanical gardens around his home, Tower Grove House. In 1859 he opened up this garden for viewing by the people of St. Louis. Be sure to visit the Climatron, which houses a tropical rain forest; don't forget the Japanese Garden, the English Woodland Garden, the Kemper Center for Home Gardening, the various well-maintained flower beds, and then walk among the galleries of giant, old-growth trees. For more information visit www.mobot.org or call (314) 577–9400.

When leaving the Missouri Botanical Garden, turn left onto Shaw Boulevard for about 3 blocks and then right on Vandeventer. If you continue on Shaw Boulevard another block, you enter **The Hill,** which is bounded by Kingshighway on the east, Hampton on the west, and Fyler on the south. The Hill, so named because it is the highest region of the city, was settled by northern Italians in the early 1900s. Throughout the neighborhood you will find great Italian restaurants and interesting Italian grocery stores.

Back on Vandeventer, head north and access I–44 West. Proceed down the interstate for 9.3 miles and take exit 277B to Lindbergh Boulevard and MO

The Missouri Botanical Garden's lily pool reflects the Climatron, which houses a tropical rain forest.

61/67. Turn left and go half a mile to Rott Road. Turn right on Rott Road and go half a mile to the entrance of **Laumeier Sculpture Park and Museum.** Founded in 1976 by Henry and Matilda Laumeier, it is considered by some to be the world's premier park for contemporary sculptures. There is a 1-mile paved loop trail that provides access to more than eighty-five sculptures in the park. The museum showcases contemporary and modern sculptures, drawings, paintings, ceramics, and photography along with a gift shop.

Return to Rott Road and turn left, then right on Geyer Road, crossing Watson Road and the bridge over I–44. Immediately after the bridge, turn left on Cragwold Road and drive to the entrance of **Powder Valley Nature Center.** The nature center, named for a Civil War munitions plant, is owned and operated by the Missouri Department of Conservation. The nature center is nestled in 112 acres of oak-hickory forest with four paved trails totaling 2.5 miles in length and exhibits that display various aspects of nature in an urban world.

Return to I–44 West, which begins the **Henry Shaw Ozark Corridor,** an area of transition from metropolitan and suburban characteristics to forested

Ozark foothills. The Henry Shaw Ozark Corridor Foundation works to protect and enhance the corridor's natural heritage while promoting sustainable economic and community activity. Noticeable results include wildflower and prairie plantings at targeted sites along the interstate. The corridor's terminus is at Gray Summit, a distance of about 20 miles. For more information about the organization, visit www.hsoc.org.

Proceeding on I–44 for 4 miles, take exit 272, which leads to MO 141 and Valley Park/Fenton. Turn right onto MO 141 and immediately take the right ramp to North Outer Road, turn left on North Outer Road West, and follow the signs to **Lone Elk Park.** The park has auto tour roads that weave through the Meramec River hills and offer opportunities to view elk, bison, white-tailed deer, wild turkeys, and other wildlife. There are cautionary signs that warn you not to approach or feed the animals because they are wild! Also in the park you will find the headquarters of the **World Bird Sanctuary,** a non-profit organization that features education programs, nature trails, and live raptor exhibits. Here you can view a wide variety of raptors, including various hawks, owls, eagles, and vultures from around the world. The sanctuary treats more than 250 raptors annually and has conducted endangered peregrine falcon and barn owl propagation and release programs over the years. Be sure to stop by the visitor center and gift shop and view the live birds. For more information visit www.worldbirdsanctuary.org or call (636) 861–3225.

One of more than eighy-five displays at Laumeier Sculpture Park.

Return to I–44 and proceed west entering a densely forested stretch bordering the interstate. In about 4 miles, exit 269, Beaumont/Antire Road, goes to **Tyson Research Center** and the **Wild Canid Survival and Research Center.** (NOTE: This is for your information only since access is limited.) Tyson Research Center, operated by Washington University, St. Louis, provides opportunities for studying plant and animal life and the habitats in which they live. Nestled within Tyson's 2,000 acres is the Wild Canid Center, a nonprofit organization founded in 1971 by Dr. Marlin Perkins and his wife, Carol. You may recall the late Marlin Perkins, former star of Mutual of Omaha's *Wild Kingdom,* among other noteworthy accomplishments. The center is a captive breeding facility for remnant wild canids including the red wolf, Mexican gray wolf, manned wolf, and swift fox. The center also has educational programs and offers guided tours on most Saturdays at 10:00 A.M. and at 1:00 P.M. Visits may be scheduled Monday through Saturday by appointment only. A fee is charged. For more information visit www.wolfsanctuary.org or call (314) 938–5900.

Beyond exit 269, another 2.5 miles takes you to exit 266 and Lewis Road, where you will find **Route 66 State Park.** Take the north frontage road west passing **West Tyson Park.** The park offers hiking trails and picnic areas. Just before the bridge over the Meramec River, stop at the visitor center on the left for maps and information on recreational activities. The building housing the center is the Bridgehead Inn, a 1935 roadhouse that welcomed travelers on the original Route 66. The 409-acre park is in the early stages of development with a boat launch, pavilions, and a playground planned for the near future. As you drive along the park roads, you will see large earthen mounds. These are the final products of a massive Super Fund site effort to remove road material that contained waste oil contaminated with dioxin, which was used to spray for dust control in the early 1970s. When the dioxin was discovered in 1982, the incorporated Times Beach residents were forced to evacuate their homes and were permanently relocated. After cleanup of the site, it was conveyed to the State of Missouri in 1997.

Continuing another 2.5 miles on I–44, exit 264 to Eureka and MO 109 provides two more areas of interest. Traveling north on MO 109 for 5.8 miles leads to the entrance to **Rockwoods Reservation.** This 1,843-acre area is owned by the Missouri Department of Conservation and contains six trails, picnicking, and an education center. Another 4 miles beyond the entrance to Rockwoods Reservation on MO 109 leads to **Babler State Park.** The park provides 13 miles of hiking trails, guided horseback trails, picnicking, outdoor sports, an Olympic-size pool, and a visitor center with exhibits illustrating the park's natural diversity.

Return to the town of **Eureka,** which got its name when on July 19, 1853, the Missouri Pacific Railroad track builders came around the bend on the east side of the present site of Eureka and looked westward at the level land with no rocks and very little dirt to move. They cried out "Eureka!," which translated from Greek means "I've found it!" The town has a wide variety of shops, restaurants, motels, and, on the west end, Six Flags Over Mid-America Amusement Park.

In about another 3 miles down I–44, take the exit 261 ramp to Business Loop 44, turn left under the interstate bridge, and then right at the next intersection. This puts you on Old Route 66. Two miles later, a side trip to **Pacific Palisades Conservation Area** offers a nice view of the Meramec River. The road sign directs you to turn left, crossing two sets of railroad tracks, then right at the intersection. The dead-end road goes 3 miles to the entrance to Pacific Palisades, a 692-acre area that offers hiking, fishing, wildlife viewing, and a boat launch.

Continuing down Old Route 66, in another mile the town of **Pacific** comes into view. Originally named Franklin, it was changed to Pacific in 1859 in honor of the Pacific Railroad. In another 1.7 miles you will notice a massive outcrop of sandstone on the right side of the road. The large entrances along the face of the cliff are from early mines that extracted the sandstone, which was ground into sand and used primarily in the making of glass. Most

Quarried sandstone hills, long abandoned, tower above Old Route 66 near Pacific.

of the mining in the area is now done by open-pit or strip mining. From the 1870s to the present, Pacific remains one of the few places in the world where the white sand, or silica, is mined. Another massive outcrop of sandstone occurs another mile or so down the road, just past the intersection of MO N and OO. It is covered by metal netting to prevent rocks from cascading down on the street. Just west of the outcrop is a small roadside park, which was donated by Mr. and Mrs. Jasper Blackburn.

Gray Summit appears in another 4.4 miles down old Route 66. Originally known as Tucker's Gap, a Mr. Daniel Gray established an inn there, and the name of the community was soon changed to Gray Summit. Continue across the three-way stop that parallels the intersection of MO 100 and I–44 and turn left at the entrance to the **Shaw Nature Reserve.** Formerly called the Shaw Arboretum, the land was acquired in 1925 and greenhouses were built to provide protection to orchids and other sensitive plants from the Missouri Botanical Garden, where the plants were being damaged by air pollution caused by coal burning in St. Louis. The 2,500-acre tract, an extension of the Missouri Botanical Garden, provides 13 miles of trails that traverse a diversity of landscapes from aquatic to desertlike glades. Staff at the visitor center/bookstore will help you plan your activities based on what you would like to see in the area. Be sure to pick up a site map. One of the highlights is the Whitmire Wildflower Garden, which contains five acres of beautifully landscaped habitats that contain hundreds of wildflowers and ferns, guaranteeing showy displays throughout the season. Adjacent to the wildflower garden, the Bascom Manor House, built in 1879, houses an array of exhibits that illustrate the history of the region over the past 12,000 years. A fee is charged, but members of the Missouri Botanical Garden enter free. For more information visit www.mobot. org/mobot/naturereserve or call (636) 451–3512.

Appendix A

FOR MORE INFORMATION

For more information on lands and events, please contact the following agencies and organizations.

Drive I

Cape Girardeau Conservation Service
    Center
2302 County Park Drive
Cape Girardeau, MO 63701
(573) 290–5730

Cape Girardeau Convention and
    Visitors Bureau
2121 Broadway
Cape Girardeau, MO 63701
(573) 335–1631
(800) 777–0068
www.capegirardeaucvb.org

Cape River Heritage Museum
538 Independence
Cape Girardeau, MO 63703
(573) 334–0405

Historic Sites Division
Illinois Historic Preservation Agency
313 South Sixth Street, 2nd Floor
Springfield, IL 62701
(217) 785–1584
www.state.il.us/hpa/ps/haargis.htm

Illinois Department of Natural
    Resources
One Natural Resources Way

Springfield, IL 62702-1271
(217) 782–6302
http://dnr.state.il.us

Jonesboro Ranger District
521 North Main Street
Jonesboro, IL 62952
(618) 833–8576

Missouri Department of Conservation
P.O. Box 180
Jefferson City, MO 65102
(573) 751–4115
www.conservation.state.mo.us

Missouri Department of Natural
    Resources
Division of Parks, Recreation, and
    Historic Preservation
P.O. Box 176
Jefferson City, MO 65102
(573) 751–2479
(800) 334–6946
www.mostateparks.com

Shawnee National Forest
Route 45 South
Harrisburg, IL 62946
(618) 253–7114
www.fs.fed.us/r9/shawnee

Trail of Tears State Forest
RR1, Box 1331
Jonesboro, IL 62952
(618) 833–4910

Trail of Tears State Park
429 Moccasin Springs
Jackson, MO 63755
(573) 334–1711

Drive 2

Fort de Chartres State Historic Site
1350 State Highway 155
Prairie du Rocher, IL 62277
(618) 284–7230

Great River Road Interpretive Center
66 South Main
Ste. Genevieve, MO 63670
(573) 883–7097
(800) 373–7007

Hawn State Park
12096 Park Drive
Ste. Genevieve, MO 63670
(573) 883–3603

Historic Sites Division
Illinois Historic Preservation Agency
313 South Sixth Street, 2nd Floor
Springfield, IL 62701
(217) 785–1584
www.state.il.us/hpa/ps/haargis.htm

Illinois Department of Natural
    Resources
One Natural Resources Way
Springfield, IL 62702-1271
(217) 782–6302
http://dnr.state.il.us

Maeystown Oktoberfest
c/o The Corner George Inn
    Bed and Breakfast
P.O. Box 103
1101 Main Street
Maeystown, IL 62256
(618) 458–6660
(The Corner George Inn acts as the
    chamber of commerce for this
    small town.)

Missouri Department of Conservation
P.O. Box 180
Jefferson City, MO 65102
(573) 751–4115
www.conservation.state.mo.us

Missouri Department of Natural
    Resources
Division of Parks, Recreation, and
    Historic Preservation
P.O. Box 176
Jefferson City, MO 65102
(573) 751–2479
(800) 334–6946
www.mostateparks.com

Drive 3

Mark Twain National Forest
401 Fairgrounds Road
Rolla, MO 65401
(573) 364–4621
www.fs.fed.us/r9/marktwain

Missouri Department of Conservation
P.O. Box 180
Jefferson City, MO 65102
(573) 751–4115
www.conservation.state.mo.us

Missouri Department of Natural
  Resources
Division of Parks, Recreation, and
  Historic Preservation
P.O. Box 176
Jefferson City, MO 65102
(573) 751–2479
(800) 334–6946
www.mostateparks.com

Drive 4
Mark Twain National Forest
401 Fairgrounds Road
Rolla, MO 65401
(573) 364–4621
www.fs.fed.us/r9/marktwain

Missouri Department of Conservation
P.O. Box 180
Jefferson City, MO 65102
(573) 751–4115
www.conservation.state.mo.us

Missouri Department of Natural
  Resources
Division of Parks, Recreation, and
  Historic Preservation
P.O. Box 176
Jefferson City, MO 65102
(573) 751–2479
(800) 334–6946
www.mostateparks.com

Drive 5
Maramec Spring Park
The James Foundation
320 South Bourbeuse
St. James, MO 65559
(573) 265–7124
(573) 265–7387 (reservations)

Mark Twain National Forest
401 Fairgrounds Road
Rolla, MO 65401
(573) 364–4621
www.fs.fed.us/r9/marktwain

Meramec Caverns
P.O. Box 948
Stanton, MO 63079
(573) 468–3166

Missouri Department of Conservation
P.O. Box 180
Jefferson City, MO 65102
(573) 751–4115
www.conservation.state.mo.us

Missouri Department of Natural
  Resources
Division of Parks, Recreation, and
  Historic Preservation
P.O. Box 176
Jefferson City, MO 65102
(573) 751–2479
(800) 334–6946
www.mostateparks.com

Drive 6
August A. Busch Memorial
  Conservation Area
2360 Highway D
St. Charles, MO 63304
(314) 441–4554
(314) 441–4669

Hermann Welcome Center
312 Market Street
Hermann, MO 65041
(573) 486–2744

Missouri Department of Conservation
P.O. Box 180
Jefferson City, MO 65102
(573) 751–4115
www.conservation.state.mo.us

Missouri Department of Natural
   Resources
Division of Parks, Recreation, and
   Historic Preservation
P.O. Box 176
Jefferson City, MO 65102
(573) 751–2479
(800) 334–6946
www.mostateparks.com

Weldon Spring Site Interpretive
   Center
7295 Highway 94 South
St. Charles, MO 63304
(636) 329–1438
www.wssrap.com

Drive 7
Arrow Rock State Historic Site
P.O. Box 1
Arrow Rock, MO 65320
(816) 837–3330

Cedar Creek Ranger District
4549 State Road H
Fulton, MO 65251
(573) 592–1400

City of Columbia Convention and
   Visitors Bureau
300 South Providence Road
Columbia, MO 65205
(573) 875–1231
(800) 652–0987
www.visitcolumbiamo.com

Finger Lakes State Park
Route 7
1505 East Peabody
Columbia, MO 65202
(573) 443–5315

The Friends of Arrow Rock [tours]
P.O. Box 124
Arrow Rock, MO 65320
(816) 837–3231

Mark Twain National Forest
401 Fairgrounds Road
Rolla, MO 65401
(573) 364–4621
www.fs.fed.us/r9/marktwain

Missouri Department of Conservation
P.O. Box 180
Jefferson City, MO 65102
(573) 751–4115
www.conservation.state.mo.us

Missouri Department of Natural
   Resources
Division of Parks, Recreation, and
   Historic Preservation
P.O. Box 176
Jefferson City, MO 65102
(573) 751–2479
(800) 334–6946
www.mostateparks.com

Drive 8
Ha Ha Tonka State Park
Route 1, Box 658
Camdenton, MO 65020
(573) 346–2986

Lake of the Ozarks State Park
P.O. Box 170
Kaiser, MO 65047
(573) 348–2694

Missouri Department of Conservation
P.O. Box 180
Jefferson City, MO 65102
(573) 751–4115
www.conservation.state.mo.us

Missouri Department of Natural
  Resources
Division of Parks, Recreation, and
  Historic Preservation
P.O. Box 176
Jefferson City, MO 65102
(573) 751–2479
(800) 334–6946
www.mostateparks.com

Ozark Caverns
Lake of the Ozarks State Park
Route 1, Box 371
Linn Creek, MO 65052
(573) 346–2500

Drive 9

Mark Twain National Forest
401 Fairgrounds Road
Rolla, MO 65401
(573) 364–4621
www.fs.fed.us/r9/marktwain

Missouri Department of Conservation
P.O. Box 180
Jefferson City, MO 65102
(573) 751–4115
www.conservation.state.mo.us

Missouri Department of Natural
  Resources
Division of Parks, Recreation, and
  Historic Preservation
P.O. Box 176
Jefferson City, MO 65102
(573) 751–2479
(800) 334–6946
www.mostateparks.com

Ozark National Scenic Riverways
National Park Service
P.O. Box 490
Van Buren, MO 63965
(573) 323–4236
www.nps.gov/ozar/

Drive 10

Big Spring Ranger District
c/o Ozark National Scenic Riverways
P.O. Box 490
Van Buren, MO 63965
(573) 323–4236

Eleven Point Ranger District
Route 1, Box 1908
Winona, MO 65588
(573) 325–4233

Mark Twain National Forest
401 Fairgrounds Road
Rolla, MO 65401
(573) 364–4621
www.fs.fed.us/r9/marktwain

Missouri Department of Conservation
P.O. Box 180
Jefferson City, MO 65102
(573) 751–4115
www.conservation.state.mo.us

Ozark National Scenic Riverways
National Park Service
P.O. Box 490
Van Buren, MO 63965
(573) 323–4236
www.nps.gov/ozar/

Van Buren Ranger District Office
U.S. Forest Service
P.O. Box 69
Van Buren, MO 63965
(573) 323–4216

Drive 11
Arkansas Game and Fish
  Commission
#2 Natural Resources Drive
Little Rock, AR 72205
(501) 223–6300
(800) 364–4263
www.agfc.com

Arkansas State Parks
One Capitol Mall
Little Rock, AR 72201
(501) 682–1191
www.arkansasstateparks.com

Eleven Point Ranger District
Route 1, Box 1908
Winona, MO 65588
(573) 325–4233

Fred's Fish House
201 Main Street
Mammoth Springs, AR 72554
(501) 625–7551

Mammoth Spring National Fish
  Hatchery
P.O. Box 160
Mammoth Spring, AR 72554
(870) 625–3912
http://mammothspring.fws.gov

Mammoth Spring State Park
P.O. Box 36
Mammoth Spring, AR 72554
(501) 625–7364

Mark Twain National Forest
401 Fairgrounds Road
Rolla, MO 65401
(573) 364–4621
www.fs.fed.us/r9/marktwain

Missouri Department of Conservation
P.O. Box 180
Jefferson City, MO 65102
(573) 751–4115
www.conservation.state.mo.us

Missouri Department of Natural
  Resources
Division of Parks, Recreation, and
  Historic Preservation
P.O. Box 176
Jefferson City, MO 65102
(573) 751–2479
(800) 334–6946
www.mostateparks.com

Drive 12
Dawt Mill
HC 1, Box 1090
Tecumseh, MO 65760
(417) 284–3540
www.dawtmill.com

Mark Twain National Forest
401 Fairgrounds Road
Rolla, MO 65401
(573) 364–4621
www.fs.fed.us/r9/marktwain

Missouri Department of Conservation
P.O. Box 180
Jefferson City, MO 65102
(573) 751–4115
www.conservation.state.mo.us

Rainbow Trout and Game Ranch
P.O. Box 100
Highway N, Road 142
Rockbridge, MO 65741
(417) 679–3619
(417) 679–4831
www.rockbridgemo.com

Theodosia Park (the specific Corps
    campground)
HC 5, Box 5030
Theodosia, MO 65761
(417) 273–4626

Zanoni Mill Inn
HC 78, Box 1010
Zanoni, MO 65784
(417) 679–4050
(877) 679–4050
www.bbim.org/zanoni

Drive 13
Ava Area Chamber of Commerce
206 East Washington Street
Ava, MO 65608
(417) 683–4594

Ava Ranger District
1103 South Jefferson
P.O. Box 188
Ava, MO 65608
(417) 683–4428

Mark Twain National Forest
401 Fairgrounds Road
Rolla, MO 65401
(573) 364–4621
www.fs.fed.us/r9/marktwain

Missouri Department of Conservation
P.O. Box 180
Jefferson City, MO 65102
(573) 751–4115
www.conservation.state.mo.us

Theodosia Park (the specific Corps
    campground)
HC 5, Box 5030
Theodosia, MO 65761
(417) 273–4626

Drive 14
Missouri Conservation Department
    Headquarters
2630 North Mayfair
Springfield, MO 65803
(417) 895–6880

Missouri Department of Conservation
P.O. Box 180
Jefferson City, MO 65102
(573) 751–4115
www.conservation.state.mo.us

Missouri Department of Natural
  Resources
Division of Parks, Recreation, and
  Historic Preservation
P.O. Box 176
Jefferson City, MO 65102
(573) 751–2479
(800) 334–6946
www.mostateparks.com

Springfield Conservation Nature
  Center
4600 South Chrisman
Springfield, MO 65804
(417) 888–4237

Table Rock Lake Project Office
U.S. Army Corps of Engineers
P.O. Box 1109
Branson, MO 65616
(417) 334–4101
(417) 271–3215 for Eagle Rock
  Campsite reservations
(417) 271–3860 for Viney Creek
  Campsite reservations
www.swl.usace.army.mil/parks/
  tablerock/history.html

Table Rock State Park
5272 State Highway 165
Branson, MO 65616
(417) 334–4704

Drive 15
Missouri Department of Conservation
P.O. Box 180
Jefferson City, MO 65102
(573) 751–4115
www.conservation.state.mo.us

Missouri Department of Natural
  Resources
Division of Parks, Recreation, and
  Historic Preservation
P.O. Box 176
Jefferson City, MO 65102
(573) 751–2479
(800) 334–6946
www.mostateparks.com

Missouri Prairie Foundation
P.O. Box 200
Columbia, MO 63144
www.mopraire.org

The Nature Conservancy
Missouri Field Office
2800 South Brentwood Boulevard
St. Louis, MO 63144
(314) 968–1105
www.tnc.org

Prairie State Park
P.O. Box 97
Liberal, MO 64762
(417) 843–6711

Drive 16
Cassville Ranger District
Highway 248 East
P.O. Box 310
Cassville, MO 65625
(417) 847–2144

Mark Twain National Forest
401 Fairgrounds Road
Rolla, MO 65401
(573) 364–4621
www.fs.fed.us/r9/marktwain

Missouri Department of Natural
  Resources
Division of Parks, Recreation, and
  Historic Preservation
P.O. Box 176
Jefferson City, MO 65102
(573) 751–2479
(800) 334–6946
www.mostateparks.com

Roaring River State Park
Route 2, Box 2535
Cassville, MO 65265
(417) 847–2330

Table Rock Lake Project Office
U.S. Army Corps of Engineers
P.O. Box 1109
Branson, MO 65616
(417) 334–4101
(417) 271–3215 for Eagle Rock
  Campsite reservations
(417) 271–3860 for Viney Creek
  Campsite reservations
www.swl.usace.army.mil/parks/
  tablerock/history.html

Drive 17

Missouri Department of Conservation
P.O. Box 180
Jefferson City, MO 65102
(573) 751–4115
www.conservation.state.mo.us

Drive 18

Norfork Lake Office
U.S. Army Corps of Engineers
P.O. Box 369
Mountain Home, AR 72653
(870) 425–2700
www.swl.usace.army.mil/parks/
  norfolk/todo.html

Norfork National Fish Hatchery
Route 3, Box 349
Mountain Home, AR 72653
(870) 499–5255
http://norfolk.fws.gov

Ozark Folk Center State Park
P.O. Box 500
Mountain View, AR 72560
(870) 269–3851 (information)
(800) 264–FOLK, ext. 3655 (lodging
  and conference facilities)
www.ozarkfolkcenter.com

Ozark National Forest
605 West Main
Russellville, AR 72801
(479) 968–2354
www.fs.fed.us/oonf/ozark

Sylamore Ranger District &
  Blanchard Springs Caverns
P.O. Box 1279
Mountain View, AR 72560
(870) 757–2211

Drive 19

Bayou Ranger District
12000 State Road 27
Hector, AR 72843
(479) 284–3150

Buffalo National River
402 North Walnut, Suite 136
Harrison, AR 72601
(870) 439–2502
www.nps.gov/buff

Buffalo Ranger District
Highway 7 North
P.O. Box 427
Jasper, AR 72641
(870) 446–5122

Jasper/Newton County Chamber of
Commerce
P.O. Box 250
Jasper, AR 72641
(870) 446–2455
(800) 670–7792
www.theozarkmountains.com

Newton County Resource Council
P.O. Box 513
Jasper, AR 72641
(870) 446–5898

Ozark National Forest
605 West Main
Russellville, AR 72801
(479) 968–2354
www.fs.fed.us/oonf/ozark

Pruitt Ranger Station
HC 73, Box 222
Dogpatch, AR 72648-9729
(870) 446–5373
Contact for river conditions and
emergencies only.

Drive 20
Arkansas Natural Heritage
Commission
1500 Tower Building
323 Center Street
Little Rock, AR 72201
(501) 324–9619
http://naturalheritage.com

Buffalo National River
402 North Walnut, Suite 136
Harrison, AR 72601
(870) 439–2502
www.nps.gov/buff

Buffalo Ranger District
Highway 7 North
P.O. Box 427
Jasper, AR 72641
(870) 446–5122

Ozark National Forest
605 West Main
Russellville, AR 72801
(479) 968–2354
www.fs.fed.us/oonf/ozark

Pruitt Ranger Station
HC 73, Box 222
Dogpatch, AR 72648–9729
(870) 446–5373
Contact for river conditions and
emergencies only.

Drive 21
Buffalo National River
402 North Walnut, Suite 136
Harrison, AR 72601
(870) 439–2502
www.nps.gov/buff

Buffalo Ranger District
Highway 7 North
P.O. Box 427
Jasper, AR 72641
(870) 446–5122

Eureka Springs Chamber of
Commerce
P.O. Box 551
Eureka Springs, AR 72632
(479) 253–8737
www.eurekaspringschamber.com

Lake Dardanelle Project Office
U.S. Army Corps of Engineers
P.O. Box 1087
Russellville, AR 72811
(479) 968–5008
www.swl.usace.army.mil/parks/
    dardanelle/faq.html

Ozark National Forest
605 West Main
Russellville, AR 72801
(479) 968–2354
www.fs.fed.us/oonf/ozark

Pleasant Hill Ranger District
Highway 21 North
P.O. Box 190
Clarksville, AR 72830
(479) 754–2864

Pruitt Ranger Station
HC 73, Box 222
Dogpatch, AR 72648-9729
(870) 446–5373
Contact for river conditions and
emergencies only.

Drive 22
Boston Mountain Ranger District
Highway 23 North
P.O. Box 76
Ozark, AR 72949
(479) 667–2191

Ozark Lake Project Office
U.S. Army Corps of Engineers
Route 1, Box 267X
Ozark, AR 72949
(479) 667–2129
(479) 667–1100 for Aux Arc Camp-
    site reservations

Ozark National Forest
605 West Main
Russellville, AR 72801
(479) 968–2354
www.fs.fed.us/oonf/ozark

White Rock Mountain
    Concessionaires
P.O. Box 291
Mulberry, AR 72947
(479) 369–4128

Withrow Springs State Park
Route 3
Huntsville, AR 72740
(479) 559–2593

Drive 23
Holla Bend National Wildlife Refuge
Route 1, Box 59
Dardanelle, AR 72834
(479) 229–4300
http://southeast.fws.gov/hollabend

Ouachita National Forest
Federal Building
P.O. Box 1270
Hot Springs, AR 71902
(501) 321–5202
www.fs.fed.us/oonf/ouachita

Petit Jean State Park
1285 Petit Jean Mountain Road
Morrilton, AR 72110
(501) 727–5441

Lodge and Cabin Reservations:
Mather Lodge
1069 Petit Jean Mountain Road
(501) 727–5431
www.petitjeanstatepark.com

Pinnacle Mountain State Park
11901 Pinnacle Valley Road
Roland, AR 72135
(501) 868–5806

Winona Ranger District
1039 Highway 10 North
Perryville, AR 72126
(501) 889–5176

Drive 24
Arkansas Natural Heritage
   Commission
1500 Tower Building
323 Center Street
Little Rock, AR 72201
(501) 324–9619
http://naturalheritage.com

Hot Springs National Park
P.O. Box 1860
Hot Springs, AR 71902-1860
(501) 624–3383
(501) 623–1433 (Fordyce Bathhouse
   Visitor Center)
www.nps.gov/hosp/

Jessieville Ranger District
P.O. Box 189
Jessieville, AR 71949
(501) 984–5313

Ouachita National Forest
Federal Building
P.O. Box 1270
Hot Springs, AR 71902
(501) 321–5202
www.fs.fed.us/oonf/ouachita.htm

Ozark National Forest
605 West Main
Russellville, AR 72801
(479) 968–2354
www.fs.fed.us/oonf/ozark

Winona Ranger District
1039 Highway 10 North
Perryville, AR 72126
(501) 889–5176

Drive 25
Magazine Ranger District
P.O. Box 511
Paris, AR 72855
(479) 963–3076

Mount Magazine State Park
16878 Highway 309 S.
Paris, AR 72855
(479) 963–8502
www.moutmagazine@arkansas.com

Ozark National Forest
605 West Main
Russellville, AR 72801
(479) 968–2354
www.fs.fed.us/oonf/ozark

Drive 26
Hot Springs National Park
P.O. Box 1860
Hot Springs, AR 71902-1860
(501) 624–3383
(501) 623–1433 (Fordyce Bathhouse
   Visitor Center)
www.nps.gov/hosp/

Lake Ouachita Project Office
U.S. Army Corps of Engineers
1201 Blakely Dam Road
Royal, AR 71968-9493
(501) 767–2101
www.mvk.usace.army.mil/map/
    ouachita.htm

Lake Ouachita State Park
5451 Mountain Pine Road
Mountain Pine, AR 71956
(501) 767–9366

Ouachita National Forest
Federal Building
P.O. Box 1270
Hot Springs, AR 71902
(501) 321–5202
www.fs.fed.us/oonf/ouachita.htm

Drive 27
Lake Ouachita Project Office
U.S. Army Corps of Engineers
1201 Blakely Dam Road
Royal, AR 71968-9493
(501) 767–2101
www.mvk.usace.army.mil/map/
    ouachita.htm

Lake Ouachita State Park
5451 Mountain Pine Road
Mountain Pine, AR 71956
(501) 767–9366

Mena Ranger District
1603 Highway 71 North
Mena, AR 71953
(479) 394–2382

Oden Ranger District
P.O. Box 332
Oden, AR 71961
(870) 326–4322
Ouachita National Forest
Federal Building
P.O. Box 1270
Hot Springs, AR 71902
(501) 321–5202
www.fs.fed.us/oonf/ouachita.htm

Poteau Ranger District
P.O. Box 2255
Junction of Highways 71 and 248
Waldron, AR 72958
(479) 637–4174

Queen Wilhelmina State Park
3877 Highway 88 West
Mena, AR 71953
(479) 394–2863
(479) 394–2864
(800) 447–4178 (reservations only)

Womble Ranger District
P.O. Box 255
Mount Ida, AR 71957
(870) 867–2101

Drive 28
Albert Pike Recreation Area
Caddo Visitor Information and
    Ranger Station
101 Smokey Bear Lane
Glenwood, AR 71943
(870) 356–4186

Caddo Ranger District
101 Smokey Bear Lane
Glenwood, AR 71943
(870) 356–4186

Lake Greeson Project Office
U.S. Army Corps of Engineers
Route 1
Murfreesboro, AR 71953
(501) 285–2151
www.mvk.usace.army.mil/map/
    greeson.htm

Ouachita National Forest
Federal Building
P.O. Box 1270
Hot Springs, AR 71902
(501) 321–5202
www.fs.fed.us/oonf/ouachita.htm

Womble Ranger District
P.O. Box 255
Mount Ida, AR 71957
(870) 867–2101

Drive 29
Choctaw Ranger District
HC-64, Box 3467
Heavener, OK 74937
(918) 653–2991

Mena Ranger District
Route 3, Box 220
Highway 71N
Mena, AR 71953
(479) 394–2382

Ouachita National Forest
Federal Building
P.O. Box 1270
Hot Springs, AR 71902
(501) 321–5202
www.fs.fed.us/oonf/ouachita.htm

Queen Wilhelmina State Park
HC-07, Box 53A
Mena, AR 71953
(479) 394–2863
(479) 394–2864
(800) 447–4178 (reservations only)

Talimena State Park
Box 318
Talihina, OK 74571
(918) 567–2052

Drive 30
Choctaw Ranger District
HC64, Box 3467
Heavener, OK 74937
(918) 653–2991

Heavener Runestone State Park
Route 1, Box 1510
Heavener, OK 74937
(918) 653–2241

Kiamichi Ranger District
P.O. Box 577
Talihina, OK 74571
(918) 567–2326

Lake Wister State Park
Route 2, Box 6B
Wister, OK 74966
(918) 655–7756

Oklahoma State Parks
500 Will Rogers Building
Oklahoma City, OK 73105
(800) 654–8240
http://touroklahoma.com

Ouachita National Forest
Federal Building
P.O. Box 1270
Hot Springs, AR 71902
(501) 321–5202
www.fs.fed.us/oonf/ouachita.htm

Talimena State Park
Box 318
Talihina, OK 74571
(918) 567–2052

Drive 31
Choctaw Ranger District
HC64, Box 3467
Heavener, OK 74937
(918) 653–2991

Fort Smith Convention and Visitors
   Bureau
2 North B Street
Fort Smith, AR 72901
(479) 783–8888
(800) 637–1477
www.fortsmith.org

Fort Smith National Historic Site
P.O. Box 1406
Fort Smith, AR 72902
(479) 783–3961
www.nps.gov/fosm/

Kiamichi Ranger District
P.O. Box 577
Talihina, OK 74517
(918) 567–2326

Oklahoma State Parks
500 Will Rogers Building
Oklahoma City, OK 73105
(800) 654–8240
http://touroklahoma.com

Ouachita National Forest
Federal Building
P.O. Box 1270
Hot Springs, AR 71902
(501) 321–5202
www.fs.fed.us/oonf/ouachita.htm

Talimena State Park
Box 318
Talihina, OK 74571
(918) 567–2052

Drive 32
Cherokee Heritage Center
P.O. Box 515
Tahlequah, OK 74465
(918) 456–6007
www.cherokeeheritage.org

Cherokee Landing State Park
HC-73, Box 510
Park Hill, OK 74451
(918) 457–5716

Oklahoma State Parks
500 Will Rogers Building
Oklahoma City, OK 73105
(800) 654–8240
http://touroklahoma.com

Robert S. Kerr Lake Project Office
U.S. Army Corps of Engineers
HC-61, Box 238
Sallisaw, OK 74955-9445
(918) 775–4475

Sequoyah National Wildlife Refuge
Route 1, Box 18A
Vian, OK 74962
(918) 773–5251
http://southwest.fws.gov/refuges/
oklahoma/sequoy.html

Tenkiller Lake Project Office
U.S. Army Corps of Engineers
Route 1, Box 259
Gore, OK 74435
(918) 487–5252

Tenkiller State Park
HCR 68, Box 1095
Vian, OK 74962
(918) 489–5643
(918) 489–5641 (cabins, RVs, and
    campsites)
(800) 654–8240 (cabin reservations)

Drive 33

August A. Busch Memorial Conserva-
    tion Area
2360 Highway D
St. Charles, MO 63304
(314) 441–4554
(314) 441–4669

Babler State Park
800 Guy Park Drive
Wildwood, MO 63005
(636) 458–3813
(800) 334–6946

Cahokia Mounds State Historic Site
30 Ramey Street
Collinsville, IL 62234
(618) 346–5160
www.cahokiamounds.com

Gateway Arch
11 North Fourth Street
St. Louis, MO 63102
(314) 655–1700
(877) 982–1410
www.gatewayarch.com
www.nps.gov/jeff

Horseshoe Lake State Park
3321 Highway 111
Granite City, IL 60240
(618) 931–0270
http://dnr.state.il.us

Laumeier Sculpture Park
12580 Rott Road
St. Louis, MO 63127
(314) 821–1209
www.laumeier.org

Lewis and Clark State Historic Site
One Lewis and Clark Trail
Hartford, IL 62048
(618) 251–5811
www.campriverdubois.com

Missouri Botanical Garden
4344 Shaw Boulevard
St. Louis, MO 63110
(314) 577–9400
www.mobot.org

Missouri Department of Conservation
P.O. Box 180
Jefferson City, MO 65102
(573) 751–4115
www.conservation.state.mo.us

Missouri Department of Natural
    Resources
Division of Parks, Recreation, and
    Historic Preservation
P.O. Box 176
Jefferson City, MO 65102
(573) 751–2479
(800) 334–6946
www.mostateparks.com

Powder Valley Conservation Nature
    Center
11715 Cragwold Road
Kirkwood, MO 63122-7015
(314) 301–1500

Rockwoods Reservation
Missouri Department of Conservation
2751 Glencoe Road
Glencoe, MO 63038
(636) 458–2236

Route 66 State Park
97 North Outer Road, Suite 1
Eureka, MO 63025
(636) 938–7198
(800) 334–6946

Shaw Nature Reserve
P.O. Box 38
Gray Summit, MO 63039
(636) 451–3512
www.mobot.org/mobot/
    naturereserve

Tower Grove Park
4255 Arsenal Street
St. Louis, MO
(314) 771–2679
http://stlouis.missouri.org/parks/
    tower-grove

Tyson Research Center
Washington University
P.O. Box 258
Eureka, MO 63025
(314) 935–8430

Wild Canid Survival and Research
    Center
P.O. Box 760
Eureka, MO 63025
(636) 938–6490
www.wolfsanctuary.org

World Bird Sanctuary
125 Bald Eagle Ridge Road
Valley Park, MO 63088
(636) 861–3225
www.worldbirdsanctuary.org

Appendix B

SUGGESTED READING

Cline, Andy. *The Floater's Guide to Missouri*. Helena, Mont.: Falcon Press, 1992.

Dufur, Brett. *The 1995 Katy Trail Guidebook*. Columbia, Mo.: Pebble Publishing, 1995.

Earngey, Bill. *Missouri Roadsides: The Traveler's Companion*. Columbia, Mo.: University of Missouri Press, 1995.

Ernst, Pam. *Arkansas Dayhikes for Kids and Families*. Cave Mountain, Ark.: Cloudland.net Publishing, 2003.

Ernst, Tim. *Arkansas Hiking Trails*. 3rd ed. Fayetteville, Ark.: Ernst Wilderness, 2003.

————. *Arkansas Waterfalls Guidebook*. Cave Mountain, Ark.: Cloudland.net Publishing, 2003.

————. *Buffalo River Hiking Trails,* 2nd ed. Fayetteville, Ark.: Ernst Wilderness, 1994.

————. *Ouachita Trail Guide*. 3rd ed. Fayetteville, Ark.: Ernst Wilderness, 2000.

————. *Ozark Highlands Trail Guide*. 3rd ed. Fayetteville, Ark.: Ernst Wilderness, 1994.

Flader, Susan, ed. *Exploring Missouri's Legacy: State Parks and Historic Sites*. Columbia, Mo.: University of Missouri Press, 1992.

Galas, Judith and Cindy West. *Walking St. Louis*. Helena, Mont.: Falcon Publishing, 1998.

Henry, Steve. *The Mountain Biker's Guide to the Ozarks*. Helena, Mont.: Falcon Press, 1993.

Kennon, Tom. *Ozark Whitewater: A Paddler's Guide to the Mountain Streams of Arkansas and Missouri*. Birmingham, Ala.: Menasha Ridge Press, 1989.

Kurz, Don. *Ozark Wildflowers*. Helena, Mont.: Falcon Publishing, 1999.

————, ed. *Public Prairies of Missouri*. Jefferson City, Mo.: Missouri Department of Conservation, 2003.

————. *Shrubs and Woody Vines of Missouri*. Jefferson City, Mo.: Missouri Department of Conservation, 1977.

————. *Trees of Missouri*. Jefferson City, Mo.: Missouri Department of Conservation, 2003.

McKee, Joan, ed. *A Paddler's Guide to Missouri*. Jefferson City, Mo.: Missouri Department of Conservation, 2003.

Rafferty, Milton D. *The Ozarks: Land and Life*. Norman, Okla.: University of Oklahoma Press, 1980.

———. *The Ozarks Outdoors: A Guide for Fishermen, Hunters, and Tourists*. Norman, Okla.: University of Oklahoma Press, 1985.

Rafferty, Milton D. and John Catau. *The Ouachita Mountains: A Guide for Fisherman, Hunters, and Travelers*. Norman, Okla.: University of Oklahoma Press, 1991.

Rossiter, Phyllis. *A Living History of the Ozarks*. Gretna, La.: Pelican Publishing, 1992.

Index

ABOUT THE AUTHOR

After completing master's degrees in botany and zoology at Southern Illinois University, Cabondate, Don Kurz spent the next thirty years working to inventory, acquire, protect, and manage natural areas, endangered species sites, and other special features. For twenty-two years he was employed by the Missouri Department of Conservation, where he held various supervisory positions in the Natural History Division, including that of Natural History Chief, which he held until his retirement from the department in 2002.

Don is now a full-time writer and nature photographer specializing in landscapes, wildlife, insects, and plants. His photos have appeared in calendars and magazines such as *Natural History* as well as numerous wildflower books, including Falcon Publishing's *Tallgrass Prairie Wildflowers* and *North Woods Wildflowers*. He is also author of Falcon Publishing's *Ozark Wildflowers* and the Missouri Department of Conservation's *Shrubs and Woody Vines of Missouri* and *Trees of Missouri*.

His countless trips into the Ozarks and Ouachitas have originated from his home on ten wooded acres outside of Jefferson City, Missouri.